2018/50/Rev.1
ST/ESA/370

Department of Economic and Social Affairs

World Economic and Social Survey 2018

Frontier technologies for sustainable development

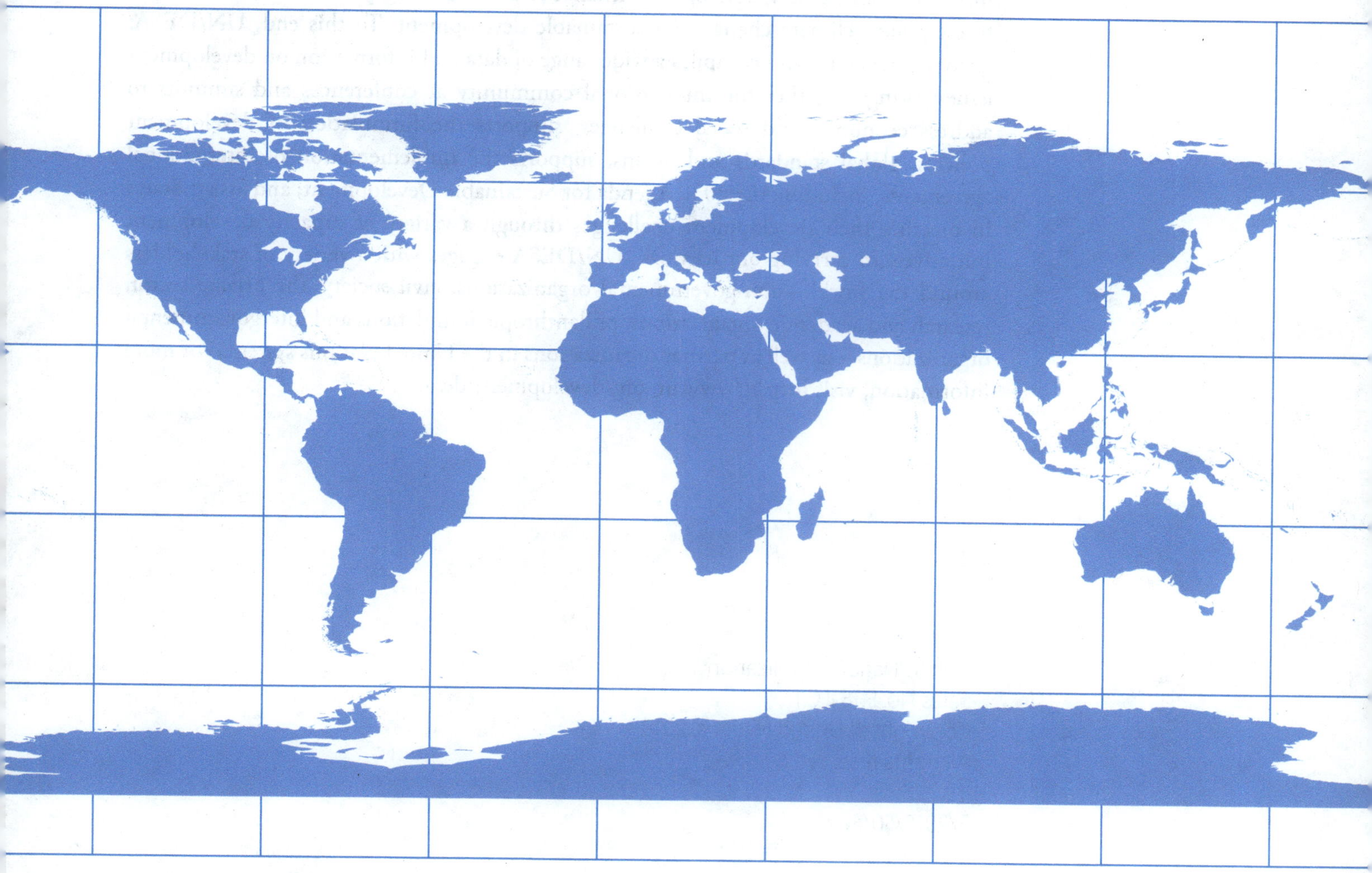

United Nations
New York, 2018

Department of Economic and Social Affairs

The Department of Economic and Social Affairs of the United Nations Secretariat (UN/DESA) is a vital interface between global policies in the economic, social and environmental spheres and national action. The Department's mission is to promote and support international cooperation in the pursuit of sustainable development for all. Its work is guided by the universal and transformative 2030 Agenda for Sustainable Development, along with a set of 17 integrated Sustainable Development Goals adopted by the United Nations General Assembly. UN/DESA's work addresses a range of cross-cutting issues that affect peoples' lives and livelihoods, such as social policy, poverty eradication, employment, social inclusion, inequalities, population, indigenous rights, macroeconomic policy, development finance and cooperation, public sector innovation, forest policy, climate change and sustainable development. To this end, UN/DESA: analyses, generates and compiles a wide range of data and information on development issues; brings together the international community at conferences and summits to address economic and social challenges; supports the formulation of development policies, global standards and norms; supports the implementation of international agreements, including the 2030 Agenda for Sustainable Development; and assists States in meeting their development challenges through a variety of capacity development initiatives. In carrying out its work, UN/DESA engages with a variety of stakeholders around the world—non-governmental organizations, civil society, the private sector, research and academic organizations, philanthropic foundations and intergovernmental organizations—as well as partner organizations in the United Nations system. For more information, visit https://www.un.org/development/desa.

United Nations publication
Sales No. E.18.II.C.1

E/2018/50/Rev.1
ST/ESA/370
ISBN 978-92-1-109179-3
eISBN 978-92-1-047224-1

Acknowledgements

The *World Economic and Social Survey* is the flagship publication on major development issues prepared by the Department of Economic and Social Affairs of the United Nations Secretariat (UN/DESA).

Under the general guidance of Liu Zhenmin, Under-Secretary-General for Economic and Social Affairs at UN/DESA, and the management of Pingfan Hong, Director, Economic Analysis and Policy Division (EAPD), the *Survey 2018* was produced by a team led by Hamid Rashid, Chief, Development Research Branch in EAPD. Core members of the team included Hoi Wai (Jackie) Cheng, Nicole Hunt, S. Nazrul Islam, Kenneth Iversen, Alex Julca, Hiroshi Kawamura, Marcelo LaFleur, Mariangela Parra-Lancourt and Sérgio Vieira. Critical overall feedback was provided by Elliott Harris, Assistant Secretary-General for Economic Development at UN/DESA.

Mohamed El Batran, Marilia Bassetti Marcato and Joshua Mask provided substantive support to the production process. Israel Machado and the Dag Hammarskjöld Library facilitated access to reference documents. Administrative support was provided by Gerard F. Reyes.

Substantive contributions in the form of background papers were made by Tatiana Falcão, Alexander Haider, Jenna Jambeck, Anselm Kamperman Sanders, Cara LaPointe, Chris Vickers and Nicolas L. Ziebarth.

Comments and inputs at various stages were provided by members of the Editorial Board at UN/DESA and colleagues—particularly the focal points—from other Divisions within UN/DESA, the United Nations Department of Management/Office of Information Communication Technology, the United Nations Office of the High Representative for the Least Developed Countries, Landlocked Developing Countries and Small Island Developing States, the International Labour Organization, the United Nations Conference on Trade and Development and the United Nations Development Programme.

The following participants at two Expert Group Meetings provided valuable comments: Diana Alarcón, Abdul Alim, Americo Beviglia Zampetti, Matthias Bruckner, Kate Crawford, Ekkehard Ernst, Chiara Farronato, Victor Gaigbe-Togbe, Kevin Gallagher, Lambert Hogenhout, Alfredo Jefferson, Lars Jensen, Maren Andrea Jiménez, Raymond Landveld, Keun Lee, Ahmed Mushfiq Mobarak, Manuel Montes, Shantanu Mukherjee, Clara Oberthür, Alberto Padova, Jonathan Perry, Michał Podolski, Aikanysh Saparalieva, Benson Soon Seng Sim, Maurice Stucke, Arun Sundararajan, Deniz Susar, Joop Theunissen, Ryosuke Ujihashi, Lisanne van Wijngaarden, Henry Wei and Fang Zhang.

Editorial and design input at the various stages of the publication process were provided by Michael Brodsky, Leah Kennedy, Gabe Scelta, Nancy Settecasi and the Branding and Graphic Design Unit in the Department of Public Information.

Explanatory notes

The following symbols have been used in the tables throughout the report:

..	**Two dots** indicate that data are not available or are not separately reported.
–	**A dash** indicates that the amount is nil or negligible.
-	**A hyphen** indicates that the item is not applicable.
–	**A minus sign** indicates deficit or decrease, except as indicated.
.	**A full stop** is used to indicate decimals.
/	**A slash** between years indicates a crop year or financial year, for example, 2017/18.
-	**Use of a hyphen** between years, for example, 2017-2018, signifies the full period involved, including the beginning and end years.

Reference to "dollars" ($) indicates United States dollars, unless otherwise stated.

Reference to "billions" indicates one thousand million.

Reference to "tons" indicates metric tons, unless otherwise stated.

Annual rates of growth or change, unless otherwise stated, refer to annual compound rates.

Details and percentages in tables do not necessarily add to totals, because of rounding.

The following abbreviations have been used:

AI	artificial intelligence
BEPS	base erosion and profit shifting
CO_2	carbon dioxide
EU	European Union
EV	electric vehicle
FAO	Food and Agriculture Organization of the United Nations
FDI	foreign direct investment
GDP	gross domestic product
GHG	greenhouse gas
GPS	Global Positioning System
GVC	global value chain
GWP	global warming potential
ICT	information and communications technologies
IEA	International Energy Agency
IIA	international investment agreement
ILO	International Labour Organization
IMF	International Monetary Fund
IPCC	Intergovernmental Panel on Climate Change
IPR	intellectual property rights
LDC	least developed country
LLDC	landlocked developing country
MOOC	massive online open course
NIS	national innovation system
OECD	Organization for Economic Cooperation and Development
PDP	plant-derived pharmaceutical
R&D	research and development
RETs	renewable energy technologies
RTA	regional trade agreement
SDG	Sustainable Development Goal
SIDS	small island developing States
STEM	science, technology, engineering and mathematics
TRIPS	Trade-Related Aspects of Intellectual Property Rights
UIS	Institute for Statistics (UNESCO)
UNCTAD	United Nations Conference on Trade and Development
UN/DESA	Department of Economic and Social Affairs of the United Nations Secretariat
UNESCO	United Nations Educational, Scientific and Cultural Organization
WHO	World Health Organization
WTO	World Trade Organization

The designations employed and the presentation of the material in this present publication do not imply the expression of any opinion whatsoever on the part of the Secretariat of the United Nations concerning the legal status of any country or territory or of its authorities, or concerning the delimitation of its frontiers. The term "country" as used in the text of this report also refers, as appropriate, to territories or areas. The designations of country groups in the text and the tables are intended solely for statistical or analytical convenience and do not necessarily express a judgment about the stage reached by a particular country or area in the development process. Mention of the names of firms and commercial products does not imply the endorsement of the United Nations.

For analytical purposes, unless otherwise specified, the following country groupings and subgroupings have been used:

Developed economies (developed market economies):

Australia, Canada, European Union, Iceland, Japan, New Zealand, Norway, Switzerland, United States of America.

Group of Eight (G8):

Canada, France, Germany, Italy, Japan, Russian Federation, United Kingdom of Great Britain and Northern Ireland, United States of America.

Group of Twenty (G20):

Argentina, Australia, Brazil, Canada, China, France, Germany, India, Indonesia, Italy, Japan, Mexico, Republic of Korea, Russian Federation, Saudi Arabia, South Africa, Turkey, United Kingdom of Great Britain and Northern Ireland, United States of America, European Union.

European Union (EU):

Austria, Belgium, Bulgaria, Croatia, Cyprus, Czechia, Denmark, Estonia, Finland, France, Germany, Greece, Hungary, Ireland, Italy, Latvia, Lithuania, Luxembourg, Malta, Netherlands, Poland, Portugal, Romania, Slovakia, Slovenia, Spain, Sweden, United Kingdom of Great Britain and Northern Ireland.

EU-15:

Austria, Belgium, Denmark, Finland, France, Germany, Greece, Ireland, Italy, Luxembourg, Netherlands, Portugal, Spain, Sweden, United Kingdom of Great Britain and Northern Ireland.

New EU member States:

Bulgaria, Croatia, Cyprus, Czechia, Estonia, Hungary, Latvia, Lithuania, Malta, Poland, Romania, Slovakia, Slovenia.

Economies in transition:

South-Eastern Europe:

Albania, Bosnia and Herzegovina, Montenegro, Serbia, the former Yugoslav Republic of Macedonia.

Commonwealth of Independent States (CIS):

Armenia, Azerbaijan, Belarus, Georgia,[1] Kazakhstan, Kyrgyzstan, Republic of Moldova, Russian Federation, Tajikistan, Turkmenistan, Ukraine, Uzbekistan.

Developing economies:

Africa, Asia and the Pacific (excluding Australia, Japan, New Zealand and the member States of CIS in Asia), Latin America and the Caribbean.

Subgroupings of Africa:

Northern Africa:

Algeria, Egypt, Libya, Mauritania, Morocco, Sudan, Tunisia.

Sub-Saharan Africa:

All other African countries, except Nigeria and South Africa, where indicated.

Subgroupings of Asia and the Pacific:

Western Asia:

Bahrain, Iraq, Israel, Jordan, Kuwait, Lebanon, Oman, Qatar, Saudi Arabia, State of Palestine, Syrian Arab Republic, Turkey, United Arab Emirates, Yemen.

South Asia:

Bangladesh, Bhutan, India, Iran (Islamic Republic of), Maldives, Nepal, Pakistan, Sri Lanka.

East Asia:

All other developing economies in Asia and the Pacific.

Subgroupings of Latin America and the Caribbean:

South America:

Argentina, Bolivia (Plurinational State of), Brazil, Chile, Colombia, Ecuador, Paraguay, Peru, Uruguay, Venezuela (Bolivarian Republic of).

Mexico and Central America:

Costa Rica, El Salvador, Guatemala, Honduras, Mexico, Nicaragua, Panama.

Caribbean:

Barbados, Cuba, Dominican Republic, Guyana, Haiti, Jamaica, Trinidad and Tobago.

1 As of 19 August 2009, Georgia officially left the Commonwealth of Independent States. However, its performance is discussed in the context of this group of countries for reasons of geographical proximity and similarities in economic structure.

Least developed countries:

Afghanistan, Angola, Bangladesh, Benin, Bhutan, Burkina Faso, Burundi, Cambodia, Central African Republic, Chad, Comoros, Democratic Republic of the Congo, Djibouti, Equatorial Guinea, Eritrea, Ethiopia, Gambia, Guinea, Guinea-Bissau, Haiti, Kiribati, Lao People's Democratic Republic, Lesotho, Liberia, Madagascar, Malawi, Mali, Mauritania, Mozambique, Myanmar, Nepal, Niger, Rwanda, Sao Tome and Principe, Senegal, Sierra Leone, Solomon Islands, Somalia, South Sudan, Sudan, Timor-Leste, Togo, Tuvalu, Uganda, United Republic of Tanzania, Vanuatu, Yemen, Zambia.

Small island developing States and areas:

American Samoa, Anguilla, Antigua and Barbuda, Aruba, Bahamas, Barbados, Belize, British Virgin Islands, Cape Verde, Commonwealth of the Northern Mariana Islands, Comoros, Cook Islands, Cuba, Dominica, Dominican Republic, Fiji, French Polynesia, Grenada, Guam, Guinea-Bissau, Guyana, Haiti, Jamaica, Kiribati, Maldives, Marshall Islands, Mauritius, Micronesia (Federated States of), Montserrat, Nauru, Netherlands Antilles, New Caledonia, Niue, Palau, Papua New Guinea, Puerto Rico, Saint Kitts and Nevis, Saint Lucia, Saint Vincent and the Grenadines, Samoa, Sao Tome and Principe, Seychelles, Singapore, Solomon Islands, Suriname, Timor-Leste, Tonga, Trinidad and Tobago, Tuvalu, United States Virgin Islands, Vanuatu.

Parties to the United Nations Framework Convention on Climate Change:

Annex I parties:

Australia, Austria, Belarus, Belgium, Bulgaria, Canada, Croatia, Czechia, Denmark, Estonia, European Union, Finland, France, Germany, Greece, Hungary, Iceland, Ireland, Italy, Japan, Latvia, Liechtenstein, Lithuania, Luxembourg, Monaco, Netherlands, New Zealand, Norway, Poland, Portugal, Romania, Russian Federation, Slovakia, Slovenia, Spain, Sweden, Switzerland, Turkey, Ukraine, United Kingdom of Great Britain and Northern Ireland, United States of America.

Annex II parties:

Annex II parties are the parties included in Annex I that are members of the Organization for Economic Cooperation and Development but not the parties included in Annex I that are economies in transition.

Non-Annex I parties:

Non-Annex I parties are mainly developing countries. Certain groups of developing countries are recognized by the Convention as being especially vulnerable to the adverse impacts of climate change, including countries with low-lying coastal areas and those prone to desertification and drought. Others (such as countries that rely heavily on income from fossil fuel production and commerce) experience greater vulnerability to the potential economic impacts of climate change response measures. The Convention emphasizes activities that promise to respond to the special needs and concerns of those vulnerable countries, such as investment, insurance and technology transfer.

The 48 parties classified as least developed countries by the United Nations are given special consideration under the Convention on account of their limited capacity to respond to climate change and adapt to its adverse effects. Parties are urged to take full account of the special situation of least developed countries when considering funding and technology transfer activities.

Sustainable Development Goals

Goal 1. End poverty in all its forms everywhere

Goal 2. End hunger, achieve food security and improved nutrition and promote sustainable agriculture

Goal 3. Ensure healthy lives and promote well-being for all at all ages

Goal 4. Ensure inclusive and equitable quality education and promote lifelong learning opportunities for all

Goal 5. Achieve gender equality and empower all women and girls

Goal 6. Ensure availability and sustainable management of water and sanitation for all

Goal 7. Ensure access to affordable, reliable, sustainable and modern energy for all

Goal 8. Promote sustained, inclusive and sustainable economic growth, full and productive employment and decent work for all

Goal 9. Build resilient infrastructure, promote inclusive and sustainable industrialization and foster innovation

Goal 10. Reduce inequality within and among countries

Goal 11. Make cities and human settlements inclusive, safe, resilient and sustainable

Goal 12. Ensure sustainable consumption and production patterns

Goal 13. Take urgent action to combat climate change and its impacts

Goal 14. Conserve and sustainably use the oceans, seas and marine resources for sustainable development

Goal 15. Protect, restore and promote sustainable use of terrestrial ecosystems, sustainably manage forests, combat desertification, and halt and reverse land degradation and halt biodiversity loss

Goal 16. Promote peaceful and inclusive societies for sustainable development, provide access to justice for all and build effective, accountable and inclusive institutions at all levels

Goal 17. Strengthen the means of implementation and revitalize the Global Partnership for Sustainable Development

Table of contents

Chapter III
Bridging the development divide

Chapter IV
Fostering innovation, diffusion and adoption

Chapter V
International cooperation for managing frontier technologies

Boxes

Figures

Tables

Foreword

Frontier technologies—from DNA sequencing to 3D-printing, from renewable energy technologies to biodegradable plastics, from machine learning to artificial intelligence—present immense potential for the 2030 Agenda for Sustainable Development. Good health and longevity, prosperity for all and environmental sustainability are within our reach if we harness the full power of these innovations.

However, these same technologies also raise serious concerns. The *World Economic and Social Survey 2018* deepens our understanding of the impact of many technological advances. Clearly, we need policies that can ensure frontier technologies—which increasingly transcend sectoral, geographic and generational boundaries—are not only commercially viable but also equitable and ethical. This will require a rigorous, objective and transparent ongoing assessment, involving all stakeholders.

The *Survey* calls for more concerted efforts to close the technology divide that persists within and between countries. In bridging this gap, governments will need to play a leading role in developing human capital and establishing institutions that can foster innovation and the diffusion and adoption of frontier technologies. Developing countries, in particular, need support to overcome systemic challenges.

No nation alone can manage the full impact of frontier technologies. The *Survey* makes a case for collective action to set standards and ethical boundaries for our shared digital future. The United Nations—with its universal membership—is in a unique position to bring people, businesses and organizations together to advance cooperation across disciplines and domains. We remain committed to facilitating global dialogue and forging commitments to ensure that frontier technologies work for all.

ANTÓNIO GUTERRES
Secretary-General

Executive summary

Frontier technologies for a sustainable future

Frontier technologies herald great hopes for humanity. They can help eradicate hunger and epidemics, increase life expectancy, reduce carbon emissions, automate manual and repetitive tasks, create decent jobs, improve quality of life and facilitate increasingly complex decision-making processes. Frontier technologies can indeed make sustainable development a reality, improving people's lives, promoting prosperity and protecting the planet. However, the rapid pace of technological change also introduces significant policy challenges, creating winners and losers in societies and presenting new ethical and moral dilemmas. Notwithstanding these challenges, societies—with the appropriate policies, institutions and international cooperation—can harness frontier technologies to achieve sustainable development, while mitigating their adverse economic and social consequences.

Frontier technologies, which encompass an array of new materials, products, applications, processes and business models, are interdependent, interconnected and mutually reinforcing. Advances in one technology foster progress in others. For example, the invention of new materials is transforming energy production and storage, additive manufacturing and 3D printing; artificial intelligence (AI) is increasingly enabling automation, online search engines and social media platforms; and rapid increases in computing power are enabling breakthroughs in genetics, nanotechnology, blockchains and cryptocurrencies. The present *Survey* focuses only on a selected set of new technologies that are deemed most pertinent and promising for sustainable development.

Frontier technologies addressing the challenges for people, prosperity and the planet

People and their well-being are often the central focus of many scientific and technological endeavours. Attesting to this, frontier technologies are generating breakthroughs in genetics, nanomedicine, personalized medication, 3D imaging diagnostics and new methods of organ development and transplantation. While those breakthroughs promise to extend longevity and transform human well-being significantly, advances in many health and genetic technologies present ethical conundrums, including the possibility of off-target genetic modifications affecting long-term health and safety considerations. Ethical standards, reflecting fundamental human values adopted and enforced globally, will be instrumental in guiding further advances in these technologies.

Concern for the state of the planet is also driving many innovations. Technological breakthroughs in carbon capture and sequestration have the potential to drastically reduce net emissions and mitigate climate change. The new materials used in photovoltaic cells have great potential for energy efficiency and renewable energy technology. Biodegradable plastic offers a means for reducing plastics pollution, which has become the second most important threat to the environment, after climate change. There are, however, no guarantees that these technological advances will protect the planet on their own. Policies and institutions will remain paramount in ensuring that these technologies are widely diffused and adopted.

The quest for prosperity is often a key driver of innovation. Humans created machines to perform tasks and improve productivity, and higher productivity in turn delivered new levels of prosperity. Frontier technologies, however, are transforming the relationship between humans and machines. Machines that are now capable of building new machines and solving complex problems, which until recently could be solved only by humans, have the potential to replace humans. Smart robots, equipped with AI, promise to raise productivity to a much higher level and enable production of many new products and services. On the other hand, robots capable of performing "mental labour" are likely to take over many tasks and occupations, potentially leading to higher levels of unemployment. The creators and owners of these robots, however, will clearly become more prosperous—at the expense of the many millions who could lose out in the process. The prosperity of nations may also be at stake, as the robotization of jobs may foreclose manufacturing and industrialization opportunities for many developing countries. Policies must therefore play a critical role in ensuring that frontier technologies leave no one behind and create prosperity for all people and all nations.

Managing the policy challenges of frontier technologies

Frontier technologies present policy challenges. The complex issues confronted by policy-makers in their efforts to maximize the potential of a new technology are well represented in the case of electric vehicles (EVs), which are already in use in many countries. With near-zero emissions, EVs have a great potential to help realize Sustainable Development Goal (SDG) 13, which is to reduce carbon emissions and combat climate change. The net emission impact of electric vehicles depends, however, on the kind of electricity that they use to recharge. Indeed, while EVs can reduce urban pollution and improve air quality, the net mitigation effect will be limited if their batteries are charged with electricity generated by fossil fuel. Realizing the full potential benefit of one frontier technology thus depends on commensurate advances in other related technologies, which, in the case of EVs, happen to be renewable energy technologies (SDG 7 aims to substantially increase the global share of renewable energy).

The future of work and inequality

Advances in automation, machine learning, and AI pose similar policy challenges. As these advances increase productivity, they are also transforming labour markets. Routine and repetitive tasks are increasingly being automated, which changes the types of demand for skills. Technology is already being held responsible for many job losses in developed economies. With automation replacing physical labour and AI taking over many analytical functions, achieving one of the targets under SDG 8 (Promote full and productive employment and decent work for all) will become increasingly difficult.

Automation is also contributing to an increase in the share of capital income, while decreasing the share of income flowing to labour, thus leading to a rise in income and wealth inequality. Unless policies are in place to redistribute some of the gains from automation, the process of skills polarization will exacerbate income inequality further and make the realization of SDG 10 (Reduce inequality within and among countries) even more daunting. Automation could also lead to re-shoring of production from developing countries back to advanced economies, potentially reducing the export earnings and gross domestic product (GDP) of many developing economies and worsening income inequality among countries.

Online technology platforms—which enable individuals or families to use their car or a spare room in their apartment as income-earning capital assets—are promoting new models of the "sharing economy" and creating new opportunities and prosperity. Similar platforms are generating new approaches to work, such as working remotely and working at multiple jobs. Social media platforms are transforming social interactions and creating new business opportunities. Blockchain technology, for example, is making it easier to verify transactions, creating decentralized financial systems and potentially increasing access to financial services. These technologies are bridging many divides—and creating new ones: While holding out great potential for achieving SDGs 3 (Ensure healthy lives and promote well-being for all at all ages) and 4 (Ensure inclusive and equitable quality education), as well as 5 (Achieve gender equality and empower all women and girls), they are also blurring distinctions between employers and employees and consequently raising concerns regarding social protection. National policies and international cooperation will therefore remain key for extracting the full development potential of these technologies.

Balancing efficiency gains and equity and ethical concerns

It is also the case that social media platforms are increasingly used to produce targeted advertisements, manipulate human emotion, and spread misinformation and even hatred. While AI-based decision-making systems can improve the efficiency of, and access to, public services, they also run the risk of reinforcing existing biases and forms of exclusion. There is thus a clear need for greater transparency and accountability for AI-based decisions. The mass volume of data generated in online platforms provides increasingly important inputs into the process of improving machine learning and artificial intelligence; data are also a critical determinant of the market power of large technology firms. Yet, responses to the questions who should own data and what their true value should be remain contentious. Online data are also increasingly susceptible to hacking and cyberattacks, raising concerns for data security and privacy. Although various policy and regulatory measures are being considered at national or regional levels, an international consensus on data ownership, security and privacy is clearly needed to address ethical concerns and mitigate potential risks, while ensuring that online platforms continue to deliver economic and social benefits.

Closing the technological gap to bridge the development divide

While developed countries—that is, countries at the technology frontier—grapple with the challenges and seize upon the opportunities associated with frontier technologies, many developing countries are yet to fully reap the benefits of existing technologies. A great technological gap persists, largely explaining the "development divide" between developed and developing countries. More than 1 billion people in the developing countries still do not have access to electricity and an additional 2.5 billion are "under-electrified", experiencing weak connections and frequent power outages. The millions who still depend on human or animal muscle power for cultivation and other forms of production remain shackled to technologies from the pre-industrial era. They also lack access to modern education and health systems, which are crucial for accumulation of a threshold level of human capital needed for the adoption of many frontier technologies. Creating enabling conditions and bridging the technology divide will remain a key development strategy for many developing countries.

Leapfrogging to frontier technologies

Frontier technologies also present developing countries with leapfrogging opportunities to achieve the SDGs. The "advantage" of backwardness is that it can enable these countries to avoid or bypass existing less efficient technologies. For example, millions of people in developing countries leapfrogged to mobile phones, without having ever owned or used landline telephones. People in many developing countries, with no electricity until now, are adopting solar electricity, bypassing fossil fuels and leaping directly to the stage of renewables (and contributing to the realization of SDG 7). In fact, many developing countries now derive higher shares of their electricity from renewables compared with many developed countries. It is possible, with appropriate policy measures and strategies, to encourage these developments and accelerate the general process of technological catch-up for many developing countries.

Notwithstanding these potentials, many developing countries—particularly countries in special situations, such as least developed countries (LDCs), landlocked developing countries (LLDCs) and small island developing States (SIDS)—face formidable barriers to leapfrogging to frontier technologies. It is almost impossible for people to secure access to digital technologies and online economic opportunities without electricity and broadband Internet connections. However, enabling physical infrastructures constitutes a necessary, but clearly not a sufficient, condition. Without a minimum level of education, it is not possible to utilize digital technologies to buy or sell goods online, for example, or offer car services or rent out an apartment, even if the requisite electricity and Internet connection are in place. It is therefore not fortuitous that the few instances of leapfrogging—through, e.g., adoption of solar energy and mobile phones—became possible for technologies that do not require high levels of human capital. This demonstrates that leapfrogging to frontier technologies also requires advances related to achieving other SDGs such as "to ensure healthy lives" (SDG 3), "to ensure inclusive and equitable quality of education" (SDG 4), and "to build resilient infrastructure" (SDG 9). In order to bridge the technology and development divides, national development strategies will therefore need to target both basic infrastructure development and human capital accumulation

National innovation systems fostering technological progress

That national innovation systems (NIS)—formal or informal—drive innovation, diffusion and adoption of new technologies is true both for countries at the technology frontier and for the technologically following developing countries. Innovation, however, is not always synonymous with a technological breakthrough, i.e., a one-of-a-kind, grand-scale invention. It can also entail small-scale, incremental—or even imperceptible—

improvements and improvisations of processes and products. National innovation systems in technologically advanced countries are generally more focused on innovation, while the NIS of technologically following countries for the most part prioritize adaptation. While infrastructure and human capital are necessary preconditions for technological catch-up, their quality and efficacy are largely determined by the NIS, which comprises interconnected institutions that create, store and transfer new technologies. More broadly, the NIS constitutes a network of universities, research institutions, and the research and development (R&D) departments of industrial firms and utilities. An NIS can drive both the creation of new methods for production of pre-existing products and services (process innovation) and the creation of new products and services (product innovation).

Aligning the national innovation system with development priorities and contexts

There is no single model of a national innovation system. Its size, scope and effectiveness are determined by country-specific priorities and contexts. The relative size and influence of various actors—public and private—are an important determinant of a national innovation system. Systems can also differ across countries depending on the relative importance they attach to basic or applied research. An NIS can prioritize indigenous research, instead of importing, or relying on, foreign technologies, or vice versa. In general, the private sector plays a more important role in the NIS of advanced countries, while the public sector usually plays a more dominant role in developing countries, simply because the private sector in those countries often does not have enough R&D capability. Similarly, the NIS in a technologically following country is likely to be more focused on application, while that of advanced countries can focus on both basic science and application. Notwithstanding these differences, it is critically important that the objectives and operations of the NIS be aligned with national development priorities.

Developing an effective NIS that fosters innovation, diffusion and adoption is particularly important for developing countries, given that the current, uneven pace of technological breakthroughs may further widen the technological divide that persists between developed and developing countries. An NIS will need to address—or may even need to overcome—continued divergences in the ability of firms and countries to innovate and adopt existing technologies; growing market power concentration, especially of firms dominating the digital sphere; and increasingly stringent and restrictive intellectual property rights (IPR) regimes. This will require revamped and scaled-up international cooperation, reflecting shared and differentiated responsibilities among all countries for managing the impacts of frontier technologies.

International cooperation for managing frontier technologies

International cooperation will remain key to bridging this persistent, and possibly growing, technology divide among countries and there is a clear need to broaden and strengthen technology transfer and diffusion mechanisms. While trade and foreign direct investment (FDI) have generally been the most important channels of technology transfer and diffusion, intellectual property rights as embedded in various trade and investment agreements are exerting an increasingly restrictive influence in this regard. While international efforts are scaled up to ease IPR restrictions, developing countries can make use of the growing number of pooled-knowledge networks—facilitated by the Internet—to accelerate the pace of their technological progress and so catch up.

The speed of diffusion and proliferation of many frontier technologies; the way they cross jurisdictional, regulatory and disciplinary borders; and how they embed, shape and exploit human values and bias render traditional and national-level regulations inadequate, if not irrelevant. The new reality ushered in by many frontier technologies calls for stronger and more effective international cooperation. As stated by the Secretary-General (United Nations, 2017a), it is crucial to avoid the naïve idea that "traditional forms of regulation" will work to address the challenges of the future. New regulatory mechanisms for managing frontier technologies must bring together all stakeholders: not only Governments, companies and scientists, but also the civil society and academia. These frameworks must strike a balance between fostering innovation and efficiency on the one hand, and fairness, equity and ethics on the other. Such a balance will be critical for ensuring that frontier technologies deliver sustainable development and leave no one behind.

Strengthening competition policy and international tax cooperation

In particular, international cooperation will be needed to address the growing and excessive concentration of market power among a few large technology firms, as a pathway towards both addressing efficiency-, equity- and ethics-related issues and bridging the technology divide among countries. The "winner-takes-most" phenomenon has allowed a small number of firms to dominate their respective industries at the global level, thereby limiting the scope of regulations at the national level. Moreover, excessive concentration of market power can hinder further innovation and diffusion of frontier technologies within and across countries. There is also a strong need to strengthen international tax cooperation so as to ensure that multinationals—particularly large technology firms operating and adding value globally—are taxed effectively. The current international tax framework—designed with the traditional bricks-and-mortar economy in mind—is often ineffective when it comes to taxing the intangible value added and digital transactions associated with many frontier technologies.

International cooperation to ensure an even playing field at the global level is imperative. For example, stringent regulations in one country will create opportunities for regulatory arbitrage if other countries do not enforce similar regulations. Furthermore, a "race to the bottom" can occur if countries use lax regulation as a strategy for attracting new businesses, getting ahead of the curve and exploiting the first-mover advantage. Absent robust international cooperation, national-level efforts to increase competition and to prevent tax avoidance and tax evasion will become increasingly ineffective. International tax cooperation will be particularly important with respect to taxing profits, which are mobile across borders and often difficult to measure. There is also a clear need for forging consensus at national levels to ensure that the new and additional tax revenues generated are utilized to minimize the short-term adverse impacts of frontier technologies on wages and income inequalities.

The role of the United Nations in forging global collective actions

The United Nations, given its legitimacy and global mandates, is in a unique position to forge a global consensus, ensuring that international cooperation for managing frontier technologies is rooted in and guided by universal values and obligations—as defined in the Charter of the United Nations, the Universal Declaration of Human Rights,[1] and the 2030 Agenda for Sustainable Development.[2] The United Nations remains a trusted venue where Governments, industry, academia, civil society and others can come together to make collective choices regarding new technologies—openly, transparently and based on shared values. Effective engagement on new technologies will clearly require close partnership with a range of government, industry, academic and civil society partners. The United Nations will also need to remain open to new ideas and new voices and engage credibly and objectively with all partners.

The United Nations can leverage its convening power to bring Member States and all relevant stakeholders together to adopt a global consensus on legal and ethical standards for guiding research and development of frontier technologies. The need for global standards is particularly acute for managing progress in AI in such a way as to increase accountability and transparency of AI-based decisions. Global ethical standards are also needed to guide current and future research on genetic technologies, especially gene editing, as they may fundamentally transform the human species.

The United Nations can play a vital role in supporting the identification and designation of certain frontier technologies that can be critical for achieving the Sustainable Development Goals. Renewable energy technologies that promote environmental sustainability, vaccines that save lives, and biotechnologies that boost food production and eliminate hunger are all critically important for achieving sustainable development and securing our common future. Building a sustainable future will require the United Nations to facilitate development, diffusion and adoption of these technologies based on shared responsibilities of all actors.

Outline of the *Survey*

Following this broad vision, Chapter I of the *Survey* presents a case for harnessing frontier technologies to achieve the shared vision of sustainable development, while minimizing their adverse and disruptive effects. The chapter highlights a few of the remaining challenges for the planet, people and prosperity as humanity strives to achieve sustainable development. It then reviews the relevance and challenges of a select set of frontier technologies in the context of the SDGs. Chapter II discusses the promises and challenges of a few frontier technologies in developed country contexts. Chapter III highlights the development divide and the difficulties—particularly the technological divide—that many low-income and vulnerable countries face in adopting frontier technologies and leapfrogging development. Chapter IV explains the role of national innovation systems and how they can bridge the persistent technological divides between developed and developing economies. Chapter V concludes the *Survey*, discussing the imperatives of international cooperation and coordination, and the special role of the United Nations, for managing frontier technologies to realize the 2030 Agenda for Sustainable Development.

1 General Assembly resolution 217 A (III).

2 General Assembly resolution 70/1.

Chapter I

Frontier technologies for a sustainable future

Introduction

The 2030 Agenda for Sustainable Development[1] unites humanity around a new, common aspiration and charts a path of action towards achieving the 17 universal and mutually reinforcing Sustainable Development Goals (SDGs). Those Goals are necessarily ambitious and reflect the challenges of addressing hunger, poverty, mortality, decent jobs, inequality and environmental sustainability, among others.

Achieving these ambitious goals—while leaving no one behind—will require new development strategies and innovative resource mobilization, as well as the creative use of both existing and emerging technologies. *World Economic and Social Survey 2018* focuses on the promise of those emerging technologies and examines how policy measures can expand their potential benefits and mitigate their potential adverse effects. It should be noted that the *Survey* is less concerned with any technology per se, but rather on how the SDGs can be impacted by rapid technological change. To the extent it discusses individual technologies, it does so to illustrate the depth and breadth of the impact possible.

Innovative and fast-growing technologies are frontier technologies that have the potential to transform societies, economies and promote environmental sustainability

The *Survey* regards as frontier technologies those technologies that are innovative and fast-growing and have the potential to exert a significant impact on societies, economies and the environment (Rotolo, Hicks and Martin, 2015).[2] The scope of frontier technologies includes advanced materials such as graphene and biodegradable plastics, scientific breakthroughs in biology and genetics, and advancements in 3D printing, robotics and artificial intelligence (AI). They are deeply interconnected and interdependent, as advances in one are likely to impact many others; and just as rapid improvements in transistor capacities enabled faster and smaller devices, advances in AI will help advance other emerging technologies. They are also interconnected through their generation of, and need for, large data sets.

Technological breakthroughs offer us the best hope for a sustainable future...

The excitement generated by many technological breakthroughs is justified as they offer us the best hope for a sustainable future. These technologies promise to help overcome some of the more intractable among existing challenges, ranging from attaining natural resource and climate sustainability to combating diseases and hunger and ensuring that education is accessible to all.

1 General Assembly resolution 70/1.

2 The terms “new technologies”, “emerging technologies”, “frontier technologies” and “technological breakthroughs” are used interchangeably throughout the *Survey*.

...but technological change is seldom neutral and cost-free, presenting new equity, ethical and moral challenges

But technological change is seldom neutral and cost-free. Previous industrial revolutions, while enhancing efficiency and increasing prosperity, came with huge environmental costs and also contributed to greater income inequality across countries and regions. History shows us that advances in a technology—automation, for example—can benefit capital owners and workers as well. Automation can free workers from inhumane toil, but in many cases it can also dislocate them, squeeze their wages and exacerbate already existing inequalities in income distribution. Clearly, then, the emergence of new transformative technologies creates major opportunities and challenges for societies. Indeed, for many developing countries, their level of access to these new and existing technologies will determine their development trajectory.

Frontier technologies also present new and unique ethical, moral and equity-related challenges, which can potentially undermine trust, cohesion, tolerance, peace and stability. The *Survey* makes a compelling case for upholding ethical standards and effective and accountable institutions as a means of guiding progress in the development and application of many frontier technologies and promoting peaceful and inclusive societies. Because frontier technologies are associated with externalities which are often global, stronger and more effective international coordination is needed to maximize the positive impacts of new technologies for sustainable development outcomes.

The present chapter examines how the shared vision of sustainable development can be realized by harnessing frontier technologies, while at the same time minimizing their adverse and disruptive effects. It highlights a few of the remaining challenges for the planet, people and prosperity as humanity strives to achieve sustainable development and then reviews the relevance of and the challenges presented by a select set of frontier technologies within the context of the SDGs.

Regarding the planet, the chapter emphasizes the need to improve the management of natural resources and the environment, which has been made urgent by the threat of climate change, the environmental impact of human activities, and the additional demand for natural resources generated by a growing and ageing population. In this regard, advances in the extraction, conversion and storage of electricity may reduce emissions and improve the environmental outlook. Regarding people, the chapter argues that, to improve health outcomes and longevity, progress in improving access to sanitation and water must continue. Technology will help enhance access to health care, and lead to better, cheaper and more innovative services and medicines, and improved health outcomes. To promote prosperity, we must achieve equitable and robust growth. The chapter discusses the economic challenges posed by low productivity growth and rising inequality in many countries. If their progress is managed appropriately with sustainable development in mind, frontier technologies like artificial intelligence, advanced automation and 3D manufacturing techniques, digital finance and blockchain technologies can create new economic opportunities and prosperity.

As the emerging technologies also raise important ethical and moral issues (as noted above), as well as issues related to equity and data ownership, the chapter discusses the need to balance the benefits of technology against the impacts of such issues. The trade-offs become particularly important within the context of the 2030 Agenda for Sustainable Development, which aims towards leaving no one behind.

Key development challenges for the planet, people and prosperity

On 25 September 2015, by its resolution 70/1, the General Assembly adopted, without a vote, the 2030 Agenda for Sustainable Development. In that resolution, Heads of State and Government and High Representatives announced the 17 Sustainable Development Goals (SDGs), galvanizing global efforts along the three dimensions of sustainable development: economic development, social inclusion and environmental sustainability. Pursuant to its universal vision of a common future based on global solidarity, the 2030 Agenda affirms the commitment to prevent degradation of natural resources and climate change; to ensure prosperous and fulfilling lives for all and that progress occurs in harmony with nature; to eradicate poverty and hunger; and to foster peaceful, just and inclusive societies free from fear and violence.

Frontier technologies can accelerate the achievement of the goals set in the 2030 Agenda

The world has seen tremendous progress in confronting many of these issues. Countries are making headway in limiting—or reversing—the human impact on climate and on natural resources. There has been progress in combating diseases and in providing access to health services and medications, with commensurate reductions in child mortality, for example. The decline of poverty by half since 2000 has helped to reduce hunger and malnutrition (United Nations, 2017c). Despite such progress, achievement of the goals set in the 2030 Agenda is still a long way off. The discussion of a few of the persisting global challenges illustrates the transformative potential of frontier technologies.

In the present section, the discussion on climate change and natural resource depletion highlights the link between progress achieved in addressing socioeconomic issues and greater environmental degradation and demonstrates how the pressure on natural resources and environment is intensified by the needs of a growing and ageing population. The discussion on people's health and well-being examines the progress achieved and the remaining challenges to combatting diseases and improving health and sanitation. The section concludes with an examination of the economic challenges of low productivity growth and rising inequality which are of concern to many countries and present a formidable challenge to achieving prosperity and sustainable development.

Combating climate change and depletion of natural resources

Climate change is perhaps the most critical existential threat facing humanity. In 2017 and 2018, the *Global Risks Report*, issued annually, ranked climate change-related events as the most likely risk facing the world and in 2017 as the second most impactful (World Economic Forum, 2017; 2018). The 2030 Agenda for Sustainable Development recognizes that climate change, whose adverse impacts undermine the ability of all countries to achieve sustainable development, constitutes one of the greatest challenges of our time.

Human activities and demographic changes continue to affect all aspects of our environment

As reported in the Fifth Assessment Report of the Intergovernmental Panel on Climate Change (IPCC), total greenhouse gas (GHG) emissions from human activity have continued to increase since 1970. Average annual growth of global emissions during the period 2000–2010 was 2.2 per cent, significantly higher than the 1.3 per cent annual growth rate observed in the period from 1970 to 2000 (IPCC, 2014b, p. 6). As continued GHG emissions will cause further warming and changes in all components of the climate system, limiting climate change will therefore require substantial and sustained reductions of those emissions.

Yet, it is not just the atmosphere that is being affected by human activity. The rise in the quantity of marine and land plastics waste is closely connected with economic growth, particularly with the rise in the use of packaging for global trade and marketing of products. Annual global plastic production increased from 1.7 million to 322 million tons between 1950 and 2015. The same period witnessed an accumulation of 6.8 billion tons of mostly non-biodegradable plastic waste. Nearly 8 per cent of this waste has been deposited in landfills or water bodies, including seas and oceans (see box I.1). Plastic waste not only continues to impact many wildlife species but also hosts microbial communities, and by transporting non-native species provides new habitats for microbes. Land-based plastic waste also creates human health problems.

Box I.1

Plastics and ocean pollution: sustainable polymers[a], bioplastics and bio-benign materials

Plastic is the major component of marine debris. Most plastic does not biodegrade, but only fragments into smaller and smaller particles. The growth of the plastics industry has been driven by the growth of the packaging industry and increasing globalization. As goods, particularly food, are transported globally, the packaging industry has embraced plastic, especially, as a useful material. Through its durability, plastic protects goods and food, and its lightness has enabled a reduction in transportation costs and carbon emissions.

Because of the popularity and durability of plastic products and, most important, the lack of proper waste management systems, microplastics (defined as being smaller than 5 millimetres (mm) in diameter) are now found in the environment—floating in lakes, rivers and oceans, and along coastlines all over the world. Impacts from plastic marine debris are wide ranging. Not only have a multitude of different species of wildlife been affected but the debris also represents a physical hazard to shipping, boating, fishing and the industrial system. Coastal tourism as well is adversely affected by marine debris and other litter. Plastic can host diverse microbial communities, referred to as plastispheres (Zettler, Mincer and Amaral-Zettler, 2013); transport non-native species; and provide a habitat for microbes that might not otherwise thrive.

New material development and product design would help eliminate the adverse impact of plastic in oceans. In 2014, however, sustainable polymers—defined as plastic materials that address "the needs of consumers without damaging our environment, health and economy" (University of Minnesota, Center for Sustainable Polymers, 2018)—made up less than 10 per cent of the total plastics market (Peplow, 2016). Further, the global production capacity of bioplastics—plastics derived from renewable biomass sources, such as vegetable fats and oils, corn starch and microbiota—was only at 1.3 per cent of total polymer production capacity. However, bioplastics and biodegradable plastics are expected to maintain high growth rates in the near future, as bioplastics are being used increasingly in several industries, such as consumer goods, automotive and transport, and construction and building.[b]

Yet, despite these positive trends, production capacities will remain marginal relative to total plastic production. The pace at which new alternative materials are replacing the current types of toxic plastics is too slow to decelerate annual flows of plastic debris into the ocean. Thus, there is a considerable need for complementary investment aimed at changing the way in which plastic products are produced, consumed and disposed of. At the same time, so-called bio-benign materials—that is, non-toxic materials that are biodegradable and recyclable—need to be promoted in the context of both production and consumption.

Source: Jambeck (2017).

a Polymers are the constituents of the plastics that we encounter in our daily lives. They are commonly used in packaging and durable goods, such as toys, cars, construction materials and furniture, as well as in textiles.

b See "Demand for bio-based plastic continues to rise despite falling oil costs", Bio-Based World News, 6 December 2016. Available at www.biobasedworldnews.com/bio-based-plastics-market-to-grow.

Human activities continue to drive an increasing demand for natural resources, as manifested in technology choices and consumption and production patterns. This trend is exacerbated by a growing and ageing population. It is expected that the world population, currently at 7.6 billion, will have reached 9.8 billion by 2050. During the same period, populations of 26 African countries are projected to double. According to the United Nations Environment Programme International Resource Panel (2017, p. 8), material resource use, which was expected to reach 89 billion tons in 2017, may more than double between 2015 and 2050. At the same time, the world's population is ageing, with the number of persons aged 80 or over expected to triple by 2050, to 425 million (United Nations, Department of Economic and Social Affairs, Population Division, 2017). Countries with ageing populations will require economic growth and higher productivity from younger workers to support the growing number of older people as they exit the workforce. For those countries, achieving this goal without raising the need for natural resources will remain an uphill battle.

Figure I.1 illustrates the link between socioeconomic progress and environmental sustainability. Several countries have made significant progress in achieving many socioeconomic goals (e.g., sanitation, access to energy, educational attainment, poverty reduction, economic prosperity and higher standards of living). At the same time, a price has been paid for such progress, namely, the crossing of biophysical boundaries related, inter alia, to CO_2 emissions, the phosphorus and nitrogen footprints, water use, the ecological and material footprints and forests.

Progress in social and economic goals in the past generally came at the expense of environmental sustainability

Figure I.1

Social thresholds achieved versus biophysical boundaries transgressed for different countries, results weighted by each country's population

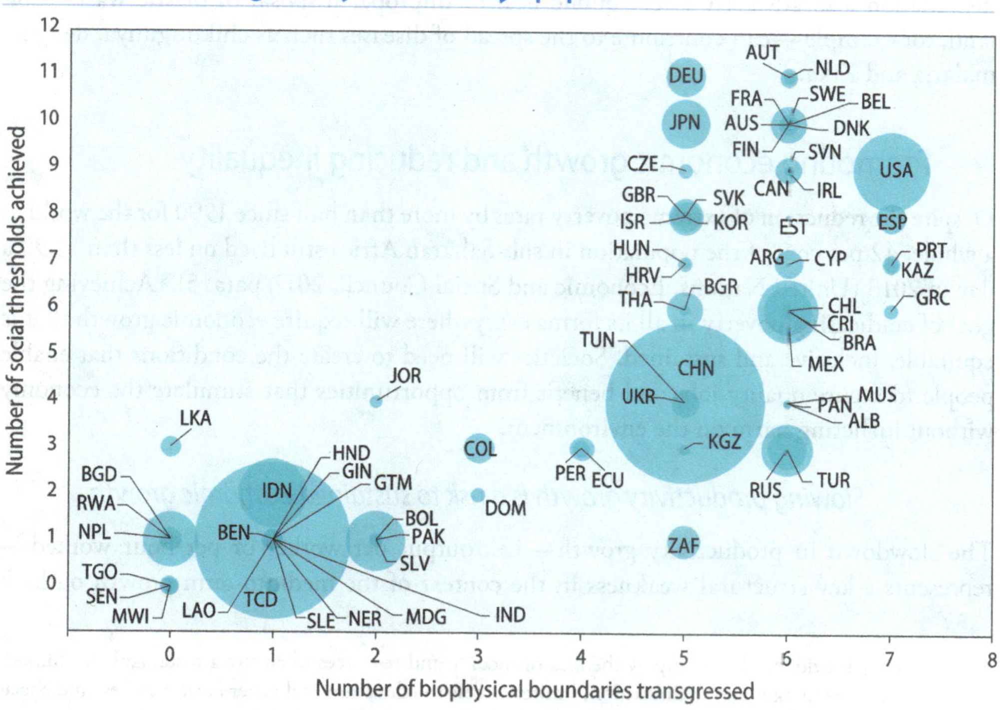

Source: UN/DESA, based on O'Neill and others (2018), figure 2.

Note: The figure includes only the 70 countries for which there are complete data on all indicators.

Achieving good health and well-being

Ensuring healthy lives and promoting well-being for all constitute a cardinal objective of the 2030 Agenda. The major health challenges facing the world, according to the World Health Organization (WHO), include reducing maternal and child mortality, improving nutrition, and combating communicable diseases such as hepatitis, HIV/AIDS, malaria, tuberculosis and neglected tropical diseases. Non-communicable diseases, mental health problems, road traffic-related injuries and environmental health are also areas of priority (WHO, 2017).

There has been significant progress in combating communicable diseases and reducing child and maternal mortality...

Despite the significant achievements in combating communicable diseases and child and maternal mortality, further efforts are needed to eradicate a wide range of diseases and to address many persistent and emerging health issues. The treatment of communicable diseases which disproportionately affect the developing world will be made more difficult by growing antibiotic resistance. Non-communicable and neurological diseases are projected to increase sharply as the population ages and as more people maintain unhealthy lifestyles. In ageing societies, infectious and parasitic diseases will continue to give way to non-communicable diseases such as heart disease, cancer and diabetes as the members of the population change their lifestyle and diet, and grow older (National Institute on Aging, National Institutes of Health and World Health Organization, 2011).

...but millions remain vulnerable to persistent health risks due to poor water and sanitation facilities

Millions of people remain vulnerable to persistent health and sanitation risks. In 2015, only 66 per cent of the population in low-income countries had access to an improved water source. In those countries, only 28 per cent use improved sanitation facilities and 12 per cent of the global population still practise open defecation. The lack of basic water and sanitation facilities has serious health risk implications, resulting in the spread of disease and affecting the physical and intellectual growth of children. The future of our planet and the future of people are inextricably interlinked. Climate change and environmental degradation also adversely affect public health. Improper disposal of plastic waste—on land, for example—can contribute to the spread of diseases such as chikungunya, dengue, malaria and Zika.

Promoting economic growth and reducing inequality

Despite the reduction of extreme poverty rates by more than half since 1990 for the world as a whole, 42 per cent of the population in sub-Saharan Africa still lived on less than $1.90 a day in 2013 (United Nations, Economic and Social Council, 2017, para. 5).[3] Achieving the goal of eradicating poverty in all its forms everywhere will require economic growth that is equitable, inclusive and sustained. Societies will need to create the conditions that enable people to secure quality jobs and benefit from opportunities that stimulate the economy without inflicting harm on the environment.

Slowing productivity growth is a risk to sustained economic growth

The slowdown in productivity growth—i.e., output per worker or per hour worked—represents a key structural weakness in the context of the medium-term growth outlook

3 Poverty is evidenced not only by the lack of income and resources to ensure a sustainable livelihood, but also by hunger and malnutrition, limited access to education and other basic services, and social discrimination and exclusion, as well as the lack of participation in decision-making.

(United Nations, Department of Economic and Social Affairs, Economic Analysis and Policy Division, 2017). In developed countries, labour productivity growth has been on a downward trend since the 1960s, briefly interrupted by the positive contributions often associated with the digital and information technology revolution. In the aftermath of the global financial crisis of 2008–2009, productivity growth declined further, and gross domestic product (GDP) per person employed has barely grown in recent years. This persistent weakness in productivity growth, as illustrated in figure I.2, has continued despite rapid advances in technology and has given rise to what is often referred to as the "productivity paradox" (LaFleur and Pitterle, 2017; Bruckner, LaFleur and Pitterle, 2017).

Figure I.2

Trends in labour productivity growth, Germany, Japan, United Kingdom of Great Britain and Northern Ireland and United States of America, 1955–2018

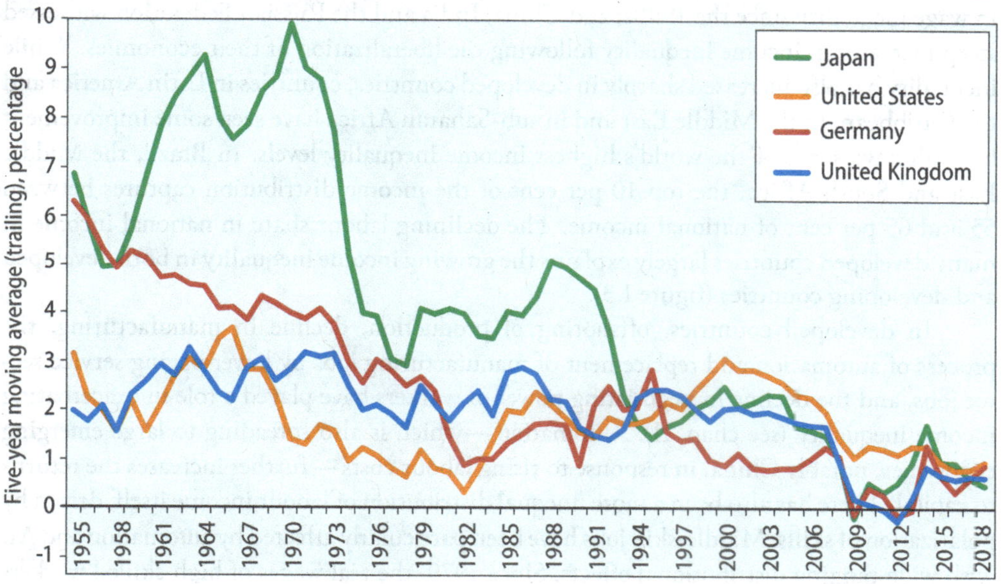

Sources: Conference Board Total Economy Database (2018); Feenstra, Inklaar and Timmer (2015), Penn World Table 9.0.

Achieving prosperity for all—and leaving no one behind—will require bridging the technology divide between and within countries

In developing countries, productivity trends are mixed. Productivity growth in East and South Asia has been on an upward trend since 1975 as countries such as China and the Republic of Korea transition from agrarian to industry-based economies. Rapid growth in productivity and income levels in some developing countries, notably China and India, has been made possible by greater manufacturing growth and trade enabled by technological progress. In contrast, productivity growth in the other developing regions has been relatively subdued. In Latin America, average labour productivity growth slowed between the 1960s and the mid-1980s and has remained weak since then. A similar trend is observed in Western Asia and sub-Saharan Africa. It will be difficult, if not impossible, to achieve prosperity for all—and leave no one behind—without boosting productivity growth, particularly in low-income, developing countries. Bridging the technology divide, as discussed in chapter III, will remain key to stimulating productivity growth in those countries.

Trends in income inequality[4]

The differences in productivity growth noted above are reflected in the distribution of income within and across countries. As noted by Milanović (2016), global inequality[5] levels remain very high but underwent some stabilization in the 1980s and began a sharp decline in 2003. This trend is attributed largely to rapid growth in productivity and income levels in China and India as these economies, supported by technological progress and trade, integrated with the global economy. As a result, the poorest half of the global population experienced strong income growth. At the same time, the top 0.1 per cent saw huge growth in their income. Those caught between the bottom 50 per cent and the top 1 per cent have seen no gain since 1980 (Alvaredo and others, 2018).

While global inequality may have declined to some extent, within-country inequality has increased in many regions of the world. Many East Asian countries, including Indonesia, the Philippines, the Republic of Korea and Viet Nam, have seen a relatively steady increase in wage inequality since the 1990s; and China, India and the Russian Federation witnessed steep increases in income inequality following the liberalization of their economies. While inequality has also increased sharply in developed countries, countries in Latin America and the Caribbean, in the Middle East and in sub-Saharan Africa have seen some improvement but still have some of the world's highest income inequality levels. In Brazil, the Middle East and South Africa, the top 10 per cent of the income distribution captures between 55 and 65 per cent of national income. The declining labour share in national income in many developed countries largely explains the growing income inequality in both developed and developing countries (figure I.3).

Globalization and automation have contributed to widening income inequality in some countries

In developed countries, offshoring of production, decline in manufacturing, the process of automation and replacement of manufacturing jobs by lower-paying service sector jobs, and the decline in negotiating power of workers have played a role in exacerbating income inequality (see chap. II). Automation—which is also spreading to large emerging economies, notably China, in response to rising labour costs—further increases the returns to capital. There has also been a more unequal distribution of labour income itself, driven by polarization of skills. Middle-skill jobs have been particularly affected by automation and AI, with wide-ranging distributional effects. Since 1970, the real wages of high-skilled workers have risen faster than those of both medium- and low-skilled workers.[6] There is therefore a need to ensure that further advances in technological progress do not worsen income inequality, especially if the overarching goal of leaving no one behind is to be achieved.

4 The focus of the present section is on productivity and economic growth. Therefore, the discussion is focused on income-related forms of inequality, particularly on how they are affected by wages. The *Survey* recognizes that inequality is a broader concept, as reflected in the SDGs, which encompass other important types of inequality, such as in economic opportunities, access to education, health and other basic services; and in political representation. However, those types are not examined here. See the 2016 edition of the *Survey* (United Nations, 2016b) for a discussion of the importance of addressing structural inequalities, including chap. II which considers how technology can worsen existing inequalities. Additional discussions on inequalities can be found in the *Report on the World Social Situation 2013* (United Nations, 2013) and the *Report on the World Social Situation 2016* (United Nations, 2016a).

5 The term "global inequality" refers to the inequalities of the income of individuals regardless of country. It contrasts with inequalities in per capita income of countries and with population-weighted international inequality (i.e., between-country inequality).

6 See chap. II and Bruckner, LaFleur and Pitterle (2017) for a fuller discussion of how automation impacts labour and income inequality.

Figure I.3
Trends of labour share of income, 1970–2015

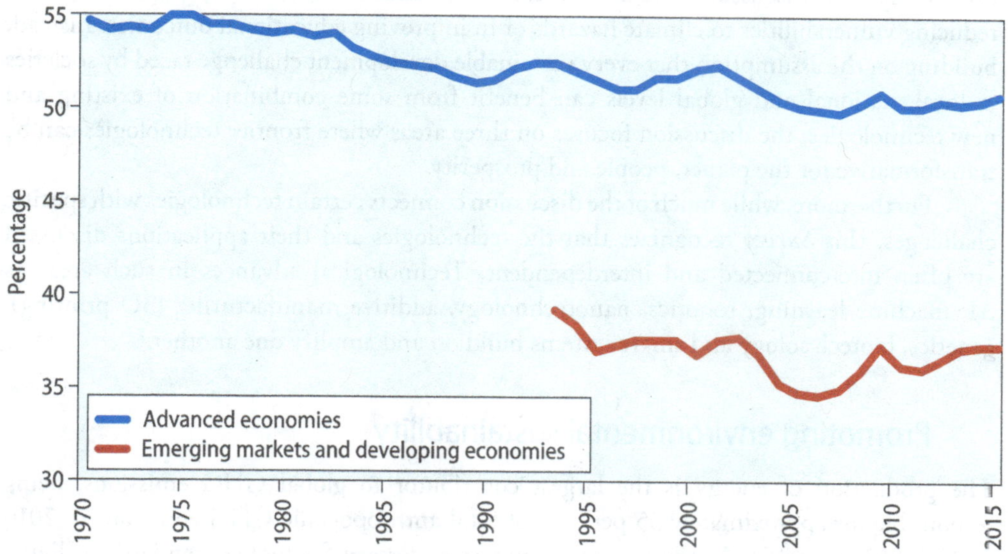

Source: IMF (2017), figure 3.1.

Potential of frontier technologies to help foster sustainable development

Technology invites us to imagine a future without poverty and hunger, with fewer diseases and higher life expectancy, greater equality of economic opportunities and universal financial inclusion. Ushering in such a future, however, will require more intensive and extensive use of natural resources, unless there are significant improvements in and use of relevant technologies. By one estimate, achieving many development goals would require a level of resource use that is 2–6 times the sustainable level (O'Neill and others, 2018).

Frontier technologies have a central role in protecting our planet and people and promoting prosperity

The present section uses challenges discussed in the previous section as the basis for illustrating the central role that frontier technologies could play in protecting our planet and people and in promoting prosperity. Specifically:

- For our planet, new advances in the extraction, conversion and storage of electricity may hold the key to making renewable energy sources competitive with fossil fuels and improving environmental sustainability.
- For improving people's lives, new technologies will continue to improve health outcomes, leading to better, cheaper and newer services, medicines and goods. Those technologies are making new methods of diagnosis and new forms of treatment possible and improving the administration and management of health care with better data and analysis.
- For prosperity, new technologies mean new products and services for a greater number of people. For example; AI is being used in a widening range of fields, from image recognition to financial analysis and scientific research; advances in automation are enabling new forms of manufacturing and self-driving drones and vehicles; and financial innovation in the form of digital payments is bringing financial services to millions.

This section is not intended to provide an exhaustive treatment of the ways in which each frontier technology can impact sustainable development in all its aspects and dimensions. The discussion does not, for example, examine the role of new technologies in reducing vulnerabilities to climate hazards or in improving educational outcomes. Instead, building on the assumption that every sustainable development challenge faced by societies at local, national and global levels can benefit from some combination of existing and new technologies, the discussion focuses on three areas where frontier technologies can be transformative for the planet, people and prosperity.

Furthermore, while much of the discussion connects certain technologies with specific challenges, this *Survey* recognizes that the technologies and their applications discussed are often interconnected and interdependent. Technological advances in such areas as AI, machine learning, robotics, nanotechnology, additive manufacturing (3D printing), genetics, biotechnology and smart systems build on and amplify one another.[7]

Promoting environmental sustainability

The production of energy is the largest contributor to global GHG emissions, being responsible for approximately 35 per cent of total anthropogenic GHG emissions in 2010 (IPCC, 2014a, p. 46). As the economic growth necessary for higher standards of living requires more energy, and hence more carbon emissions, limiting climate change requires a fundamental transformation of the energy supply system entailing a shift towards low GHG emissions.

Cleaner renewable energy technologies have opened the door to a sustainable future

The challenge posed by energy scarcity and climate change has spurred the development of new, cleaner energy technologies and opened the door to a possibly sustainable future. The threat of climate change and the demand for new energy sources have changed the economics of existing energy systems and spurred a new wave of green technology-based manufacturing and trade.

Rapid technological advancements are driving this transformation by improving low-emission energy technologies such as renewable energy and nuclear power, and carbon dioxide capture and storage. Only a small proportion of the potential for renewable energy has been exploited with current technology, but this proportion has been increasing as the performance of many renewable energy technologies advances and their costs decrease. (Bruckner and others, 2014; World Energy Council, 2016). These developments are expanding the access of renewable energy technologies in poorer and remote locations, making off-grid installations scalable and economically feasible.

The pursuit of renewable energy generation goes hand in hand with the need for advances in energy storage to prevent energy from being wasted. The supply of renewable energy from wind, solar and other sources fluctuates depending, e.g., on the time of the day and weather conditions. The ability to secure the supply of a steady, large quantity of electricity generated from renewable sources, and to transmit it as needed to meet demand, calls for advances in storage technology.

7 The appendix to this chap. provides a more detailed discussion of how specific technologies work. While the discussions here and in the appendix do not encompass every technology that may be categorized as a frontier technology, they do illustrate the potential of frontier technologies to help resolve some of humanity's biggest challenges.

Improvements in the energy density and recharging speed of batteries are making electric vehicles (EVs) viable alternatives to traditional vehicles that use internal combustion engines. As a result, a wider variety of EVs have become available at more affordable prices. The stock of EVs is forecast to reach between 40 million and 70 million by 2025 and new types of batteries are being developed which will continue to tip the scale in favour of EVs. For example, Toyota has plans to develop all-solid-state batteries by 2022. The aim of Samsung Electronics, a major producer of auto batteries, in working on lithium-air cells is to double the capacity of today's mainstream lithium-ion batteries.

Since EVs require electricity, the key to their reduction of energy consumption and emissions over the entire lifetime of the vehicle (i.e., from the generation of electricity to the use of electricity by EVs while running) lies with the energy sources that charge the EV batteries. Replacing internal combustion engine-based vehicles with EVs will not be of much help if the electricity used by those EVs is produced from fossil fuels, emitting high volumes of GHG emissions.[8] EVs have the potential not only to reduce lifetime emissions but to transform the entire auto manufacturing industry, as new companies and new production chains are created around frontier technologies.[9]

Improving health outcomes[10]

Humanity has reason to be tremendously hopeful regarding the ability of emerging technologies to help save lives, improve health outcomes and extend life expectancy. The present section focuses on health outcomes, highlighting digital technologies, genetic technologies, and drug and vaccine delivery—frontier technologies that are exerting a transformative impact on health care. These technologies will prove especially important for developing countries, helping them to expand the reach of existing and new health services to those most at risk. Another set of frontier technologies (a few of which are examined in chapter III) can be equally impactful with regard to educational outcomes.

Digital technologies: artificial intelligence, communications and robotics

Artificial intelligence presents an immense potential for improving health care

Artificial intelligence (AI)—encompassing machine learning and deployment of algorithms for data processing and pattern recognition—possesses an immense potential for improving health care. AI can help to achieve the goal of turning personalized medicine and outcome-based public health into a clinical reality (*The Lancet*, 2017). Together with other technologies, AI will make it possible to better calculate and manage risk and to better evaluate policies and intervene with those that are appropriate. Innovative means of detecting public-health risks employing cell phone and other consumer data and machine learning are already being used. They can, for example, help WHO identify and respond

8 EVs embody technologies that are very different from those employed in vehicles with internal combustion engines. The main components of electric vehicles are motors, batteries, power inverters and the controlling software. The parts are connected via electrical wires within a structure that is much simpler than the complex mechanical system required by internal combustion engine-based vehicles.

9 See chap. II and Kawamura (2017) for further discussions on the importance of electrical vehicles for economies and societies.

10 This section is based on a presentation by Henry Wei (Google's Medical Director for Benefits) made at the Expert Group Meeting on Emerging Technologies and Sustainable Development, held in New York on 14 and 15 December 2017, at which the background, objectives and outline of the 2018 *Survey* were discussed.

to health emergencies by facilitating better prediction, scenario modelling, resilience-hardening, and response planning.

Algorithms can improve medical diagnoses and extend the capabilities of medical professionals

Image analysis algorithms can help identify skin malignancies, breast cancer, pneumonia and other diseases. AI-enabled continuous speech recognition can improve medical record-keeping, a time-consuming task which in the United States of America currently consumes over half of a physician's time. Better medical records can be used to assist AI systems in predicting readmission rates, infection risks and other treatment complications. This tool complements human judgment and thus helps minimize preventable errors.

Improvements in digital technologies and human interfaces combined with machine learning can extend the capabilities of community health workers, thereby helping to mitigate the shortage of expert workers. For example, those workers can be given live instructions through augmented reality techniques on how to administer wound care under the remote supervision of a more experienced medical professional. Conversational AI systems can alleviate the shortage of psychiatrists and provide limited help to those sufferers from depression or anxiety who cannot access trained professionals (ibid.).

Advances in communications technology can further improve knowledge dissemination among health providers and patients and improve behavioural interventions for the prevention of diseases, including chronic conditions such as obesity, cardiovascular disease and cancer. For example, SMS text-based health education and treatment compliance, medical appointment reminders, and health surveys and surveillance can improve access to and effectiveness of health-care services, particularly for those in remote areas (Schwebel and Larimer, 2018). Further, social networks and mobile connectivity, coupled with data analytics, can help to strengthen public-health campaigns designed to increase awareness, influence cultural norms and improve sanitation practices.

Frontier technologies can facilitate improvements in the hardware needed for health care. New manufacturing methods like 3D printing can lower the cost of precision medicine and medical devices. Technologies available in widely used consumer devices, such as modern smartphones, can serve as low-cost substitutes for expensive medical devices, such as portable ultrasounds. Smartphones, tablets, cameras and audio sensors, among other devices, are becoming consistently more powerful and cheaper. Robots are already performing certain routine but highly technical surgical procedures, which is reducing risks of human error and infection. Autonomous surgical robots are already able to perform better than human surgeons in stitching together segments of the intestine. Assistive robots, which include exoskeletons, permit those who are paralyzed or disabled to walk.

Genetic technologies

New genetic technologies can address some of our greatest medical challenges

The development of powerful gene-editing tools and a growing capability with respect to altering biological systems, including those of humans, unveil huge possibilities for meeting some of the greatest medical challenges, including how to produce new treatments for many of the diseases which humankind has been combating for decades.

New or "next-generation" DNA sequencing technologies have drastically reduced the cost and time needed for sequencing DNA. Between 2007 and 2017, the cost of sequencing a genome declined from nearly \$9 million to just \$1,100 per genome.[11] The drastic reduction in cost has led to a "genomics race" between countries looking to establish themselves as

11 See https://www.genome.gov/sequencingcostsdata/.

leaders in the field of precision medicine. For example, following the announcement of a precision medicine initiative in the United States, China followed suit in 2016 with its own 15-year initiative.

This is an area, however, where the technological divide may lead to a growing inequality in terms of access to precision medicine. Despite the decline in costs, next-generation sequencing remains quite costly for developing countries. As next-generation sequencing facilities require capital investments in the range of $100,000–$700,000 in developed countries and even greater investments in the developing world, such facilities are rare worldwide (see figure I.4). Limited availability of skilled personnel and training and limited access to the scientific community and data are other factors that prevent many countries from reaping the benefits of next-generation sequencing technologies.

High costs limit the access to genetic technologies and may lead to a growing inequality in health outcomes

Participants in the Human Heredity and Health in Africa (H3Africa) initiative, which represents an attempt to overcome the constraints on the development of knowledge and technical capacity in the continent, work to establish research infrastructure and expertise, to foster pan-continental collaboration, to nurture research and, in general, to support African scientists. The initiative directs funding from the National Institutes of Health and the Wellcome Trust to research sites across Africa, where genomics, environmental determinants of common diseases, disease susceptibility and drug responses in African populations are being studied.

Figure I.4
Genome sequencing centres per country

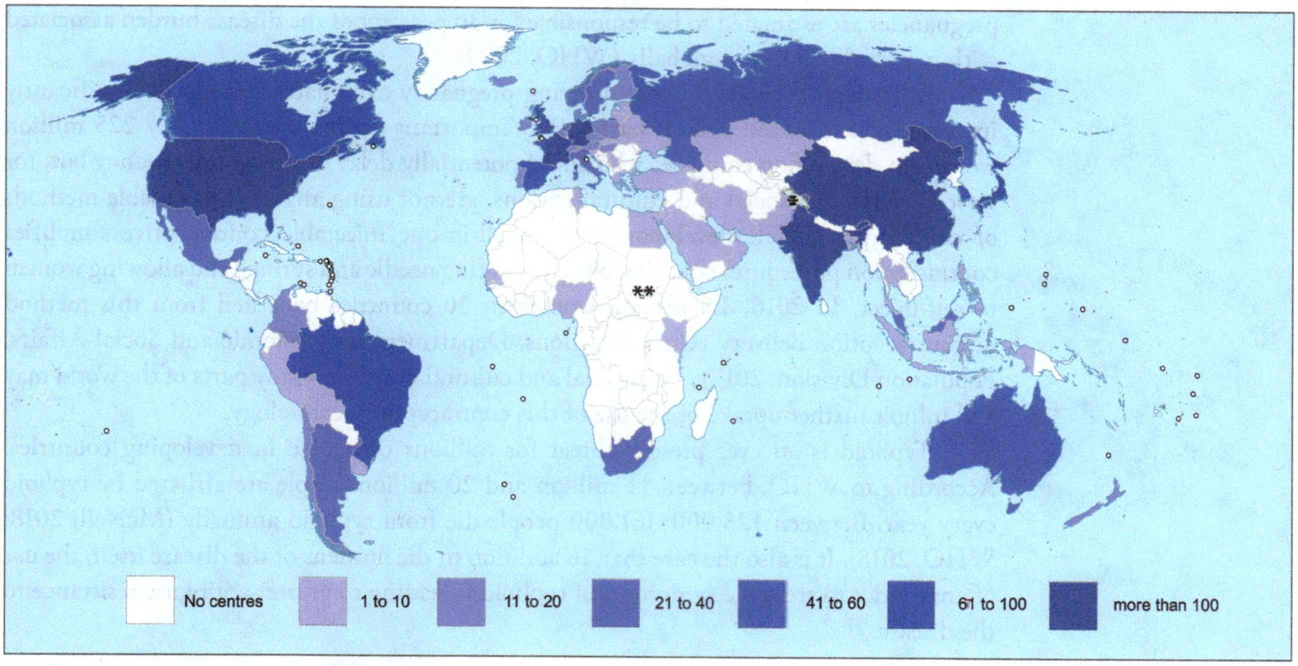

Source: Helmy, Awad and Mosa (2016), figure 1.C.

Note: The boundaries and names shown and the designations used on this map do not imply official endorsement or acceptance by the United Nations.

* Dotted line represents approximately the Line of Control in Jammu and Kashmir agreed upon by India and Pakistan. The final status of Jammu and Kashmir has not yet been agreed upon by the parties.

** Final boundary between the Republic of Sudan and the Republic of South Sudan has not yet been determined.

As the cost of DNA sequencing declines, the advances in gene editing and genetic therapies are accelerating. New genetic treatments for, e.g., HIV, beta thalassemia and cancer, are showing promise. Immunotherapy is another area of technology that shows promise—immense promise—for health outcomes, particularly in combating cancer. Still another promising technology—chimeric antigen receptor (CAR) T cell therapy—entails extracting a patient's own T cells and exposing them to a disarmed virus. Through exposure they are engineered to locate and attach themselves to tumor cells and subsequently destroy them.[12] The cost of the treatment, about $475,000 per year with current methods, remains prohibitive, however.

New technologies for drug delivery and vaccines

Technologies are improving access and delivery to medicines, improving the wellbeing of the most vulnerable

Drug delivery is another area where the new technologies can positively impact health outcomes. The polypill, which combines multiple drug products in a single pill, has been used successfully to decrease the incidence of cardiovascular events. Similar advances were seen in the treatment of HIV patients with the "quad pill", which has simplified treatment regimens and improved adherence. New advances in the manufacturing of pills will involve 3D printing, with medication and dosage appropriate for each individual patient.

Universal access to sexual and reproductive health-care services is a basic right, as measured by SDG indicator 3.7.1, and is vital to improving lives and livelihoods. Technological advances in drug delivery will significantly improve family planning and contraception and overall health. For example, an estimated 20 per cent of all obstetric deaths could be prevented each year if all women desiring no more children used modern contraceptives (Collumbien, Gerressu and Cleland, 2004). Moreover, unplanned pregnancies are estimated to be responsible for 30 per cent of the disease burden associated with maternal conditions globally (WHO, 2009).

It has also been found that delaying pregnancy can enable women to significantly increase their incomes. This is particularly important for the approximately 225 million women in developing countries who could potentially delay or prevent pregnancy but, for various economic, social and cultural reasons, are not using any of the available methods of contraception. The development of an all-in-one injectable contraceptive simplifies contraception procedures considerably, eliminating needle and syringe and allowing women to self-inject. In 2016, 1.5 million women in 20 countries benefited from this method of contraception delivery (United Nations, Department of Economic and Social Affairs, Population Division, 2017);[13] but social and cultural norms in many parts of the world may still inhibit further uptake of the use of this contraception technology.

Typhoid is an ever present threat for millions of people in developing countries. According to WHO, between 11 million and 20 million people are afflicted by typhoid every year. Between 128,000–161,000 people die from typhoid annually (McNeil, 2018; WHO, 2018). It is also the case that, in addition to the burdens of the disease itself, the use of antibiotics to treat the symptoms of typhoid is leading to greater antibiotic resistance to the disease.

12 T cells are white blood cells that are important for adaptive immunity. Their unique cell surface receptors enable T cells to sense and respond to diverse forms of infection.

13 Technologicaly innovative forms of contraception may be cheaper than traditional methods, but uptake could still be hindered by the same social and cultural constraints that currently prevent many women from accessing contraception and other forms of family planning.

The control of typhoid through improved water quality and adequate sanitation has been highly effective in Northern America and Europe over the past century. In developing countries, however, the infrastructure required to break the transmission cycle of typhoid is often inadequate. While immunization programmes remain an important component of disease control, current vaccines are unfortunately not effective and cannot be administered to children under age 5.[14] However, a new type of vaccine, has recently been approved by WHO for global use. Referred to as the typhoid conjugate vaccine (TCV), it will transform typhoid vaccine delivery for children under age 5.

Achieving equitable economic growth

Frontier technologies have opened up new opportunities for economic growth, jobs and wealth creation. They continue to expand productive capacities and productivity of firms and individuals based on utilization of better machines and information, enabling new business models and creating entirely new industries. In the last 30 years, technology has been a contributing factor to the halving of the rate of global poverty since 2000; to the reduction of hunger, malnutrition and child mortality; to the combating of infectious diseases; and to progress in achieving most of the other Millennium Development Goals (United Nations, Economic and Social Council, 2017).

Developing countries have the most to gain, and also the most to lose, from the new opportunities offered by frontier technologies

Frontier technologies are rapidly changing industries and sectors, creating opportunities for competition in new markets with new production capacities (see chap. IV for a comprehensive discussion on the importance of technology for structural economic change). Countries leading the innovation of many frontier technologies will enjoy a competitive edge over those that are lagging in innovation and technology development. Closing the technological divide will remain critical for achievement by many developing countries of higher, sustained economic growth and for their reduction of economic inequalities.

On the other hand, those developing countries enjoy certain advantages during periods of rapid technological change, since they are not saddled with what are known as legacy investments in technologies, i.e., investments in technologies whose time has now passed (Gerschenkron, 1962). For example, countries may not necessarily need a twentieth century industrial base to build a twenty-first century bio-, nano- or information economy. It may be easier for a firm without large capital investments to undertake manufacturing with a 3D printer, thereby skipping all the steps needed to make the same part in the traditional way. Innovations in algorithms and data analysis, new manufacturing methods and new digital financial systems will generate new sources of growth, create new jobs and open up new opportunities for entrepreneurship.

Machine learning and artificial intelligence have wide applications

Artificial Intelligence could fundamentally reshape our economy and society

The growing ability of AI systems to solve complex problems autonomously could fundamentally reshape our economy and society, for example, through development of new forms of transportation or a revolution in health care. Whereas the steam engine was deployed in tasks that required muscle power, AI is being applied to tasks that require brainpower (Furman and others, 2016, p. 8). The World Economic Forum characterized AI as the cornerstone of the so-called fourth industrial revolution (4IR), and its growing

14 The oral typhoid vaccine, which is effective for children, is formulated in capsules that cannot be swallowed by children.

ability to mimic aspects of human intelligence as a historic development in the automation process (Schwab, 2016).

Machine learning has enabled AI to defeat the best human in a number of contests (chess and Go being the most known examples) and has proved useful in industrial automation, in better communication around the world, and in improving our ability to interpret medical data. AI capabilities have also greatly enhanced computer vision, speech recognition, motor control (of robots), language translation, and decision-making processes in science, finance and other fields.

The layers of abstraction underpinning AI—building upon deep (machine) learning of trends, patterns and scenarios—can turn it into a black box. Efforts to understand the reasoning process governing an AI system, in particular how and why it reached a particular decision point, often meet with obstacles. In health care, for example, those obstacles can make integration of AI systems into routine clinical care a difficult task. The broader use of data and algorithms also raises ethical concerns and legal issues related to data privacy, transparency and the need for an institutional framework of accountability (see chap. II).

3D printing (additive manufacturing) and digital fabrication

Advances in technologies such as additive manufacturing (the industrial version of 3D printing), which are drastically altering the way physical goods are produced, promise to transform the economics of manufacturing.[15] 3D printing offers many benefits over traditional forms of manufacturing, including the ability to generate faster design prototypes; produce complex, customized items; and change a design quickly (*The Economist*, 2017). In addition to additive manufacturing, innovations in fabrication, such as laser cutters, 3D milling machines and programmable electronics, together with advances in computer-aided design and manufacturing software, are bringing the benefits of the digital revolution to factories. Neither additive manufacturing nor digital fabrication requires economies of scale to make production profitable. With respect to metal parts, for example, 3D printing and laser cutting allow for a level of complexity in shapes which may be nearly impossible to achieve with traditional methods, and reduce the need for welding, which facilitate customized and niche applications. Additionally, 3D printing facilitates just-in-time inventories and reduces waste in manufacturing.

Currently, 3D printing is used extensively to build prototypes, but technological development continues to improve the manufacturing machinery and software and expand the range of materials that can be produced with additive manufacturing, including composites and functionally graded materials (OECD, 2016). As this technology continues to mature, it will become exploitable for new industrial, consumer and medical uses, especially when low-volume, complex and customized solutions are needed. In health care, 3D printing is used to manufacture prostheses and implants and to prototype robotic exoskeletons. Clearly, digital fabrication, offers an opportunity for developing and least developed countries (LDCs) to bridge the technological divide, kick-start manufacturing and build a new industrial base.

The environmental impact of 3D printing and digital fabrication is not yet clear. The process can decrease waste and emissions by reducing the number of steps and the energy

15 Construction of an object through the process of 3D printing entails addition of material one layer at a time based on a digital set of instructions. By contrast, construction of an object through the process of traditional (subtractive) manufacturing entails either moulding or removing material by cutting, drilling or milling.

needed to produce, transport, assemble and distribute products. Often, raw materials used in additive manufacturing are recyclable or biodegradable, as is the case for some commonly used plastics. On the other hand, certain 3D printing processes use ultrafine particles which may pose health risks. Consequently, the energy and carbon footprints of 3D manufacturing need to be studied more thoroughly (ibid.).

Digital finance technologies

Many households and small businesses, often operating in the informal sector, have no access to formal financial services and therefore rely on cash. The lack of physical availability of financial service centres means that many of those affected must travel long distances to access financial services. Globally, about 2 billion people lack a formal financial services account, of whom 1.4 billion reside in low- or lower middle income countries (Jensen, 2018).

Mobile technologies and innovations in digital finance have made financial services accessible to millions in developing countries

Mobile technologies have opened the door for a growing number of people in developing countries to access digital financial services. According to estimates by McKinsey Global Institute (2016), 80 per cent of adults in emerging markets have a subscription with mobile phone providers. This enables mobile operators to facilitate financial transactions for mobile customers for as little as $10 per year, 90 per cent lower than the fee charged by conventional banks. In 2015, there were 271 mobile money services in 93 countries, managing an average of 33 million transactions per day, including payments, deposits, microloans, insurance and pension-related transactions—and even investments in treasury or government infrastructure bonds (Suri and Jack, 2016). People are using digital financial systems to receive wages, pay school fees and utilities bills, buy groceries, save for emergencies, and send remittances. Digital finance has also helped spur new models of service delivery and payment, such as Pay-As-You-Go solutions in the utilities sector, improving the feasibility of infrastructure and other investments.[16] In lending, digital finance is helping to facilitate access of households and small and medium-sized enterprises to credit and insurance products. With regard to the impact of services, in the recent study by Suri and Jack (2016), cited directly above, it was estimated that access to the mobile money system in Kenya increased per capita consumption levels and lifted 194,000 households (2 per cent) out of poverty, a result of more efficient allocation of labour, savings and risk.

Digital finance can help to drastically lower fees for remittances, and directly help meet target 10.c under the SDGs, which aims at the reduction of the costs of sending remittances. In 2016, the global average cost of sending remittances was 7.3 per cent, with rates in sub-Saharan Africa averaging 10 per cent (Jensen, 2018).

Cryptocurrencies represent a new frontier in digital finance and their popularity is growing.[17] The decentralized networks for cryptocurrencies, bitcoin being a well-known example, can keep track of digital transactions. They enable value to be exchanged and can give rise to new business models which would otherwise require significant regulatory and institutional commitments. For example, a value token called climatecoin is being considered as a basis for creating a global market for carbon emissions, allowing peer-to-peer exchange of carbon credits and a direct connection with the Internet of Things. It

16 Because this model is metered, it can be utilized in the utilities sector. Under such an arrangement, consumer payments are a function of careful measurement and monitoring.

17 See the appendix to this chapter for a description of how cryptocurrencies work and their relationship to the traditional financial system.

would then be possible for devices to calculate their own carbon emissions and purchase carbon credits to offset those emissions.

There are also proposals for using blockchain technology as a distributed ledger of real-world information on property registration, personal identity, and provenance of food and medicines, among many other types of data. The United Nations and the World Identity Network are exploring ways to register the identities of children on a blockchain as a means of combating child trafficking.

The path of technology development towards broad-based efficiency, equity and ethics

There is no guarantee that new technologies will serve the most pressing needs of humanity

While technological progress is fundamental for achieving the SDGs, there is no guarantee that this progress will be aligned with the most pressing needs of humanity: eradicating poverty and hunger, reducing inequality, generating shared prosperity and building resilience against climate change. The *Survey* recognizes the need for balancing efficiency and cost effectiveness against equity considerations and ethical standards to facilitate development, diffusion and adoption of appropriate technologies for sustainable development. Firms may innovate the products, services and business models that will maximize profit in the short run even if those innovations do not ensure equity and meet ethical standards. However, a narrow, short-term profit-driven commercialization of technology may not always be compatible with sustainable development outcomes (figure I.5). The process of technology development—ensuring transparency, accountability and participation—matters as much as the final outcome. Effective institutional mechanisms can ensure that the new technologies entering the market meet socially agreed efficiency, equity and ethical goals and standards.

Frontier technologies also have unforeseen and unintended consequences for planet, people and prosperity

The use of AI-driven robots exemplifies how technological progress may have unintended consequences which undermine other development objectives. While this type of automation can help raise output and minimize manual and routine work, it can also cause significant job loss and thereby adversely impact the goal of achieving greater social equality. In a global context, automation may trigger a process through which manufacturing is reshored in developed countries, making it difficult for developing countries to industrialize through the expansion of labour-intensive manufacturing that has relied on the offshoring of manufacturing from developed countries.

Online social platforms—which have become an inevitable feature of modern existence, bringing individuals and communities together in the digital space—provide another example of the unintended consequences of technological progress. These networks can be used to disseminate information on environmental and sustainability options and best practices and to widen the range of consumer choices to include sustainable goods and services. However, they may also enable the spread of misinformation and become weaponized to influence political processes and undermine vulnerable institutions where governance is weakest. Along similar lines: while the Internet of Things and the use of more advanced algorithms to analyse big data can transform entire sectors (including improvement of health care, as discussed above), they can also radically reshape the concept of privacy; and while gene editing, for example, may save many lives, it may also open up a Pandora's box of dangerous pathogens.

It is therefore not sufficient for a new technology to be efficient—it must also be deployed in a way that is sufficiently equitable and ethical to support the realization of the

Figure I.5
The development process for frontier technologies

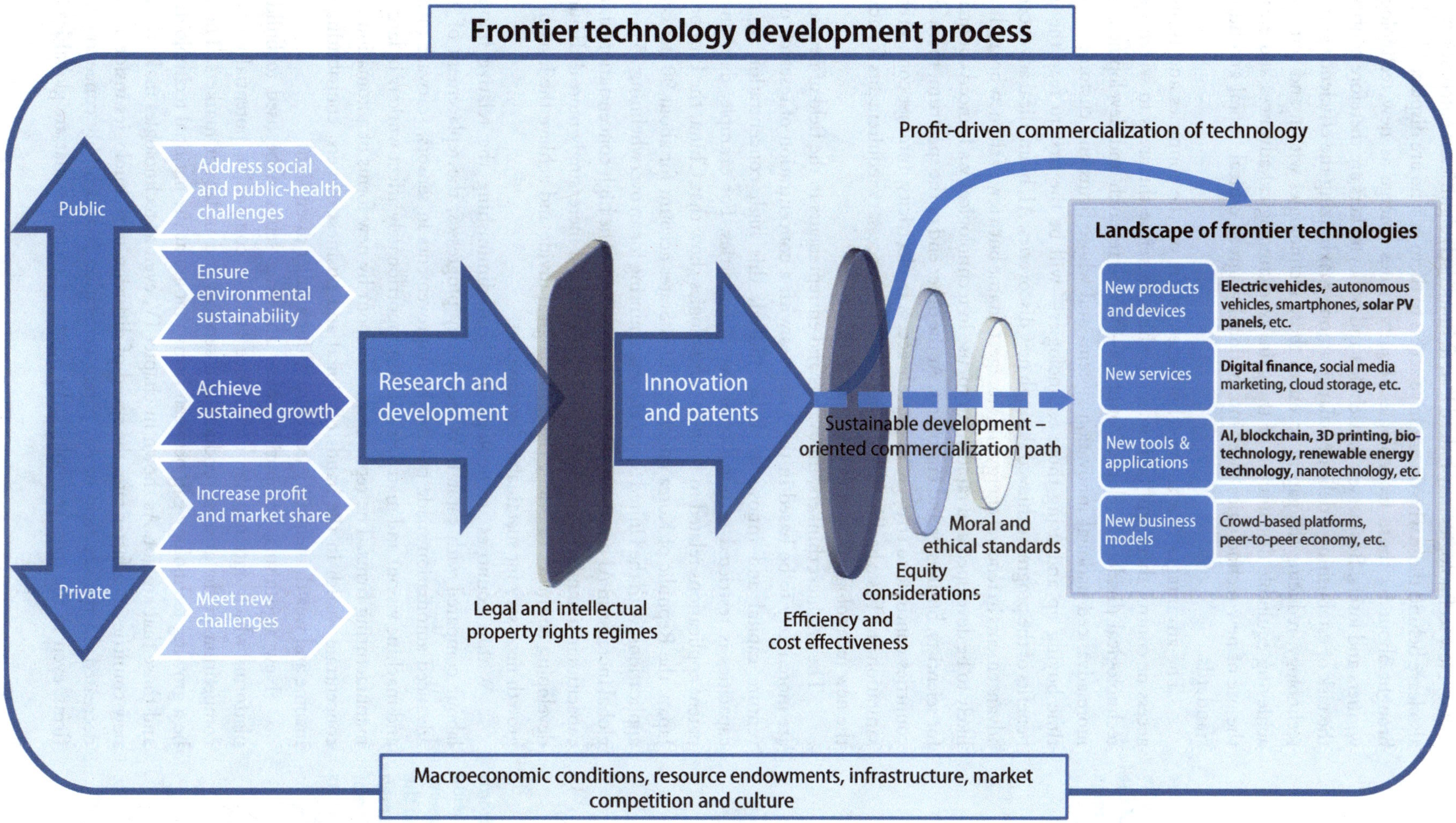

Source: UN/DESA.
Note: In the right-hand box, entitled "Landscape of frontier technologies", the names of technologies discussed in this *Survey* are in bold.

SDGs. New technologies may indeed lead to immensely significant outcomes, but they may also leave behind those who do not have access to them or who are displaced by the changes brought about by those technologies. Equity issues emerge as new technologies create winners and losers. Businesses, households and policymakers are therefore confronted with the task of establishing a delicate balance among maximizing the efficiency gains of a new technology, reducing the gap in access to those technologies within and across countries, achieving equitable distribution of the gains of technological advances and ensuring that the use of new technologies meet internationally agreed ethical, moral and human rights standards.

Countries and firms controlling access to, and use of, many of the frontier technologies stand to gain immensely

The advantages that such technologies confer on the countries and firms that can access or control them will be immense, which therefore threatens to widen the existing technological divide. Developed countries—whose research and development are led by more advanced national innovation systems and whose firms and customers will lose no time buying up and using those technologies—will be the first to reap the immediate benefits of the progress achieved through new discoveries. AI, biomedical advancements and advancements in renewal energy and storage, to name but a few of the new breakthroughs, are likely to be developed and rapidly put to use in technologically advanced countries as tools for scientists, businesses and customers. At the other end of the spectrum, many developing countries continue to struggle to provide access to electricity, Internet connectivity, water, sanitation and basic health technologies, which are necessary requirements for advancing to the new technological frontier (see chap. III).

The brightest thinkers, innovators and entrepreneurs in the field of new technologies are more likely to be based in the countries with a concentration of research universities, venture capital and innovation hubs. Indeed, this high concentration of innovation capacities is restricted to but a small set of countries. For example, data on European patent applications related to frontier technologies show that China, the European Union, Japan, the Republic of Korea and the United States account for about 90 per cent of such applications, with the United States alone accounting for an overwhelming 75 per cent of the global increase in AI patents between 2010 and 2016. The high concentration of innovation capacities in a handful of countries is likely to make it increasingly more difficult for many developing countries to bridge the technological divide and achieve the level of economic growth necessary for sustainable development.

Automation, algorithms and ever-increasing computing power have diminished the importance of human labour in production of goods and services

Within countries, technology has been diminishing the relative importance of labour compared with capital. As technology progresses, the replacement of workers by advanced automation made possible by improvements in sensors, software (including AI and machine vision) and materials will disproportionately affect workers in large advanced manufacturing firms. The replacement of labour by new forms of automation can further concentrate wealth in the hands of capital and business owners, contributing to greater income and wealth inequality (see chap. II for a fuller discussion).

New algorithms, computing power and data sets can be used to build so-called platforms which entrench the dominance of large companies, potentially undermining competition in the area of products and services and in labour markets. The result will be a growing technology gap between firms that are at the national technological frontier and those that are not. As shown in chapter IV, even as technologies make their way into new countries at a faster rate, the speed of diffusion of technologies inside a country has decreased. In the key field of AI, patent generation is also highly concentrated in a few firms, even in the most technologically advanced countries that are global leaders in the

Box I.2

Data as a common factor in frontier technologies

Data is the common thread connecting many of the frontier technologies and their applications. Data are generated every time, for example, we click on a digital device, make a phone call, swipe a credit or electromagnetic card, or use a vending machine. We leave digital footprints everywhere, often without realizing that the footprint contains a valuable piece of information. In this digital era, firms have increasingly recognized the value of data, pursuing new ways to capture the information generated by activities and contained in places and things. Digital data are now collected from, e.g., Global Positioning System (GPS) trackers in vehicles and phones, social media, commercial transactions, and medical information. The value of these data is enormous. Data generate additional data through analysis, enable network effects and platforms, and are the key input for building algorithms, improving machine learning and creating AI which already competes with human intelligence. As factor inputs for analytics and AI, data constitute valuable capital.

While the data economy transcends political and sectoral boundaries, an appropriate framework for establishing ownership rights over data are still lacking. In this economy, individuals are both producers and consumers—but are not the owners—of data,. Data have become increasingly essential as capital in the provision of many products and services (MIT Technology Review Custom and Oracle, 2016). Individuals, however, do not participate in this market as suppliers and users. Rather, as they generate data to be mined and analysed, their role is largely that of a resource to be exploited.

In the existing digital economy, the firm—which can range from anything from a social media platform to a rideshare service—that collects the data owns the data, without necessarily compensating the individuals who created those data. An asymmetric relationship therefore exists between individual creators of data and the firms that collect, compile and analyse those data. This is a relationship in which the firms amassing the data enjoy an undue advantage over the individuals that are the source or producers of the data. The fact that those firms are able to collect what are in fact huge economic rents without the explicit consent of those individuals creates a significant distortion in the marketplace.

Because of the value of data as capital and as personal information, the security, privacy and ownership of data are important considerations for ensuring the integrity of the digital economy. The rise of a data-driven economy therefore requires laws and regulations that clearly establish a basis for the ownership of data and for the recognition of data as an asset that is economically valuable. Countries and country groups have begun to set boundaries regarding how data can be collected and used. For example, in April 2016, the General Data Protection Regulation (GDPR) was agreed by the European Parliament and the Council of the European Union. The regulation, which entered into application in May 2018, brings all data of residents of the European Union that is being processed within the scope of the European Union's data protection law. GDPR specifies the rights of individuals and the obligations placed on organizations covered by the regulation, that is, those organizations must, inter alia, grant persons easier access to their data, as held by those organizations; comply, under a new fines regime, with severe penalties for infringement, of up to 4 per cent of worldwide turnover, or €20 million, whichever amount is higher; and secure the consent of individuals before collecting data on them. The European model for ensuring the rights of individuals as related to their personal data represents a step in the right direction and the start of a conversation on how the multilateral system can go about creating global standards for data privacy and rights.

Source: UN/DESA.

domain. Addressing such large and growing divides requires a broad understanding of the key dynamics driving the processes of technology innovation and diffusion.

Frontier technologies raise new concerns over safety and ethics

Frontier technologies present new and unique challenges to ethics and morality

Frontier technologies present new and unique ethics- and morality-related challenges, which can potentially undermine trust, cohesion, tolerance, peace and stability. These concerns arise with the emergence of new technologies, either as societies determine how to cope with those technologies' intended disruptions or as they set the boundaries of acceptable use, as in the case, e.g., of genetic engineering (see chap. II for a more detailed discussion on the ethical implications of digital technologies).

Gene editing poses a risk of off-target edits which could lead to mutations and other problems in the targeted genome. In addition to these safety risks, there are ethical concerns raised by the use of germline editing (gene editing for reproductive purposes), especially if it is applied to address the genetic diagnosis of an unborn child, a situation where off-target edits can evolve quickly. Other issues include lack of the informed consent of the future person, greater accessibility to the technology by the rich, and moral and religious objections.

The rise in importance of artificial intelligence opens up the possibility of new forms of discrimination which may be harder to identify and address (see chap. II). Machine learning algorithms by their very nature defy our ability to understand how and why a decision has been made, thereby limiting our ability to evaluate that decision within the context of ethical and other societal norms.

The growing importance of data in economic, social and political activities merits appropriate and acceptable legal and ethical boundaries that respect the fundamental rights of individuals

The rise in the importance of data as an input into economic activity raises important ownership issues; and how data are being collected and, in some cases, misused is a growing privacy concern. Breaches and leaks have occurred in the databases of financial institutions, credit-rating agencies, email providers, social networks and health facilities, among many others. Some leaks are made public, while others become the basis for criminal activities such as identity or financial fraud or for exerting political influence on a massive scale. It has recently been discovered that a research group made use—legally—of data extracted from the social media platform Facebook to help create targeted political campaigns, which has ushered in a whole new era of political campaigning.

As data become increasingly valuable to businesses for what they reveal about individuals, the world must strive to set appropriate and acceptable legal and ethical boundaries, while respecting the fundamental rights of individuals. Through work on regulation, the rights of consumers as the targets of data collection can be clearly established (see chap. V for a discussion of the policy implications in this regard).

Policies for harnessing the potentials of frontier technologies

Policies should ensure that technological breakthroughs serve the overarching goal of leaving no one behind

Considering the potential of frontier technologies to help achieve the SDGs as well as their potential to generate unintended adverse effects, proactive and forward-looking policy measures are required for managing progress in the development of many frontier technologies. There is a need to ensure that further advances in technological processes do not lead to a worsening of income inequality, especially if the overarching goal of leaving no one behind is to be achieved.

Technological breakthroughs should be embraced and promoted, while balancing efficiency, equity and ethical considerations

On the one hand, technological breakthroughs should be embraced, and continued progress should be promoted. On the other, it should be recognized that realizing the vision of the 2030 Agenda for Sustainable Development without leaving anyone behind will require a balance to be struck among efficiency, equity and ethical considerations. In this regard, countries can adopt a range of policies to ensure that frontier technologies are deployed to facilitate attainment of national and global development objectives.

Proactive and effective policies are needed to reduce the pains of adjustment to new technologies and economic structures

At the national level, policies and institutional context play a major role in determining who benefits and who loses from the adoption of new technologies. In some countries, the ushering in of new technologies will lead to changes in the demand for skills and in the nature of work. This phenomenon is already being observed in many developed economies and in the large manufacturing sectors of developing economies. Hence, policies must be proactive so as to facilitate the transition and reduce the pains of adjustment to new economic structures, ensuring that workers are employable, adaptive and competitive. Given the potential for a widening gap between winners and losers in the technological race, competitiveness and inequality effects will also require policy solutions.

Bridging the technological divide is a necessary condition for closing the development divide

The ability of developing countries to access new technologies will determine whether they will be able to keep up with and catch up to countries closer to technological frontiers. Knowledge begets knowledge and for a country and its firms to produce more and better products, that country must have the capacity to make full use of its existing resources and capabilities and develop new ones. Therefore, bridging the technological divide is an important precondition for closing the economic divide between countries. Periods of rapid technological change create opportunities for those developing or otherwise "latecomer" countries that are seeking to catch up with more advanced countries. However, seizing these opportunities to catch up can occur only with a strong national system of innovation in place to identify key challenges, direct a research agenda, provide funding requirements, and establish intellectual property and patent rights regimes (see chap. IV).

International cooperation can help facilitate access to technologies most needed for sustainable development

The immense scope of frontier technologies and the rapid pace of their diffusion across national boundaries—affecting efficiency, equity and ethical standards—demand global collective action. While national responsibilities will remain paramount, no nation alone can harness the full potential of emerging technologies and mitigate associated risks. More effective international cooperation for managing advances in frontier technologies is essential. Greater international cooperation with regard to their generation, diffusion and adoption—reflecting shared and differentiated responsibilities among all actors—can bring frontier technologies to those who lack the means to access them. This will require (a) revisiting intellectual property rights regimes that govern technology transfers among countries and firms within and across countries and (b) rethinking competition policies and creating incentives for innovation that are potent enough to ensure profitability, while at the same time fostering sustainable development. Further, international cooperation will also be needed to ensure that the advances in frontier technology meet universal ethical and moral standards and that competition in the technology sector is fair. New standards of corporate governance, corporate social responsibility and consumer protection can help ensure that frontier technologies promote equity and social justice.

A more development-oriented intellectual property rights (IPR) regime—one that balances incentives for innovation with the greater need for technology diffusion—will be critically important for sustainable development. Greater international cooperation on taxation as it relates to the digital economy can play a vital role in generating new revenues for those adversely affected by frontier technologies, although this would require a concurrent commitment to ensuring that those revenues are directed towards redressing some of the distributional impacts of frontier technologies (see chap. V).

The role of the United Nations in forging global collective action

The United Nations can facilitate a global dialogue on the risks and opportunities associated with frontier technologies

There is a need for a global dialogue, involving all stakeholders, on how to identify and manage the risks and opportunities associated with frontier technologies. The United Nations can serve as an impartial facilitator, among Governments and private sector and civil society organizations, of an objective assessment of the impact of emerging technologies on sustainable development outcomes, including on employment, wages and income distribution. One issue in this regard is how to define the rights of individuals in the context of the collection and use of their digital data. The new realities reflecting the importance of data for identification and security, and for the design of new products and services (especially in the realm of artificial intelligence) require a reconsideration of how data fit within the existing framework of principles underpinning human rights and responsibilities.

The present *Survey* constitutes one small contribution to the efforts to facilitate international cooperation and global action on frontier technologies, but many other kinds of efforts exist. The fruit of those efforts include the Technology Facilitation Mechanism, established in the 2030 Agenda for Sustainable Development under SDG 17.6, to foster collaboration and partnerships among Member States, civil society, the private sector, the scientific community, United Nations entities and other stakeholders. Other important United Nations initiatives for facilitating understanding and diffusion of relevant technologies and bridging some dimensions of the technology divide include the work of the Commission on Science and Technology for Development and the Technology Bank, first proposed in paragraph 52 ("1. Joint action") of the Programme of Action for the Least Developed Countries for the Decade 2011–2020.[18]

Given its universal membership and unwavering commitment to human values, the United Nations is also uniquely positioned to facilitate a dialogue among all stakeholders on the elaboration of a global ethical compact to guide research and development of frontier technologies, so as to ensure that they conform to universally held ethical standards. Efforts need to be directed towards forging a global consensus on the important ethical challenges. These include setting limits to bioengineering and the use of automated weapons. Indeed, the global community, and the United Nations in particular, have a unique responsibility to address these two issues (see chap. V for a more comprehensive discussion).

18 *Report of the Fourth United Nations Conference on the Least Developed Countries*, Istanbul, Turkey, 9–13 May 2011 (A/CONF.219/7), chap. II

Appendix

Frontier technologies discussed in this *Survey*

The present annex contains concise discussions on a set of technologies that are examined throughout the *Survey*, as well as technologies that are deemed important based on a review of the literature on economic and social issues, including the results of foresight exercises conducted by some Member States, identifying key or emerging technologies for policy attention (OECD, 2016).[a]

Artificial intelligence and machine learning

Since the dawn of research in artificial intelligence (AI) in the 1950s, scientists have worked to create a system capable of intelligent behaviour indistinguishable from that of a human being. Rudimentary AI systems have been used commercially since the mid-1990s to assist in a variety of decision-making tasks, such as fraud detection.

Progress in AI has accelerated rapidly since around 2010, driven by the confluence of the growing availability of large data sets from commerce, social media, science and other sources; continued improvements in computational power; and the development of better machine learning algorithms and techniques (such as "deep learning").[b] Systems are now capable of learning how to accomplish a task without having been provided with explicit steps for doing so. Once designed and deployed, the neural network that underpins modern AI can formulate its own rules for interpreting new data and designing solutions, with minimal—or no—human participation.

AI algorithms have outscored humans in identifying objects and faces in two popular tests (Aron, 2015). On the other hand, their performance is limited to certain categories, and humans can still identify a much larger number of categories and infer context and other aspects of images. The challenge in further developing AI lies in building algorithms that can draw inferences about wider contexts, including what the images convey regarding what may happen next.

It is also important to understand the limitations of this technology. AI has proved to be transformative in many areas, but deployment of the techniques currently in use result in a form of AI that is "narrow" in its applications, allowing algorithms to achieve mastery in only a single domain each time. Some visible examples of mastery include winning at a game

a Of the 10 technologies identified in the study by OECD (2016), 8 are discussed in this *Survey*: the Internet of Things; big data analytics; artificial intelligence; neuro-technologies; additive manufacturing; advanced energy storage technologies; synthetic biology; and the blockchain. The only ones not discussed are nano/microsatellites and nanomaterials. The literature review included the results of foresight exercises conducted by Canada (2013), the European Union (2014), Finland (2014), Germany (2015), the United Kingdom of Great Britain and Northern Ireland (2012) and the Russian Federation (2014), as reported in the OECD study.

b Machine learning involves algorithms whose performance improves through experience in identifying patterns from data and continuously testing and adjusting solutions. This requires large data sets and computational power.

like chess, maximizing accuracy in translating a text or understanding speech, and even the safe manoeuvring of a car. Existing techniques allow for the optimization of defined tasks, but the development of a general-purpose AI—capable of creativity, planning and other inherently human activities—remains a distant possibility. According to one expert (Lee, 2017): "[t]here are simply no known engineering algorithms for [general-purpose AI]". And he doesn't "expect to see them any time soon."[c]

There are also concerns regarding information security, as algorithms and robots insinuate themselves into our newsfeeds and election campaigns; and physical security, as lethal autonomous weapons make their way onto the battlefield and into the skies (see chap. II).

Nevertheless, applications for AI-equipped robots are being found in various fields, including manufacturing. Going forward, and in combination with 3D manufacturing, these applications may have an important impact on the current processes of offshoring and the operations of global value chains.

Renewable energy technologies

Following recent technological breakthroughs, a growing number of current and emerging technologies in the area of renewable energy generation have achieved a sufficient level of technical and economic maturity to render them ready for large-scale deployment.

In terms of maturity level, solar energy technologies ranges from those in the R&D stage (e.g., fuel production from solar energy), to those in the maturing stage (e.g., concentrated solar thermal power) and on to technologies that are technically mature (e.g., solar heating and photovoltaic (PV)). The result intended through achievement of technological progress in solar PV is the development of commercial-scale production technology for PV that has low capital intensity, high conversion efficiency, an exemplary relationship with the environment and long module lifetime. New materials such as organic solar cells and graphene are central to achieving these objectives. At the same time, researchers continue to improve the efficiencies of silicon solar cells through engineering breakthroughs.[d] Improvements in PV technologies and manufacturing processes, along with the change in manufacturing capacity and reduced non-hardware costs, have substantially reduced PV costs and prices (see chap. III for an examination of the use of PVs in developing countries).

Traditional land-based wind technologies are mature. As for the use of wind energy in offshore locations, it is increasing but is typically costlier than land-based wind energy. Turbines currently extract nearly 50 per cent of the energy conveyed by wind, just below the theoretical maximum of nearly 60 per cent.[e] The aim to be achieved through technological progress on materials, mechanical engineering and wind forecasting is to reduce cost and increase the availability of wind power. Individual wind turbines are increasing in size, helping to reduce the cost of wind energy, particularly for offshore wind farms.

Bioenergy technologies are diverse and span a wide range. Examples of mature technologies include conventional biomass-fuelled power plants and heating systems as well as ethanol production from sugar and starch. Technological progress has been made in

c See Artificial Intelligence Index (2017) for a complete discussion on the technical possibilities of ongoing research on AI.

d See www.nrel.gov/pv.

e https://www.worldenergy.org/wp-content/uploads/2017/03/WEResources_Wind_2016.pdf.

the area of conversion systems that use more sustainable fuel sources (advanced biomass). Performance improvements have also been effected in cropping systems, logistics and multiple conversion technologies for bioenergy. Technological advances have been witnessed in the area of geothermal energy as well.

Energy storage technologies

The technology of utility-sized energy storage has been advancing and becoming more economical. The appropriate method of storing energy depends on the resources available to the local power producer. The existing technologies for storing energy include: (a) hydropower and compressed air storage; (b) molten salt thermal storage; (c) the redox flow battery; (4) the conventional rechargeable battery; and (e) thermal storage.[f]

Storage of hydropower, e.g., through pumped storage, represents 99 per cent of the world's operational electricity storage capacity.[g] Pumped hydro-storage plants work through gravity, by pumping water up into a reservoir when electricity is in surplus, "charging" the system. When the electricity is needed, the water is allowed to flow down to another reservoir through a hydroelectric generator. As of 2015, global pumped storage capacity was 144.5 gigawatts (GW). East Asia and Europe accounted for 108 GW.

Compressed air storage works in a similar way, pumping ambient air into a storage container and releasing it through electrical turbines when needed. Special arrangements must be made for such systems to enable them to deal with the heat of the air as it compresses, which adds to the cost.

Heat generated by solar thermal plants, when not used immediately to generate electricity, can be stored in molten salt. This heat storage extends the hours of solar plants into the evening. There is ongoing research on the use of molten metal as a replacement for salt, which would further increase the efficiency of these systems.

Redox flow batteries store energy in the form of electrolytes and release energy as the different electrolyte solutions are made to interact and generate an electrical charge. These batteries require large quantities of electrolyte tanks, which is not a barrier to utility-level installations. They also have a longer service life and are less prone to fires. Increasing their capacity requires only larger storage tanks.

Conventional rechargeable batteries are making their way from personal electronics into vehicles and utility-size applications. Companies are also exploring the viability of pairing wind turbines with batteries to store excess energy. In November 2017, the State of South Australia installed the world's largest battery, with the capacity to power 30,000 homes. The installation, which was carried out in less than 100 days by Tesla, will help the State balance the supply-and-demand problems that have resulted in regular blackouts for its residents and the world's highest electricity prices (Baidawi, 2017).

A less traditional form of energy storage is thermal storage, where excess electricity is used to freeze water. The "ice battery" then provides cooling without the use of traditional air-conditioning systems when demand for electricity is high.

---

f See https://arstechnica.com/information-technology/2017/10/a-world-tour-of-some-of-the-biggest-energy-storage-schemes/.

g See https://www.worldenergy.org/wp-content/uploads/2017/03/WEResources_Hydropower_2016.pdf.

Autonomous vehicles and drones

Autonomous vehicles are perhaps the most visible applications of advanced algorithms, sensors and powerful computing power. Five levels of automation exist for vehicles (excluding zero automation), ranging from basic driver assistance (level 1: "hands on") to full automation (level 5: "steering wheel optional") (see figure A.1). The most successful automation system currently available, offered by Tesla in its passenger cars, provides level 2 automation ("hands off"), where the driver can rely on the vehicle to steer and control speed but must be attentive and ready to intervene when required. A significant amount of research is being conducted whose aim is to allow vehicles to operate at level 3 ("eyes off") and higher automation levels. While some automakers are announcing plans to market level 3 automation capabilities in the next two years,[h] level 5 automation is, by some estimations, decades away.[i]

In a recent study on the potential benefits of autonomous vehicles, it was estimated

Figure A.1
Six stages of automation

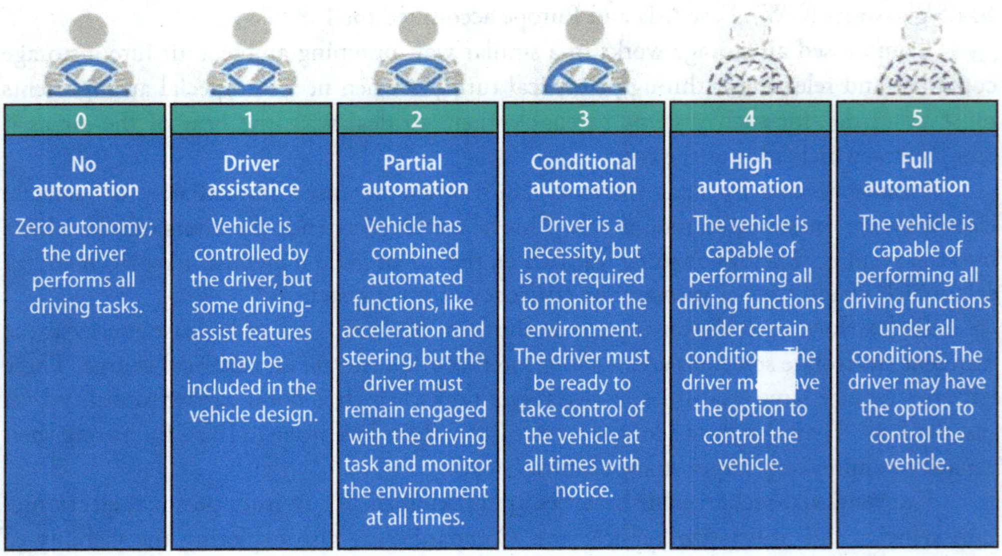

Source: www.nhtsa.gov/technology-innovation/automated-vehicles-safety

that their use could reduce accident rates by 90 per cent in the United States, potentially saving 30,000 lives and $190 billion in associated health-care costs.[j]

Automation also has applications in the development of unmanned aerial systems (UAS), or drones. These systems are used for surveillance, operations, entertainment and advertising, signal emission, and the movement of people or goods (Cohn and others, 2017). The most mature use of drones involves surveillance (using photographs and video applications without analytics). Drones that can assist with labour-intensive and dangerous

---

h See https://www.slashgear.com/2019-audi-a8-level-3-autonomy-first-drive-chasing-the-perfect-jam-11499082/.

i See https://spectrum.ieee.org/cars-that-think/transportation/self-driving/google-selfdriving-car-will-be-ready-soon-for-some-in-decades-for-others.

j See https://www.mckinsey.com/industries/automotive-and-assembly/our-insights/ten-ways-autonomous-driving-could-redefine-the-automotive-world.

tasks and those that can be leveraged for entertainment (e.g., advertising and light shows) are beginning to enter into commercial use. Drones are also planned to provide radio, video and Internet connectivity in remote areas. Transporting objects is another logical future use of this technology. In October 2016, a company called Zipline began using drones to deliver medical supplies (medicines and blood) to health clinics in remote locations of Rwanda. In 2017, the Government of the United Republic of Tanzania announced its partnership with Zipline to "provide emergency on-demand access to critical and life-saving medicines" in the country.[k]

Cryptocurrencies and blockchain technology

In any monetary transaction, it is required that the buyer of a product have sufficient funds and that the funds be used only once (i.e., there is no "double spending"). Electronic transactions require special attention, since it is easy to copy and alter digital information. The traditional financial system verifies the ownership of funds and checks for any double spending by means of ledgers, or records of the balance in every account and in every bank. The transaction then modifies the appropriate ledgers to reflect the withdrawal and deposit of funds. The functioning of this system requires trust in formal institutions and regulatory systems.

In 2009, a person or persons going by the name of Satoshi Nakamoto proposed a public distributed ledger system which would rely on cryptography and self-interest to enable electronic transactions. This notable innovation, in the form of a system underpinned by incentives and mathematical proofs, would obviate the need for trust in any one actor or central institution as the basis for preventing fraud and ensuring that the ledgers were kept up to date. Within such a system, every participant therefore works to build a single public ledger of transactions and constantly verifies its validity. That ledger is known as the blockchain.

The blockchain works through a competitive process whereby the first to successfully validate a block of transactions and broadcast the solution to the network wins a monetary reward. The proposed block is quickly and independently verified by every participant. If a majority of the network agrees that the block is valid, the block and the transactions it contains become part of the consensus blockchain (see figure A.2).

Figure A.2
Anatomy of a blockchain

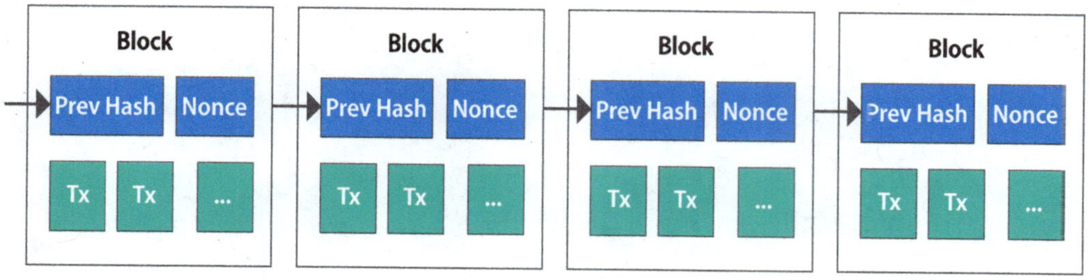

Source: Nakamoto (2008).
Note: A block represents data which include descriptive information such as unique identifiers (hash) and counters (nonce) as well as transactions that have been validated (Tx). The connection between blocks (the chain) is the unique identifier of the previous block. Any change in the previous data will change all subsequent identifiers.

k See http://www.flyzipline.com/uploads/Tanzania%20Announcement%20Press%20Release%20vFinal.pdf.

The innovativeness of this system lies in the way in which the various parts combine to create the trust and guarantees that the traditional financial system derives from institutions and regulation. The incentives align the interest of participants towards contributing to the system's security. In contrast, the traditional system relies on a complex armature of reporting, oversight and implicit or explicit guarantees, ultimately backed by the reputation of the central authority. As such, the blockchain technology presents the possibility—a first in the field of finance!—that trust in institutions backed by government can be replaced by trust in computer code.

Chapter II

Managing the promises of frontier technologies

Introduction

Emerging technologies—as introduced in chapter I—will have a profound impact on sustainable development. The present chapter assesses the impact of a few emerging technologies within the contexts of specific countries where they have been developed and deployed in recent years. While these technologies are redefining work, promoting prosperity, improving environmental sustainability and transforming social interactions, they are also presenting equity-related and ethical challenges and are likely to have large direct and spillover effects on the rest of the world as well.

New technologies possess immense potential for achieving sustainable development, but...

New technologies and products possess immense potential but inevitably bring with them uncertainties, risks and unintended and unanticipated consequences. For example, while the discovery and use of fossil fuels have led to a revolution in transportation and a manifold increase in the speed of travel, those fuels have also contributed to global warming and climate change. Similarly, plastics have transformed storage but remain a major source of pollution; processed sugar has expanded our dietary options but its use has led to a higher prevalence of obesity; and the use of fertilizer has resulted in an improvement in crop yields but also in the contamination of rivers and oceans. Indeed, technologies, as these examples illustrate, are seldom neutral—they solve certain problems but create others.

...they also generate uncertainties, risks and unintended consequences

This chapter identifies the opportunities and challenges associated with the advances produced by a few frontier technologies (but whose selection in no way diminishes the importance of other such technologies). The focus is on a specific product, namely, the electric vehicle (EV), and automation and digital technologies, which encompass suites of applications. The aim is to illustrate their promise, their impact in terms of economic and social trade-offs, and their potential spillover effects across sectors and countries.

This chapter identifies the potentials and challenges associated with EVs, automation and digital technologies

While EVs offer a viable alternative to conventional cars with respect to reducing CO_2 and other greenhouse gases emissions, this technology is not yet a viable alternative to conventional vehicles in terms of price and convenience. EVs are unlikely to contribute significantly to reducing CO_2 emissions without a more dramatic shift away from the fossil fuels that they use to recharge their batteries. The promise of a frontier technology may therefore remain unfulfilled without the requisite shift from fossil fuel to renewable energy technologies.

Automation promises to increase labour productivity, income and prosperity. However, its actual and potential impacts on labour demand, production of goods and services, concentration of market power, and wealth and income distribution raise economic and social concerns. The level of apprehension regarding the future of work appears to be growing particularly high in industries and economies where the speed and spread of technological changes have been rapid. Anxieties in this regard are driving social and political discontent, as manifested in many advanced economies, with significant spillover effects on the rest of the world.

Also explored in this chapter is the promise embodied by digital technologies and artificial intelligence (AI)—possibly the final frontier of new technologies—which possess the immense potential to minimize human errors and biases in decision-making processes. On the other hand, AI-powered social platforms are also used to produce targeted advertisements which manipulate human behaviours or spread misinformation, so as to undermine social cohesion, peace and stability. While an automated decision system can improve the efficiency of public agencies, it also runs the risk of reinforcing existing biases and exclusion.

Technological change is inevitable, but humanity can still become better prepared to manage its benefits and risks

The solution, however, is not to steer clear of or to stifle technological progress. Technological change is inevitable, but humanity can become better prepared to manage this inevitability. For example, there need to be more concerted efforts to reduce our dependence on fossil fuels and transform EVs into a more substantive tool for achieving environmental sustainability. Appropriate investments in human capital—through which to foster the acquisition of new skills and knowledge not just by a few privileged groups but by all—can help enable societies to create new jobs and embrace automation without unwarranted fear. Strengthening institutions and mechanisms that play a key role in the determination of wages and benefits—including labour unions, collective bargaining processes and labour regulations (e.g., minimum wage legislation)—can help ensure a more equitable and balanced distribution of gains between labour (employees) and capital (employers), translating into wage growth and robust social protection. Complementary investments are also needed to redefine property rights or even create new ones for the various forms of digital content (Vickers and Ziebarth, 2017) and to develop new ethical, legal and regulatory frameworks for managing algorithms, machine learning and artificial intelligence.

Actions taken by the Governments of the technological frontier countries shape global standards for managing frontier technologies

While the opportunities and challenges discussed in this chapter are related mainly to technologies developed and used in countries at the technological frontier, they are increasingly becoming universal opportunities and challenges, affecting all of humanity. The chapter underscores the special role of Governments in those frontier countries, which are leading innovation in technologies that will affect people and prosperity—indeed, the entire planet. Governments in the handful of developed countries and the few large developing countries that are innovating new technologies and rolling out their applications for businesses and consumers will need to encourage and incentivize innovations that are critical for humanity, while minimizing their unintended adverse economic and social effects. The actions taken by those Governments will shape global standards for managing frontier technologies. The countries that, while not leading innovation, are adopting and using those technologies, will be able to learn from the successes as well as the failures of the frontier countries and in turn pursue national policymaking on appropriate and complementary investments in institutions, regulations and standards so as to achieve their own development objectives.

Electric vehicles: panacea or target of misplaced hope?

Massive consumption of fossil fuels has improved the quality of our lives, but it has also led to global warming and climate change

The twentieth century witnessed a massive increase in the consumption of fossil fuels to power transportation, machines and electricity generation. In essence, fossil fuel now underpins human existence. But while improving the quality of life, it has also emerged as the largest contributor to greenhouse gas (GHG) emissions, global warming and climate change—an adverse (and unanticipated) consequence of meeting the needs of the modern world. Although this adverse climatic impact has become more evident, efficiency- and profit-related considerations are perpetuating the dependence on fossil fuel in the absence of viable alternatives.

There is a growing recognition that humanity must reduce its dependence on fossil fuel to achieve environmental sustainability. Increasingly, many developed countries, and a few large developing countries such as Brazil, China and India, are taking concrete steps to reduce CO_2 emission and enhance environmental sustainability, in line with their commitments to the Paris Agreement[1] adopted under the United Nations Framework Convention on Climate Change.[2] The quest for environmental sustainability is driving technological breakthroughs in (a) energy efficiency and conservation practices, (b) carbon-free or reduced-carbon energy resources and (c) carbon capture, either from fossil fuels or from the atmosphere, and carbon storage.

Electric vehicles (EVs) hold out hope for reducing GHG emissions

Electric vehicles—using carbon-free or reduced-carbon energy resources—represent a technological breakthrough, and a possible small step towards achieving the larger goal of environmental sustainability.[3] EVs replace internal combustion engines with battery-powered or battery-assisted engines which emit significantly fewer or no tailpipe greenhouse gas emissions. Requiring less or no fuel combustion and relying for the most part on electricity, EVs also boost energy efficiency for road transport and thereby contribute to the attainment of a wide range of transport policy goals, such as national energy security, especially for countries that import fossil fuels; and noise reduction and improved air quality, particularly in large cities. Given that the transport industry accounts for 23 per cent of global energy-related GHG emissions (International Energy Agency (IEA), 2016), policy support for EVs, which is growing, represents the kind of urgent action to combat climate change envisaged under Sustainable Development Goal (SDG) 13. EVs may also contribute indirectly to reducing inequality among countries (as envisaged under SDG 10) by reducing the high costs of climate change imposed on those that are both climate-vulnerable and low-income.

While EVs hold out hope for reducing CO_2 and other GHG emissions at the consumer level, their widespread use may not necessarily lead to a significant reduction in those emissions—especially if the breakthrough they represent remains an isolated phenomenon. Use of these vehicles might lead to a reduction in CO_2 emissions in large cities, improving air quality and yielding other benefits to urban residents; but if their batteries continue to be recharged with fossil fuel-generated electricity, overall emission levels could very well remain largely unchanged. For EVs to deliver on their full potential to reduce emissions and generate environmental sustainability, a fundamental shift to renewable energy sources will be needed.

1 See Adoption of the Paris Agreement in United Nations Framework Convention on Climate Change (2015).

2 United Nations, *Treaty Series*, vol. 1771, No. 30822.

3 EVs include battery, plug-in hybrid, range-extended and fuel cell electric vehicles.

EVs are making inroads

It is hard to imagine that the comforts and conveniences of modern life could have emerged in the absence of the automobile. However, the significant expansion of the use of automobiles during the twentieth century occurred without much consideration being given to their impacts on the Earth's atmosphere. Indeed, large quantities of GHG emissions arising from the use of automobiles (as well as from other uses of fossil fuels) have contributed to significant levels of air pollution, global warming and climate change.

At the same time, the adverse impacts of climate change are distributed unevenly across countries and across population groups within countries. While the poorest people, communities and countries are disproportionally affected by climate change-induced extreme weather events, such as tropical cyclones, and long and frequent drought spells (United Nations, 2016b), it is the developed countries and some large developing countries that have been largely responsible for GHG emissions. This reflects what is often referred to as the inequality of climate change (Lowrey, 2013).

In 2017, about 1.1 million EVs were sold worldwide, with the global stock surpassing 3 million

About 1.1 million electric cars were sold worldwide in 2017, with the global stock surpassing 3 million vehicles. China had the largest electric car stock: constituting about 40 per cent of the global total (IEA, 2018b, p. 9). With a nearly 40 per cent market share in 2017, Norway achieved the highest market penetration of EVs in the world (see figure II.1). Further, the number of public charging stations in the world has continued to increase: from 322,000 in 2016 to 430,000 in 2017.[4]

Figure II.1
Market share of electric cars (battery electric and plug-in hybrid), selected countries, 2017

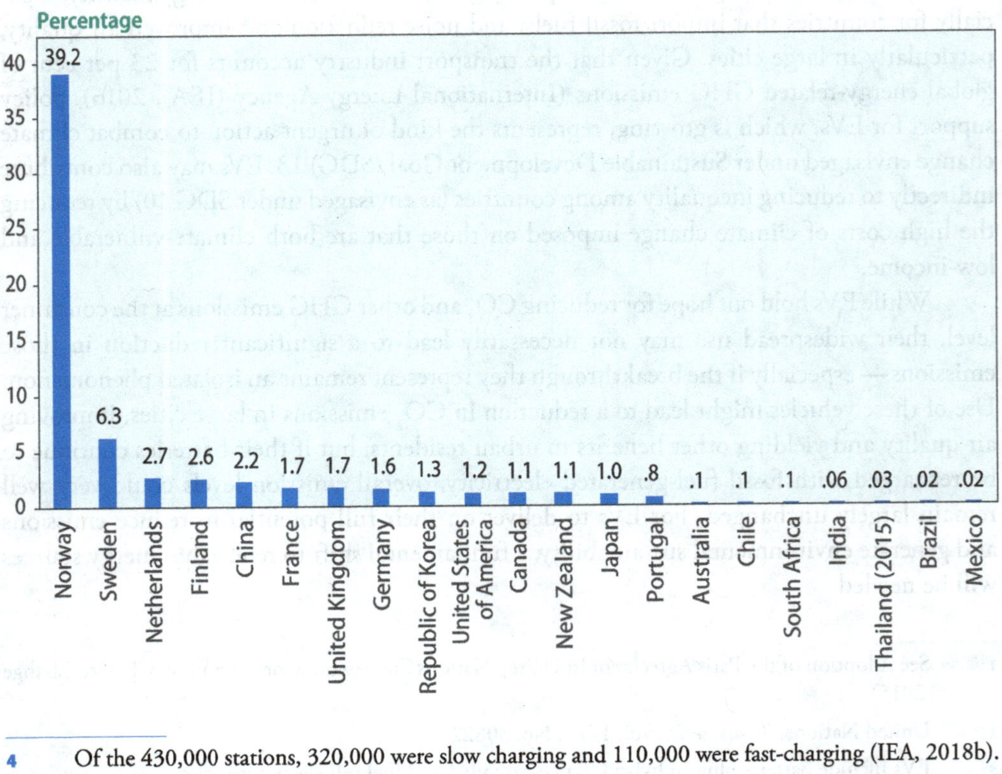

Source: UN/DESA, based on IEA (2018b), table A.7.

4 Of the 430,000 stations, 320,000 were slow charging and 110,000 were fast-charging (IEA, 2018b).

A wider variety of EVs—with high-energy batteries and improved operating software—are now available at more affordable prices. Based on increasing public and private expenditures on research and development (R&D) on EV-related technologies—particularly on safer batteries with higher energy density—EVs are expected to become more attractive, with an increase in the variety of vehicle types and sizes in the near future, and, again, at affordable prices. The stock of light EVs is forecast to reach 125–220 million by 2030, but this will largely depend on the level of policy ambition directed towards achieving climate goals (IEA, 2018b, p. 11). UN/DESA predicts that the market share of EVs in the new car market reaches between 5 and 17 per cent in 2025 amid a high level of uncertainty regarding battery capacities, public support measures, oil prices and public acceptance of EVs as the prime mode of transportation, as well as the total demand for all types of vehicles.

With improving technologies, EVs will become more affordable and the stock is forecast to reach 125 million–200 million by 2030

EVs may not reduce economy-wide emissions

Replacing internal combustion engine cars with EVs will not lead automatically to the reduction in CO_2 and other GHG emissions at national and global levels, for that reduction depends not on tailpipe emissions of vehicles but rather on so-called total life-cycle emissions and electricity generation structures at national or local levels.

Replacing conventional cars with EVs will not automatically lead to CO_2 emissions reduction

The total life-cycle emissions (also known as well-to-wheel emissions) of an EV include the emissions derived from its manufacture, battery production, operation, maintenance and disposal, and all of its energy consumption. Lang and others (2013) estimate that, from the perspective of the life cycle, the fuels usage phase (i.e., operation) accounts for most of the total energy consumption of a single EV, followed by the fuels production and transportation stage. That is, the key determinant for reducing GHG emissions is the share of electricity obtained by EVs from renewable sources, including hydro sources, to charge their batteries.

What matters is the life-cycle emissions, not the tailpipe emissions, of vehicles

Hawkins, Gausen and Strømman (2012) estimate that the life-cycle global warming potential (GWP)[5] of EVs whose batteries are powered by coal electricity falls somewhere between that of small and large fossil fuel-driven vehicles. On the other hand, the GWP of EVs powered by natural gas or low-carbon energy sources is lower than that of the most efficient internal combustion engine vehicles. A related study focusing on three regions of China (Beijing-Tianjin-Hebei, Yangtze River Delta and Pearl River Delta) found that the benefits of switching to EVs are maximized in regions with high proportions of hydropower generation and that, where the proportions of hydropower are nil or small, the per-kilometre consumption of EVs are lowest over their life cycles when the batteries were recharged from natural gas-fired sources, compared with coal-, oil-, biomass- and garbage-fired sources (see Lang and others, 2013). A more recent study in which the total life-cycle emissions of EVs were evaluated found that, even where high volumes of coal are used, EVs produce one quarter fewer emissions than diesels.

5 The global warming potential (GWP) has been developed to allow comparisons of the global warming impacts of different gases. It is a measure of how much energy the emission of one ton of a gas will absorb over a given period of time, relative to the emissions of one ton of CO_2. The GWP of CO_2 is set at 1, regardless of the time span used. See United States Environmental Protection Agency, "Greenhouse gas emissions: understanding global warming potentials", available at www.epa.gov/ghgemissions/understanding-global-warming-potentials.

CO_2 emissions reduction is maximized when EVs use renewable energy sources to recharge their batteries

These studies indicate that the reduction of CO_2 emissions through replacement of internal combustion engine cars with EVs is maximized when those EVs use only renewable energy sources to recharge their batteries (see table II.1). In other words, it is the structure of electricity generation that is the most important determinant of the capacity of EVs to produce positive environmental impacts. Thus, the deeper penetration of EVs into the auto market will not lead automatically to significant reductions of GHG emissions.

Table II.1
Total lifecycle and tailpipe emissions: Internal combustion engine vehicles and EVs

	ICEVs	EVs
Tailpipe emissions	Yes	No
CO_2 tailpipe emissions (grams/kilometre)[a]	255	0
Estimated CO_2 reduction if there is an all-car switch from internal combustion engine vehicles to EVs in the United States (percentage)	16.2	
Life-cycle emissions if batteries are charged with electricity produced from coal	Quantity lies between the quantities for small and large internal combustion engine vehicles	
Life-cycle emissions if batteries are charged with electricity produced from natural gas and renewable resources (including hydropower)	Fewer emissions than from the most efficient internal combustion engine vehicles	

Source: UN/DESA, based on national and international sources.
a For the average-sized passenger car in the United States of America.

Whether EVs contribute to a meaningful reduction in carbon footprints will also depend on how quickly consumers accept EVs as their preferred mode of transportation. In the rural areas of countries covering a large territory—e.g., Australia, Canada and the United States of America—EVs are not yet viable options for many users owing to (a) the relatively short distance that can be travelled by a EV with a single charge and (b) the unavailability of EV charging stations in remote areas. Because of their high prices, EVs are currently affordable only by affluent households but the demand for EVs even among the affluent is highly sensitive to factors such as tax incentives and subsidies. EVs have yet to become a financially viable option for middle-income households. Furthermore, the remarkable growth in shale oil and gas production could halt the future growth of oil prices, making internal combustion engine cars more attractive choices to the user. With the United States accounting for 80 per cent of the increase in global oil supply to 2025, users "are not yet ready to say goodbye to the era of oil" (UBS Limited, 2017).

Policies for making EVs a viable alternative

Policies play a key role in making EVs a reasonable alternative to conventional cars

Policies and incentives have played a key role in making EVs a reasonable alternative to conventional vehicles. Since 2010, Governments in both developing and developed countries have been offering potential EV buyers various incentives. The financial incentives include zero or lower taxes. The non-financial incentives include exemptions from access restrictions to urban areas, dedicated parking opportunities, and preferential access to bus lanes and high-occupancy vehicle lanes.[6] Public R&D expenditures on EVs will continue to play a critical role. The International Energy Agency (IEA) has identified Brazil, Canada, China, India, Japan, the Republic of Korea, South Africa, the United States of America and 20 European countries as having implemented at least one of these incentives to popularize EVs.

Quantitative targets are encouraging EV production and deployment

Policies include setting up long-term targets for EV production, sales or imports, and mandates and regulations

Several Governments announced medium- to long-term targets for EV production, sales or imports, as well as mandates and regulations aimed at achieving those targets. In July 2017, the Government of France announced that it would end the sale of petrol and diesel vehicles by 2040. In October 2017, the city of Paris announced its plan to ban all petrol and diesel cars from Paris by 2030, underscoring that large cities like Paris will need speedier phase-outs of cars with internal combustion engines because of rising levels of nitrogen oxides, a major risk to public health. At the same time, the United Kingdom of Great Britain and Northern Ireland announced its plan to ban all new sales of petrol and diesel cars (including all types of hybrid cars) and vans from 2040. Almost every car and van on the road will need to produce zero emissions by 2050 (United Kingdom, 2017a; 2017b).[7]

In September 2017, the Government of China announced that it is developing a long-term plan to phase out vehicles powered by fossil fuels, but without setting a timeline for a ban. It is considering a dual-credit scheme for manufacturers for their production of more fuel-efficient gasoline cars and new energy vehicles—EVs, including plug-in hybrid and fuel cell models. The scheme is complex and is undergoing changes, but automakers whose annual production is over 50,000 will be assessed as regards new energy vehicle production (International Council on Clean Transportation, 2016; IEA, 2018b, pp. 23–25). The 2020 target translates into about a 4–5 per cent market share in annual car sales.

At least 12 countries have set EV deployment targets and introduced mandates and regulations

At least 12 other countries—including Austria, Denmark, Germany, India, Ireland, Japan, the Netherlands, Norway, Portugal, the Republic of Korea, Spain and the United States—have set EV deployment targets as part of their clean energy and mobility plans. In the United States, 10 States have set their own targets, although there are no national targets. The cumulative assessment of these targets (as developed by the Electric Vehicles Initiative (EVI)), if achieved, suggests the deployment of 13 million EVs in these countries by 2020 (IEA, 2017, EV support policies annex and p. 23).[8]

In 2009, the EVI was established at the intergovernmental level under the Clean Energy Ministerial. As at May 2017, the Initiative had 10 member Governments: Canada, China, France, Germany, Japan, the Netherlands, Norway, Sweden, the United Kingdom and the United States. In 2017, it launched the EV30@30 campaign, which set the collective goal for all EVI member countries of achieving a 30 per cent market share for EVs in the total of all passenger cars, light commercial vehicles, buses and trucks by 2030. IEA is coordinating this important initiative (IEA, 2017, pp. 9–10).

Despite these initiatives, EVs have still a long way to go before they can exert a significant impact on global CO_2 emissions. The global stock of EVs is estimated to have accounted for only about 0.2 per cent of the total number of passenger cars and light trucks

6 Both financial and non-financial incentives change from year to year and are too numerous to list. For details, see Thiel, Krause and Dilara (2015).

7 It should be noted that in 2011, the United Kingdom became the first country to announce its intention that fossil fuel car and van sales should end by 2040.

8 The figure should be considered as only tentative, since national plans of these countries are frequently revised and other countries may join this group of countries.

in 2016; hence, policy support will remain critical for further encouragement of wider use of EVs.

Major global auto makers made important announcements on EV deployment in response to government initiatives

In response to these government initiatives, major global original equipment manufacturers also made important announcements on EV deployment targets. The announcement by Volvo — the Swedish auto brand which is currently owned by Zhejiang Geely Holding Group, a Chinese multinational automaker — of its plan to manufacture only EVs and hybrid cars from 2019 onward has been hailed as the beginning of the end of internal combustion engines' dominance of motor transport after more than a century.

Governments will need to further expand tax, monetary and other incentives in order to render EVs more attractive

Given the prevailing high prices of EVs, Governments will need, increasingly, to provide and expand tax and monetary incentives and other benefits in order to make EVs more attractive. The availability of publicly accessible fast chargers is still limited across countries, with drivers of EVs typically preferring home or workplace chargers (IEA, 2018b, chap. 3). Hence, Governments will also be required to encourage the private sector to improve the charging infrastructure, so that the recharging of EV batteries becomes as convenient and rapid as the refuelling of tanks at conventional gas stations. Furthermore, there is the need for increasing R&D investments in EV research to render them commercially viable for middle-income households without the support of tax subsidies. More importantly, Governments in both developed and developing countries must intensify efforts to shift their energy source from fossil fuels to renewables in order to establish EVs as an important innovation within the context of reducing GHG emissions and improving environmental sustainability.

Is automation a double-edged sword — promoting growing prosperity while fostering growing inequality?

AI, machine learning and robotics have expanded automation to new areas of work

Advances in the field of artificial intelligence (AI) offer the opportunity to expand automation to new areas of work, which has the immense potential to generate productivity gains and economic growth. Such technological advances can also have beneficial impacts on working conditions and health by sparing human labour from having to carry out physically and psychologically demanding tasks.

Historically, automation has created winners and losers, necessitating adequate policies and institutions

The history of automation suggests that technological change typically generates a trade-off between efficiency and equity. That trade-off, which creates winners and losers, requires adequate policies and institutions to minimize the impact on those adversely affected. On this depends the achievement of the Sustainable Development Goals (SDGs), particularly the promotion of sustained, inclusive and sustainable economic growth, full and productive employment and decent work for all (Goal 8) and reduction of inequalities (Goal 10).

However, the potential to automate certain tasks — and possibly entire occupations — does not signify a commensurate disappearance in the aggregate number of jobs, since the automation process will also create new tasks and offer productivity gains, which in turn will spur additional demand for labour. These new employment opportunities could offset the number of jobs lost to automation. On the other hand, the adjustment will not be guaranteed without the aforementioned adequate policies, and may also turn out to be too slow and painful for workers adversely affected by automation. Moreover, the types of new jobs created, especially in the service sector, may not be as well paid as, or of similar quality to, those eliminated by automation.

Ongoing automation could represent a continuation of the automation process that began in the late 1980s with the onset of computerization and a more intensive use of robots. The challenges to average workers and to income distribution that automation may pose therefore need to be considered in the context of the challenges and long-term trends observed since the 1980s.

AI, machine learning and robotics, in expanding to new domains, offer huge opportunities for automating work processes both manual and cognitive (Brynjolfsson and McAfee, 2011; 2017).[9] Routine tasks entail predictable procedures framed by specific rules and are therefore easy to automate; and the automation process which began (as noted above) with computerization in the late 1980s had largely been confined to routine tasks (Autor and Dorn, 2013). However, the use of industrial robots, which accelerated during the 1990s and 2000s in advanced economies (Graetz and Michaels, 2015), has led to the disappearance of many routine tasks in the automotive, electronics and metal product manufacturing industries, which were traditionally performed by low- and medium-skilled workers. Computerization and automation are no longer confined to routine jobs (Brynjolfsson and McAfee, 2011). Deep learning algorithms, for instance, can now outperform humans in detecting patterns in big data. In a new automation age, engagement in cognitive tasks will no longer be the exclusive prerogative of humans.

A debate persists on the extent to which jobs could be automated and replaced by machines

An intense debate persists on the extent to which jobs could be automated and replaced by machines (Bruckner, LaFleur and Pitterle, 2017) — a debate that is centred on analysing potential impacts on specific tasks versus entire occupations. The analytical results for tasks are different from those for occupations and both sets of results are not always comparable. The estimated impacts on the tasks tend to be lower than those estimated for entire occupations. Notwithstanding these differences, the new wave of automation will extend to many non-routine tasks, putting low and medium skills more at risk than higher ones.

Many technological, economic and social factors determine the extent and pace of automation

Many factors will determine the extent and pace of automation and its impact on tasks and occupations (McKinsey Global Institute, 2017a), including technical feasibility, advancements of AI in speech and sensory perception, the cost of automation, wage and labour-market flexibilities, potential productivity gains, and improvements in quality and convenience of automation, as well as regulatory frameworks and behavioural factors. There will be a need to differentiate between the labour saving and labour augmenting

9 Artificial intelligence (AI), one of the most significant and potentially disruptive technological developments observed in recent years, encompasses technologies as diverse as "intelligent" stock trading, human speech recognition and self-driving vehicles. At the core of current AI applications, is machine learning—where machines become capable of learn from large amounts of data—and whose development has been very rapid. This has been made possible through the evolution of the Internet and the increase in the availability of large amounts of digital data for analysis. In machine learning, rather than learn from human beings, machines utilize all available information, to achieve the ability to perform a wide range of activities. Often cited in this regard are the advantages machine learning offers in the health sector. A computer can make use of 600,000 medical reports or millions of patient records for pattern recognition and compare the results with a specific case to determine the best treatment plan. In the financial industry, automation is also being taken seriously, as both an opportunity and a threat. Analysts, for example, are becoming redundant, given that new algorithms—often performed by small start-up companies—have the potential to automate a large part of their work. Decisions regarding loans are now being made by software which can take into account a wide variety of detailed data on a borrower, instead of simply using the classic credit score.

effects of automation: While labour saving automation may increase unemployment, labour augmenting technologies may increase the demand for high-skilled workers, leading to the polarization of labour markets and an increase in wage inequality. In less developed economies, where the levels of both wages and adoption of frontier technologies are low, automation will likely take root at a slower pace (World Bank, 2016).

Slow adjustment in labour markets

Automation displaces labour in some tasks, but creates demand for labour to perform non-automated tasks

Automation will require adjustments in labour markets, and adjustment costs may be particularly onerous for less skilled workers. A new wave of automation, which will cause displacement of labour in some tasks, is expected to result in a reduction of wages and, ultimately, of the share of labour in national income. However, this initial displacement effect can be offset by productivity gains (Acemoglu and Restrepo, 2018a), entailing a reduction of production costs and an increasing demand, as the economy expands, for labour to perform non-automated tasks (either in the same sector or other sectors), including those requiring adaptability, common sense and creativity (Autor, 2015). During the early stages of the computerization process, for example, the task composition in the United States reflected a shift towards more interpersonal and communication-intensive activities (Michaels, Rauch and Redding, 2013). This computerization process, which started in the 1980s, generated demand for analytical and interactive work, as routine tasks became automated (Autor, Levy and Murnane, 2003).

The impact of automation on employment growth will vary across sectors. The increased use of information and communications technologies (ICT) in the manufacturing sector, for example, is associated with slower growth in manufacturing jobs, but greater use of ICT in the service sector has had little or no negative impact on employment growth. However, concerns remain regarding whether automation will create a sufficient number of new jobs to compensate for the jobs lost owing to automation. When computer spreadsheets began to replace manual bookkeeping, and the bookkeepers were replaced by data-processing staff as well as software and hardware professionals in the same sector or industry, the impact on the total number of jobs was minimal. Ongoing AI-led automation, especially automation of non-routine tasks, is likely to have a larger negative impact, on both routine and non-routine jobs.

A study shows that each high-tech job creates 4.9 additional jobs in other occupations…

The silver lining is the potential spillover effects of automation on other sectors, generating additional demand for goods and services (Acemoglu and Restrepo, 2018a). There are estimates suggesting that each high-tech job creates 4.9 additional jobs in other occupations (Moretti, 2010, as cited in Berger and Frey, 2016) which explains partly why recent job growth in countries that are members of the Organization for Economic Cooperation and Development (OECD) has been largely concentrated in non-technology sectors (Berger and Frey, 2016).

The pace of adoption of emerging technologies will determine the time required for labour-market adjustments. Adjustments to new tasks will require new skills, which the workforce may lack, especially when technology requires higher skills and when the educational system cannot anticipate future demand for skills. The mismatch between skills and new tasks not only slows down employment and wages adjustments, but can also undermine potential productivity gains (Acemoglu and Restrepo, 2018a).

…but automation is likely to affect low-skilled, low-wage workers, exacerbating income inequality

Even when automation leads to higher productivity and increased demand for goods and services from non-automated sectors, aggregate demand in an economy may still stagnate or even fall. Automation is likely to adversely affect low-skilled, low-wage workers, who tend to have a higher propensity to consume than high-skilled, high-income workers. A permanent decline in labour income of low-skilled workers may therefore depress economic growth. Automation in developed countries may also reduce imports from low-income countries which rely on relatively low-cost labour, displacing workers in their export sectors and potentially exacerbating income inequality among countries.

Automation and the future of work

The empirical evidence since the 1980s has illustrated how automation has led to a reduction in jobs in routine intensive occupations and to the polarization of labour markets, which contributed to a significant increase in wage inequalities. Computerization and robotization in the 1980s and 1990s reduced the demand for labour that performed routine tasks (Autor, Levy and Murnane, 2003). Industrial robots, introduced in late 1980s, automated many of the labour-intensive tasks in manufacturing, including machining, welding, painting, palletizing, assembly, material handling and quality control (Graetz and Michaels, 2015). This led to a long-term secular decline in the share of labour in routine-intensive occupations. For instance, in OECD countries, the share of employment in the manufacturing sector decreased from about 25 per cent in the 1970s to about 10 per cent in 2013 (OECD, 2015) (see figure II.2). While various factors contributed to the decline in manufacturing jobs in OECD countries, automation is considered a key underlying factor (OECD, 2012).

Parallel to the elimination of routine tasks, job growth in OECD countries slowed down in the medium-skill category over the past 20 years (see figure II.3). On the other hand, job opportunities increased at both ends of the skill spectrum in those countries (OECD, 2017e), suggesting increased polarization of skills.

The introduction of automation slowed down job growth in the medium-skill job category

Figure II.2

Decline in manufacturing jobs in OECD countries and China, 1970–2013

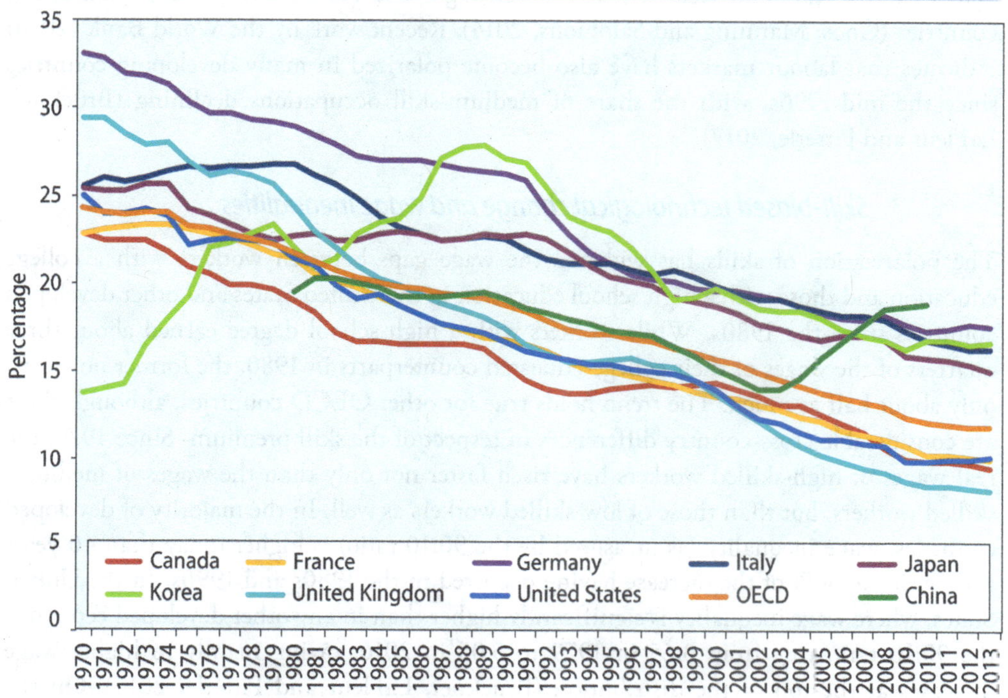

Source: OECD (2015).

Figure II.3
Polarization of labour markets in OECD countries, 1995–2015

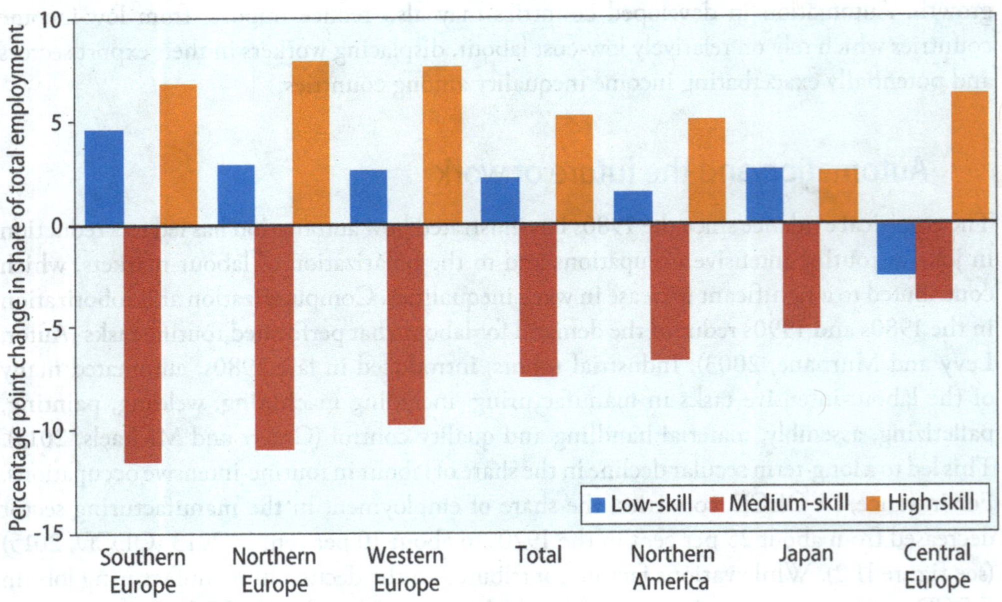

Source: OECD (2017e).

At the same time, the number of jobs increased in both the high- and low-skill categories

This polarization of skills can be explained largely by computerization which has favoured relatively higher-skilled labour. On the other hand, the increase in incomes for higher-skilled workers led to an increased demand for goods and services in other sectors, performed largely by low-skilled labour. There was a surge in low-skill service jobs as well as in work involving manual non-routine tasks, which were not susceptible to computerization. This hollowing out of the middle of the wage distribution is well documented for the United States (Autor, Katz and Kearney, 2006; Acemoglu and Autor, 2011) and for European countries (Goos, Manning and Salomons, 2014). Recent work by the World Bank (2016) indicates that labour markets have also become polarized in many developing countries since the mid-1990s, with the share of medium-skill occupations declining (Bruckner, LaFleur and Pitterle, 2017).

Skill-biased technological change and wage inequalities

Job polarization has widened wage gaps among workers with different levels of education and…

The polarization of skills has widened the wage gaps between workers with a college education and those with a high school education in the United States and other developed countries since the 1980s. While workers with a high school degree earned about three quarters of the wages of their college-educated counterparts in 1980, the former now earn only about half as much. The trend holds true for other OECD countries, although there are considerable cross-country differences in respect of the skill premium. Since 1970, the real wages of high-skilled workers have risen faster not only than the wages of medium-skilled workers, but than those of low-skilled workers as well. In the majority of developed countries, wage inequality (as measured by the 90:10 ratio) is higher today than 40 years ago, with the bulk of the increase having occurred in the 1980s and 1990s. In the United States, where wage inequality is significantly higher than in any other developed economy, the 90:10 ratio rose from 3.65 in 1979 to 5.05 in 2016, owing mainly to higher wage increases at the top of the distribution (Bruckner, LaFleur and Pitterle, 2017). On the other hand, there is growing evidence that differences in labour-market institutions, as reflected, for example, in union density, employment protection and minimum wage laws, play an important role in containing wage gaps and skill premiums (Koeniger, Leonardi and Nuziata, 2007; OECD, 2017e; Bruckner, LaFleur and Pitterle, 2017).

With further automation, the polarization of labour markets is expected to continue, which would potentially further aggravate wage inequalities. In this regard, the International Federation of Robotics estimates that the number of robots in advanced economies could increase fourfold by 2025. Should the spread of robots be as rapid as anticipated by several analysts, the negative consequences for the aggregate employment and wage will be significantly stronger than those that have been observed so far (Acemoglu and Restrepo, 2017).

...polarization is expected to continue in the future, further aggravating wage inequalities

Declining share of labour income

An automation process can further increase income and wealth inequalities through its effect on the distribution of income between capital and labour. Automation is inherently capital-intensive. Increased capital intensity in production of goods and services typically increases the total return on capital and the share of capital income in gross domestic product (GDP). As discussed above, AI, machine learning and robots are expected to lead to a substitution of labour by capital for certain skills, with direct and severe consequences for income distribution.

Automation has also reduced the labour share of national income in developed countries since the 1990s

The labour share of income was stable in developed economies until the 1980s, despite important variations in the short and medium terms. Since then, however, the share of labour income has been declining consistently across advanced economies for several decades (OECD, 2012; IMF, 2017), contradicting the notion of a stable labour share of income in the long term. For example, between 1990 and 2009, the labour share of national income declined in 26 out of 30 advanced countries for which data were available (see figure II.4). During that period, the median (adjusted) labour share of national income across these countries fell from 66.1 to 61.7 per cent (OECD, 2012).

In some emerging and developing economies, the decline in the labour share of national income is even more pronounced than in advanced economies, with considerable declines in Asia and Northern Africa (ILO, 2011). In a recent study, Karabarbounis and Neiman (2013) found that labour share in GDP had declined in 42 out of 59 countries, including China, India and Mexico, and concluded that, as advances in information technology reduced the cost of plants, machinery and equipment, firms became more capital-intensive and reduced the number of employees. A high degree of substitution between capital and labour—particularly less-skilled labour (Brynjolfsson and McAfee, 2011)—explains the declining share of labour income.

The labour share also declined in some developing countries, particularly in Asia and Northern Africa

Further, there is evidence that wage and productivity growth diverged during the same period in most advanced economies. In the majority of G20 countries for which data are available, the aggregate growth of real wages was significantly slower than that of aggregate productivity (see figure II.5), even taking into account the dynamics of relative prices, which thus accounted for the decline in the labour share (ILO and OECD, 2015). However, the divergence between productivity growth and wage growth is presumably less pronounced for high-skilled workers because of the skill premium received by those workers. This notwithstanding, increasing productivity is not a sufficient condition for an increase in the real wages of the average worker.

Since 2000, wage and productivity growth have diverged, particularly for lower-skilled workers

Figure II.4

Decline of labour share in OECD countries, 1990–2009[a]

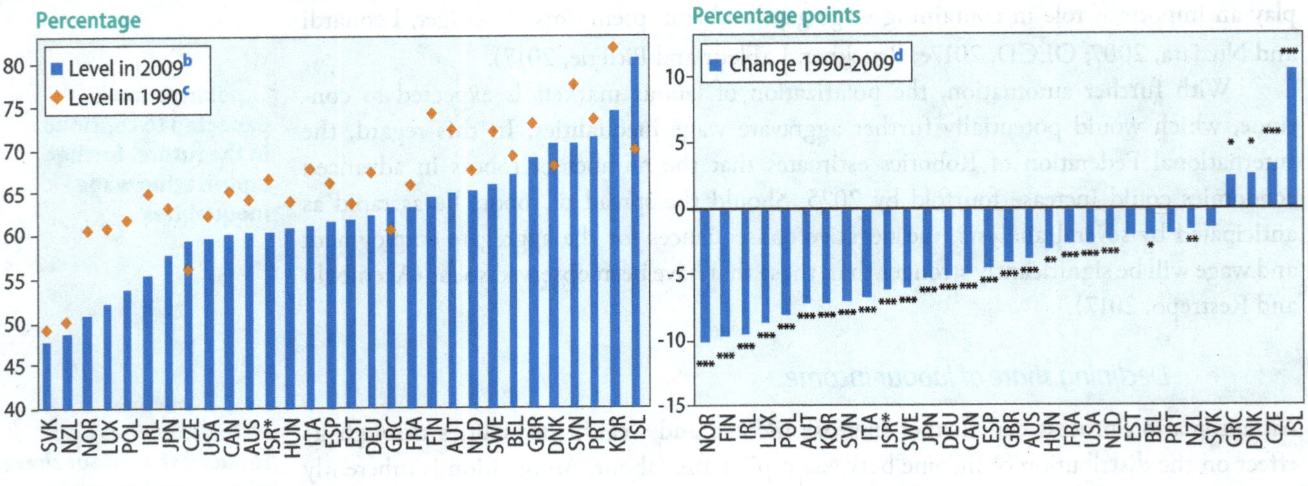

Source: OECD (2012), figure 3.1.

Notes:

a Graphs represent three-year averages, starting and ending with indicated years.

b Germany and Iceland: 1991; Estonia: 1993; Poland: 1994; Czech Republic, Greece, Hungary, Slovak Republic and Slovenia: 1995; Israel: 2000.

c Portugal: 2005; Canada and New Zealand: 2006; Australia, Belgium, Ireland, Norway and Sweden: 2007; France, Iceland, Israel, Poland and the United Kingdom: 2008.

d ***,** and * indicate significance at the 1 per cent, 5 per cent and 10 per cent levels, respectively. Statistical significance refers to the coefficient of the time trend in a bivariate regression on annual data with the labour share as dependent variable. The wage of the self-employed is imputed assuming that their annual wage is the same as for the average employee of the whole economy.

Declining labour-force participation

Automation is also partly associated with the declining labour-force participation observed in OECD countries

Declining labour-force participation—that is, decline in the proportion of people who are employed or looking for work—across advanced economies is a concerning labour-market trend. The declining labour-force participation rate has been associated partly with the automation process, entailing a painful adjustment by workers whose skills became redundant. In OECD countries, labour-force participation has trended downward, particularly for members of the prime male labour force between the ages of 25 and 64. This decline became more pronounced starting in the 1990s and, later, with the unfolding of the global financial crisis.

Reductions in the demand for labour, especially for lower-skilled men, appear to be another critical component of the decline in prime-age male labour-force participation in developed economies. This is consistent with the observation that technological change weakened demand for less-skilled labour, principally in the manufacturing sector, making job polarization a major contributor to the declining labour-force participation rates (Krause and Sawhill, 2017). There is also evidence that prime-age men often choose not to work under a given set of labour-market conditions. For example, supply-side factors, such as increased participation in social programmes (e.g., those offering disability insurance or food stamps) and the setting of a high reservation wage, contribute to low labour-force participation in the United States (ibid.).

Figure II.5
Average wages and labour productivity in selected G20 countries, 1999–2013

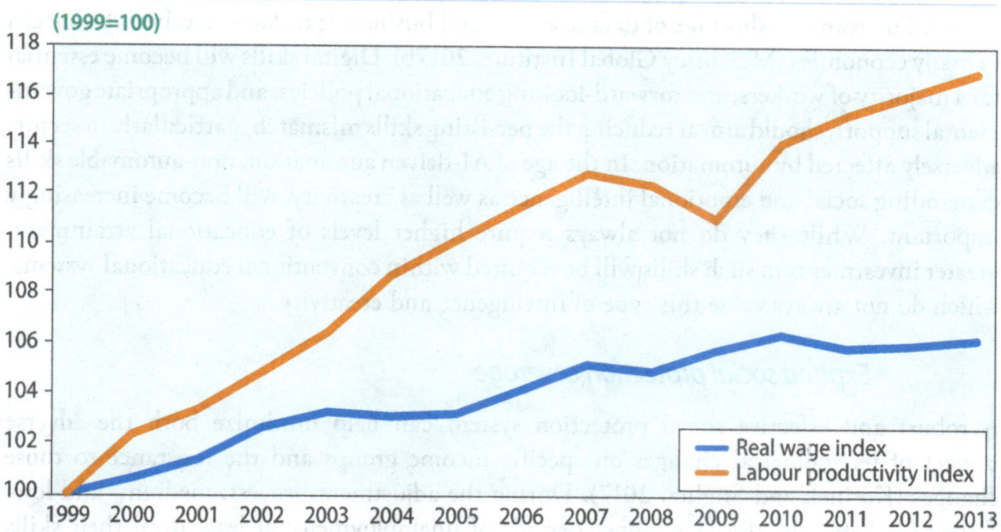

Source: ILO and OECD (2015).
Note: Data refer to Australia, Canada, France, Germany, Italy, Japan, Republic of Korea, the United Kingdom of Great Britain and Northern Ireland and the United States of America. Real wage growth is calculated as a weighted average of year-on-year growth in real average monthly wages in the advanced G20 economies. For a description of the methodology, see ILO (2015), appendix I.

Policies for protecting employment and wages

Policymakers need to minimize the adverse impact of automation

AI, machine learning and the new age of robotics present a number of policy challenges to minimizing their potential negative impact on employment, wages and inequalities. Political reaction to frontier technologies can, in theory, slow down or even prevent their adoption and development if they do not promote shared prosperity (Acemoglu and Restrepo, 2018a). It is therefore important to focus on policies that have the potential to minimize the impact of these emerging technologies on employment and income distribution.

Build forward-looking and inclusive education systems

The education system should be more inclusive, particularly for disadvantaged groups, including youth

Automation will require a constant upgrading of workforce skills. However, many workers whose jobs are partially or fully automatable lack the skills and ability they would need to switch to the higher-skill jobs created by automation. There are considerable cross-country variations in the impact of automation on wage inequalities since the 1980s, which is partly explained by differences in terms of the availability of educated and skilled workers. Given that access to higher and better education is often determined by the socioeconomic background of parents, the educational system needs to be more inclusive in the age of automation so as to ensure that socioeconomically disadvantaged population groups have opportunities to acquire the skill sets that are relevant in markets for increasingly automated jobs.

As unemployment and the risk of falling below a poverty line are particularly high for youth, whose education and career choices have yet to be made, younger generations need to be made aware of the potential of automation, including the changes that it will generate in the labour market. In this regard, Governments could contribute to developing an educational system that facilitates the acquisition of basic skills and capabilities which are adaptable and less at risk of becoming automatable, thereby helping youth identify the skills that will be complementary to the automation process (Brynjolfsson and McAfee, 2014).

Private firms and workers have roles to play in reducing the persisting skills mismatch

Governments could implement policies that encourage private firms and workers to invest in continuous learning and development of skills in areas where demand remains unmet. For example, shortage of data scientists and business translators has been a concern in many economies (McKinsey Global Institute, 2017b). Digital skills will become essential for a majority of workers; and forward-looking educational policies, and appropriate governmental support, should aim at reducing the persisting skills mismatch, particularly in sectors adversely affected by automation. In the age of AI-driven automation, non-automable skills demanding social and emotional intelligence as well as creativity, will become increasingly important. While they do not always require higher levels of educational attainment, greater investments in such skills will be required within conventional educational systems, which do not always value this type of intelligence and creativity.

Expand social protection coverage

A robust and effective social protection system should be in place

A robust and effective social protection system can help minimize both the adverse impact of technological changes on specific income groups and the resistance to those changes (Korinek and Stiglitz, 2017). During the adjustment process, medium- and low-skilled workers typically face longer periods of unemployment, at least until their skills are upgraded. Social insurance programmes can be critical in providing affected workers with sustenance during these transitional periods involving joblessness. In addition, there will be a clear need for coverage by targeted social protection schemes of specific sectors and locations where the displacement effect is stronger. Active labour-market policies—including, e.g., job placement services, special labour-market programmes and wage subsidies—can help facilitate adaptation during the transition period, especially of less-skilled workers. Automation may create jobs in one region, while eliminating them in other regions; and if the workers affected are to avail themselves of new job opportunities, they may be faced with high search and relocation costs. They would therefore require help in relocating to those areas where employment growth is faster. Policies to facilitate such geographical mobility could target housing and moving costs, among others (Berger and Frey, 2016).

Social protection schemes in developed countries will need to evolve if they are to confront the new realities of non-standard employment conditions. In many advanced economies, work under temporary contracts, part-time jobs and self-employment often do not qualify for full social protection. As frontier technologies increasingly favour self-employment, part-time work and new types of employment based on sharing-economy models, there will be a need for the extension of social protection coverage, funded with tax revenues, to workers whose conditions of employment are non-standard.

The universal basic income, which would provide a regular unconditional cash grant to every individual, has gained fresh importance in this new age of automation, given the risks it presents of loss of employment and decline in wages. The empirical evidence needed to assess the impact of such an initiative is still lacking. In addition, Governments will need to increase tax revenues substantially in order to cover all of the population with a UBI high enough to tackle poverty.

Build stronger labour-market institutions

Stronger labour-market institutions should be (re)built

Empirical evidence suggests that labour unions can play a major role in ensuring a fair distribution of national income (OECD, 2012). They give workers, in particular less-skilled workers, a stronger bargaining power in negotiating wages that match their productivity and ensure minimum labour standards. Since the 1970s, the density of labour unions has decreased considerably in developed economies; and de-unionization, along with automation, has been considered an important factor in the decline in the wages of lower-skilled workers (Acemoglu, 2000). As AI and other similar technologies are expected to exert pressure on wages, especially on the wages of medium- and low-skilled labour, workers will need more effective representation.

Introduce progressive and innovative taxes

Income tax schemes should be more progressive towards the very top of the income distribution

Reducing income inequalities will also require more progressive income tax schemes. Disposable income has increased much faster at the top of the income distribution, owing not only to skill- and capital-biased technological change, but also to the less progressive taxation that was introduced during the past three decades. Income tax schemes are needed to become more progressive, especially towards the very top of the income distribution. By reducing the accumulation of capital and wealth of top income-earners—and consequently the return on accumulated wealth-tax schemes of this type reduce not just post-tax income inequality, but future pre-tax income inequality as well.

Taxing robots and taxing capital returns from patent monopolies to reduce income inequality have been suggested

The concept of taxing *robots* has gained traction (Guerreiro, Rebelo and Teles, 2018), as suggested in a 31 May 2016 report of the Committee of Legal Affairs to the European Parliament. In that report, the Committee introduced a motion for a European Parliament resolution in which the Parliament would emphasize that "consideration should be given to the possible need to introduce corporate reporting requirements on the extent and proportion of the contribution of robotics and AI to the economic results of a company for the purpose of taxation and social security contributions". Taxes of this type could generate the resources required to retrain workers and expand employment in the health-care and education sectors. While a number of entrepreneurs have supported such a requirement and while some countries have taken concrete steps in this direction, developing a common understanding of the definition of "robot" remains a challenge. If such a definition is not clearly established, a tax on robots may simply induce their producers to bundle the components of this new technology with other types of machinery. It has also been suggested that a robot registry be created to keep an accounting of the loss of jobs performed by humans and facilitate compensation for the loss of revenues through a supplementary tax, which could be levied at the corporate or the robot level. As indicated above, the speed at which automation is being introduced poses a challenge. Hence, slowing down automation and creating tax disincentives to counter technology's displacement effect on employment could be sensible policy options and serve as the basis for a policy that is suitable for some countries. However, the effect might be only temporary, inasmuch as countries will need to keep pace with technological development if they are to compete in international markets.

The returns on capital earned by innovators are an important source of income inequality (Korinek and Stiglitz, 2017). Taxing return on capital—especially excess return earned from patent monopolies—may be more conducive to a balancing of income distribution. A suggestion in the same vein has been to shorten the term of patents, which would accelerate the entry of innovations into the public domain and their accessibility and limit monopolistic income advantages.

Digital technologies: a Pandora's box?

Social media and online platforms, backed by AI, may have opened a Pandora's box of ethical issues

AI, powered by algorithms and machine learning, is defining the future of digital technologies, with economic and social activities increasingly being shifted from the physical world to the digital space. Computer codes and algorithms are the key drivers of various applications of the technologies in that space—ranging from activities on social media and other online platforms to automated decision systems used in public agencies. While advances in digital technologies offer great benefits in terms of efficiency and information sharing, they may have also opened up a Pandora's box of ethical issues related to fairness and inclusion, privacy and autonomy, and accountability and transparency.

Addressing ethical issues is crucial to ensuring social inclusion and cohesion, and political stability

Deployment of the algorithms driving social media and other online platforms may lead to discrimination against specific groups of people and an undermining of informed decision-making. Addressing these concerns is crucial to ensuring social inclusion, social cohesion and political stability, as envisaged under Sustainable Development Goals 16 and 17. The increasing use of automated decision systems in the areas of job recruitment and criminal justice also runs the risks of further reinforcing biases against minority groups and exacerbating social inequalities. Fulfilling the imperatives of leaving no one behind—the cardinal objective of the 2030 Agenda—and of reducing inequality, promoting social inclusion and eliminating discriminatory practices, as envisaged under SDG 10, requires urgent action to address these challenges.

Rapid advances in various digital technologies, increasingly underpinned by artificial intelligence, render existing regulatory frameworks, social norms and ethical standards inadequate. Societies must develop new ethical standards on the use of those technologies; and policymakers and the public must reflect concretely on the meaning of fairness and accountability as they will apply in digital space. While ethical and social norms vary across countries, the new standards should be grounded in internationally agreed instruments, such as the Charter of the United Nations and the Universal Declaration of Human Rights,[10] which provide the framework for the protection of and respect for human rights.

The need to address the undesirable impacts of digital technologies, as already manifested on social media platforms and in algorithmic decision systems—and to avert even more negative consequences as applications of those technologies proliferate more widely—puts every society at a critical juncture. Through an examination of the issues at hand, the present section charts a way forward towards enabling a society to benefit from the efficiency gains to be achieved through digital technology while addressing collateral equity and ethical challenges. There is a clear need for policymakers to step in and for public debate to determine the appropriate balance among efficiency, equity and ethics.

Online platforms: connecting or disconnecting people?

Social media have changed the way we interact with each other

Social media and other online platforms have greatly changed the way social interactions and the spread of information are carried out. It is increasingly obvious that the use of social media and other online platforms—which have remained unregulated for years—can have negative societal consequences. Those platforms have facilitated the spread of misinformation and hate speech and created so-called echo chambers which have contributed to the polarization of society and have possibly influenced elections. Further,

10 General Assembly resolution 217 A (III).

they have collected massive amounts of data which are used by the platforms themselves, by advertisers and by other third parties, with ramifications extending to privacy, freedom and, potentially, to the very foundations of democracy. While disruptions of this type are not a new phenomenon, the ease of communication on social media and the ability to deploy big data-driven algorithms to sway or rouse large population groups have caught policymakers by surprise.

Echo chambers and the spread of misinformation

The Internet, while creating a global village, is also increasingly fostering the formation of isolated digital communities through use of algorithms to shape social media interactions (El-Bermawy, 2016). People form these "islands" to interact with other people who possess and share similar views. This dynamic, which locks participants into personalized feedback loops or the above-mentioned echo chambers, has arguably widened societal divides, allowing different groups to live in their own cognitive bubbles and reinforcing confirmation biases. Those algorithms also have an enormous impact on how the information consumed by people is selected. Algorithms take advantage of human vulnerabilities: they can manipulate a user by presenting content that may either reinforce or contradict that user's opinions.

Echo chambers have been cited as one of the key contributors to the political polarization experienced by many developed countries in recent years. Recent studies have revealed how Facebook users come to inhabit highly polarized closed communities (Quattrociocchi, Scala and Sunstein, 2016) and how people who communicate on Twitter become disproportionately exposed to the tweets of like-minded users (Halberstam and Knight, 2014). This can propel people towards ever more extreme viewpoints, a tendency referred to as algorithmic radicalization and also as enclave extremism (Sunstein, 2007). Such online platforms are well suited to the amplification of the voices of a small group, a process in which algorithms play a key role. For example, when a user engages with a certain type of content, the algorithm-based recommendation system will pull that user towards more extreme or more radical content (Nicas, 2018).

Echo chambers have also contributed to the undermining of objective expertise and the spreading of misinformation (OECD, 2017c). These platforms favour content that grabs the user's attentions and maximizes engagement, regardless of its accuracy, and whatever users see in their newsfeeds has been algorithmically curated. The algorithms, combined with automated accounts (so-called bots), ensure that false information spreads fast (Vosoughi, Roy and Aral, 2018).

Social media have disseminated hate speech and content that incites violence

These issues are being confronted not only in developed countries but in many developing countries as well. Hate speech, content that incites violence, and disinformation targeting specific minority groups have been disseminated rapidly on social media in several developing countries, often with devastating consequences.[11] False information is disseminated differently in developing as compared with developed countries. This is due to limited availability of official information for fact-checking and the lack of public confidence in news media sources. Language barriers, higher illiteracy rates and the relative higher cost of securing Internet access serve to limit the amount of time people can devote to obtaining truthful information (World Wide Web Foundation, 2017).

11 See, for example, the statement by the Chairman of the Independent International Fact-Finding Mission on Myanmar, Marzuki Darusman, at the thirty-seventh session of the Human Rights Council on 12 March 2018.

It is important that the spread of misinformation and hate speech on social media platforms be addressed, while at the same time respecting freedom of speech and avoiding undue censorship. The clear need to ensure accountability for content and to apply content moderation should be balanced by an awareness of the dangers of surveillance, censorship and suppression of free speech.

Targeting advertisements, discrimination and manipulation

Digital technology firms generate revenue by selling ads based on personal information

The largest digital technology firms generate revenue by selling advertisements based on personal information collected on online platforms or by search engines. The reliance on advertising as the primary business model for revenue generation creates adverse incentives for online platforms, which are often faced with a trade-off between protecting user privacy and generating ad revenue. While users have benefited from free access to these platforms, they bear the hidden cost of ceding control of their personal data.

The consent agreements governing the operation of these data exchanges are often opaque and their terms are consequently unclear to users. Consumers have come to trust companies with vast amounts of data of a highly intimate nature, which can result in the loss of ownership of those data. It is particularly difficult for users to anticipate the ways in which the personal information that is extracted might be used and reused by third parties. Intense data collection can enable advertisers to increase consumer satisfaction by targeting relevant advertisements to specific user groups. However, targeted advertisements also raise many ethical issues, with implications for consumers related to privacy, manipulation and potential discrimination (Plane and others, 2017).

Advertisers can target specific groups of people to view, or to be excluded from viewing, their ads

Their ability to identify specific users has made it possible for advertisers to target specific groups of people to view—or to be excluded from viewing—their ads. Not only is this practice questionable from an ethical perspective but it sometimes runs counter to certain civil rights laws (Angwin and Paris, 2016). ProPublica has demonstrated that it is indeed possible for advertisers to exclude certain categories of users when placing a housing advertisement on Facebook, which may constitute a violation of United States federal legislation, namely, the Fair Housing Act (Angwin, Tobin and Varner, 2017). Both Facebook and Google subsequently disallowed advertisers the use of characteristics such as ethnic "affinity" as a means of preventing ads related to housing, employment or financial services from being seen. However, Speicher and others (2018), investigating the different targeting methods offered by Facebook, have shown that even without relying on sensitive attributes, an advertiser can still create highly discriminatory ads.

Targeted ads can have implications for democratic processes and elections

The potential of targeted advertisements can have implications as well for democratic processes and elections. The massive amounts of data derived from social media platforms have enabled researchers to build accurate psychological profiles of individuals, which enable personalized political advertising. This entails tailoring messages to the specific interests and vulnerabilities of particular voters in order to manipulate them, invade their privacy and undermine their agency, autonomy and freedom. Personalization algorithms of this type must strike an ethical balance between coercion and support for the decision-making autonomy of users (Lewis and Westlund, 2015).

Those who own and control this kind of information and data wield real power over people. The accumulation of personal data by credit agencies, social media companies and other entities has significant implications with respect to who has the right to own and monetize personal data. Even if, technically speaking, people are the owners of their personal data, they may not be able to exercise control over those data, and this has important implications. A key means of preserving the ability of people to exercise that control is to ensure that, for example, they have the right to data portability, and hence the ability to transfer their data from one service provider to another.

The data collection that facilitates targeted advertising is underpinned by an opaque surveillance infrastructure, which enables platforms to exercise immense power over individuals and, potentially, over the whole of society. To the extent that people are unaware of their rights and the options available for protecting their privacy, they are understandably surprised when confronted by the magnitude of the data concerning them that are available on those platforms (LaFleur, Iversen and Jensen, 2018). Data security and protection of privacy are factors critical to ensuring that social media and other online platforms can be trusted and held accountable. Lack of data protection has, in several instances, compromised the personal information of users. The lack of adequately enforced contractual restrictions on third-party users of data is an issue that must be addressed.

An opaque surveillance infrastructure enables platforms to exercise power over people

Automated decision systems: addressing human bias or reinforcing it?

Automated decision systems, based to varying degrees on AI, are being used increasingly for decision-making in many domains. In the private sector, automated systems are being deployed to facilitate hiring practices, and in the provision of loans. Public sector automated systems contribute to decision-making in the criminal justice system, the education sector and the system of social and children's protection services. While in some cases automated decision systems have improved efficiency, consistency and fairness, in others, they have reinforced historical discrimination and obscured undesirable behaviour (Rieke, Bogen and Robinson, 2018).

Automated decision systems are now being used for decision-making in public and private domains

Replacing human judgment with machines: issues of efficiency, explainability and bias

Automated decision systems can improve efficiency by enabling firms and public institutions to make more informed decisions in a shorter period of time. Indeed, Brynjolfsson and McAfee (2017) argue that in conducting various tasks, machines outperform humans in minimizing bias and error. They contend that while people should remain in the loop for the purpose of common-sense checking, most decision-making should be assigned to algorithms. The belief in the superiority of machines over human judgment is shared by Kahneman (2011), who argues that the decision-making process of humans is "noisy". Especially when the amount of information is large and it is costly for humans to process that information, algorithms will outperform humans. Kahnemann therefore argues that humans should be replaced by algorithms "whenever possible".[12]

Proponents of automated decision systems claim that they not only increase efficiency, but also reduce human bias. However, there are many counter-examples which demonstrate how machine learning reinforces existing bias, discrimination and prejudice, and leads to further social exclusion. Data can be biased, as they are often incomplete, skewed or drawn from non-representative samples, and algorithm developers can encode the bias, consciously or unconsciously, when programming the machine learning processes (Campolo and

Automated decision systems can reinforce existing human bias

12 Remarks by Nobel laureate Daniel Kahneman made at the National Bureau of Economic Reseaech inaugural conference on the Economics of AI, held in Toronto in 2017.

others, 2017). The harms inflicted by such bias can be categorized as either (a) harms of *allocation*, arising when a system allocates a certain opportunity or resource to, or withholds it from, a specific group or (b) harms of *representation*, arising when, through technology, the subordination of some social and cultural groups becomes entrenched (see box II.1).

While an individual can be held accountable for a decision, there is no mechanism for ensuring the transparency and accountability of opaque, "black-box" automated decision systems. Machine learning has created a fundamentally different approach to programming (discussed in more detail in chapter I). While this approach has increased programming efficiency, it has also contributed to greater opaqueness. According to Brynjolfsson and McAfee (2017), "machine learning systems often have low interpretability, meaning that humans have difficulty figuring out how the systems reached their decisions".

Greater explainability is required, given the difficulty of deconstructing how an automated system has reached its decisions

In consequence, there is an increasingly loud call for explainability with respect to automated decision systems. However, people in the technology field fear that requiring this technology to be explainable will only slow down progress, reducing the potential of machine learning to address important challenges, such as diagnosing diseases (Weinberger, 2018). To fully tap the potential of machine learning, it is necessary to relinquish the need to understand the systems involved, as it is often literally impossible to explain their operation to the human mind. In this sense, there is a clear trade-off between progress in machine learning as measured by accuracy and efficiency, and the need for explanations and transparency.

Automated decision systems in public agencies

Automated decision-making processes in the public sector can disproportionally affect disadvantaged people

Automated decision systems have radically changed decision-making processes in many public agencies. However, as those systems are being used in high-stakes domains, issues of bias and discrimination have advanced to the forefront of the public debate. Not only are there inherent biases in the data and algorithms used, but automated decision systems are more often deployed in domains of society where they will affect disadvantaged people. According to Eubanks (2018), many of these systems are first tested on low-income households where there is less of an expectation of respect for privacy. Moreover, the increased prevalence of algorithms in the decision-making processes of public agencies can lead to a decrease in their visibility and, at the same time, an amplification of their effects through layering.

Two applications of machine learning in the criminal justice system—namely, as tools for risk assessment and for predictive policing—have been heavily debated. The United States criminal justice system uses a machine learning tool to calculate what is referred to as a risk score, which is then considered by judges in making pretrial, parole and sentencing decisions. In analysing the efficacy of this tool, Angwin and others (2016) found that the predictions were racially biased and that the predictions made by the system affected black and white defendants differently. While the data used by the software do not include an individual's race, there are other elements of the data that correlate to race, which leads to racial disparities in terms of predictions. Predictive policing provides another powerful example of how algorithms can amplify historical bias. Using machine learning techniques, police departments try to predict the locations of future crimes. Historically, crime data are biased against certain minorities. As a result, the algorithms driving this type of program—which entails learning from previous crime reports—are sometimes trapped within a vicious feedback loop, which results in the over-policing of certain neighbourhoods (Lum and Isaac, 2016).

Box II.1

Two types of potential harm arising from automated decision systems

Harms of allocation — inflicted when a system allocates a certain opportunity or resource to, or withholds it from, a specific group — are well known within the context of automated decision systems. For example, banks using automated systems to evaluate mortgage applications have ended up unfairly denying mortgages to certain minorities or people from a specific geographical area (Harney, 2008).

Recently, more attention has been given to problems related to harms of representation including social stigmatization, where technology reinforces the subordination of some social and cultural groups. In recent examples of such harm, an image recognition programme labelled the faces of several black people as belonging to gorillas; and in a Google Images search for "CEO", the first woman to appear was Barbie! While these "errors" were quickly fixed by the companies and characterized as simple glitches within the systems, they highlight a deeper problem associated with bias in automated systems. Noble (2018) has explored, in particular, how negative stereotypes of black women are codified in search engine algorithms.

In many cases, representational harm can have allocative consequences. For example, the perpetuation of stereotypes regarding a certain group can reduce the employability of the members of that group. Use of automated decision systems in public agencies poses this risk, as the historical data often reinforce past representational harms, which generates economic or identity-based impacts (Reisman and others, 2018).

Table II.1.1

Potential harms arising from algorithmic decision-making

	Example	Impact
Harms of allocation		
Credit discrimination	Withholding specific credit offered to members of certain groups	Economic loss and loss of opportunity
Employment discrimination	Filtering candidates by geographical proximity, leading to exclusion of minorities	
Insurance and social benefits discrimination	Increasing auto-insurance prices for workers on a night shift	
Housing discrimination	Housing advertisement displayed only to certain groups	
Education discrimination	Ads for only for-profit colleges presented to low-income individuals	
Harms of representation		
Confirmation bias	Image search results for "CEO" consist only of male images	Social stigmatization
Increased surveillance	Use of predictive policing which results in the presence of more police in minority neighbourhoods	
Stereotype reinforcement	Word-embedding models reveal gender stereotypes	
Dignitary harms	Emotional distress arising from bias or from a decision based on incorrect data	

Source: UN/DESA, based on Future of Privacy Forum (2017).

Automation must guarantee key values of society, such as fairness, justice and due process

While it is reasonable, in some cases, for public institutions to employ automated decision systems, and private and public information utilized in the systems, to increase efficiency, it is important to understand that both data and algorithms encode bias. As a result, minorities and vulnerable groups can end up being affected disproportionately; and as long as these systems are not built to explicitly dismantle structural inequalities, they are more likely to intensify those inequalities dramatically (Eubanks, 2018). While some have argued that technological fixes to the bias and explainability challenge posed by automated decision systems are available, those fixes remain largely theoretical. Indeed, addressing bias requires more than a technological fix: it requires an understanding of the underlying structural inequalities. In essence, the use of automated decision systems has outpaced the development of the frameworks required to understand and govern them. Given these concerns, there have been serious calls for a cessation of the use of unaudited black box systems in core public agencies, at least until key values such as fairness, justice and due process are guaranteed (Campolo and others, 2017).

Policies for producing socially responsible digital technologies

While the benefits of digital technologies are significant, it is important for policymakers and other stakeholders to proceed with adequate caution in this domain. Rather than accept decisions made by machines uncritically, society needs to construct the mechanism best suited to combine machine intelligence with human wisdom. There is a tendency of many in the technology industry to highlight the negative consequences of "dumbing down" AI for the purpose of providing transparency. Notwithstanding their concerns, it is imperative that a full understanding of the implications of automated decision-making be achieved, even if this entails a slower pace of progress in the field of AI.

It is important that the debate focused on ethical norms and regulatory architecture be shaped not only by leading technology companies but by public debate and Governments as well. Policymakers have a significant and proactive role to play in developing the legal and ethical frameworks needed to govern the evolution and use of digital technologies.

Make privacy laws fit for the digital age

More extensive privacy protection for consumers and the promotion of a data ownership model are needed

Consumers are in need of more extensive privacy protections. The current system, which relies on individualized informed consent, is problematic, as people often do not understand the privacy-related consequences of providing their data. It is increasingly difficult to perceive those consequences since, through the advances in machine learning, seemingly superficial data can be linked with other data in such a way as to reveal highly private information. A third-party rating agency can help protect privacy by offering consumers the opportunity to better understand the consequences of data sharing and thereby enable them to make more-informed decisions on whether or not to share their data.

There are also calls for the promotion of a data ownership model under which people can share or sell their own data if they so desire. However, this could enable firms to take advantage of a consumer's financial situation to secure access to their personal data. One alternative would be the adoption of a data protection law providing individuals with more fundamental rights regarding the processing of all personal data. This would be crucial to ensuring that data privacy is understood to be a right, not a luxury affordable only by some. A balance must be sought, however, with regard to the ethical responsibility to share data for the common good. By sharing data, people will enable technology to attain long-standing goals for the public good, such as achieving a cure for cancer (Domingos, 2015). Hence, it might be important to strike a balance between respecting the need for privacy and making data available as a public good.

The European Union (EU) is at the forefront of the discussion on privacy and data protection. The General Data Protection Regulation (GDPR),[13] which was agreed by the European Parliament and the Council of the European Union in April 2016 and became enforceable in Europe in May 2018, will require social platforms to change the way that they collect data from their customers and store and deploy them. The predictions are mixed, however, regarding the societal and ethical impacts of the Regulation, as the cost of compliance for companies may be so high as to limit innovation and access to technology within the EU. Some argue that the GDPR will have a negative effect on AI innovation while at the same time failing to protect—or even potentially harming—consumers (Wallace and Castro, 2018). However, the proponents of the Regulation predict that it will provide valuable protections for consumers which will produce a ripple effect extending beyond the EU (Susswein, 2018).

The European Union is at the forefront of the discussion on privacy and data protection

Since all companies with a presence in Europe must implement the rules set out in the Regulation to cover their operation there, it should also be possible for companies to put a system in place for extending the same protection to users elsewhere in the world (as Facebook has hinted that it will strive to do). However, the potential voluntary geographical extension of the GDPR by some technology companies, for the purpose of covering other countries, would not eliminate the need for an international standard on data protection and regulation.

Encourage diversity and ethics education in the technology field

There is a disconnect between people who develop technologies and the communities that are affected by those technologies. Since technology is not value-neutral, it needs to be built and shaped by diverse communities so as to minimize adverse social consequences, such as bias, prejudice and discrimination. Indeed, women and minority groups remain underrepresented in the technology field, and policymakers need to be proactive in transcending this status quo.

As technology is not value-neutral, it needs to be shaped by diverse communities in order to reduce adverse impacts

Some technology industry leaders warn that studying subjects other than science, technology, engineering and mathematics (STEM) would be a mistake for anyone seeking a job within the digital economy. While it is true that advancing artificial intelligence will require greater numbers of people who have digital skills and training in data science, the fact remains that tackling many of the adverse social impacts highlighted above will entail more than just a proficiency in STEM: Not just technical skills will matter, but how one thinks. Critical thinking, cognitive flexibility and creativity will remain important assets in the future. It is also crucial that a greater focus on ethics be incorporated in data and computer science education. There is after all an urgent need in this age of big data for clearer ethical guidelines on research and experimentation that are applicable to both universities and private companies.

13 Regulation (EU) 2016/679 of the European Parliament and of the Council of 27 April 2016 on the protection of natural persons with regard to the processing of personal data and on the free movement of such data, and repealing Directive 95/46/EC (General Data Protection Regulation).

Prevent the spread of misinformation and false news

Social media have been under increased scrutiny for their failure to remove misinformation, hate speech and other such content

Social media platforms have come under increased scrutiny for their failure to remove misinformation, illegal content, discriminatory ads and hate speech, as well as for their tolerance of fake accounts. There is a widespread belief within the technology community that artificial intelligence will be the panacea for these technological ills. AI, however, is inadequate for addressing a problem that is so complex and so entangled with its economic, psychological and political roots. Regulation is needed to compel those platforms to take the steps necessary to prevent the dissemination of the fabricated, false and misleading content on their sites. Policymakers in some countries have started to target these issues and make firms accountable for such content. For example, in Germany, under the new Network Enforcement Act ("NetzDG"), which entered into law in June 2017, online platforms face fines of up to 50 million euros if they do not remove "obviously illegal" hate speech and other postings within 24 hours of receiving a notification.

Promote fair, accountable and transparent automated decision systems

Governments and other stakeholders should ensure ethical use of digital technologies

Governments and other stakeholders should apply the foundational principles of fairness, transparency and accountability so as to ensure ethical use of digital technology. Algorithmic fairness is important for ensuring that automated decision-making does not exert discriminatory or unjust impacts across different demographics such as race and gender. Accountability is important for establishing avenues of redress for adverse effects of an algorithmic decision system on individuals or societies. Assigning responsibility, especially in cases of technological redlining, is vital for the rapid redress of discrimination.

Building transparent algorithms capable of explaining their own reasoning can promote transparency. That most automated decision systems are little more than black boxes for the people affected by them is an issue that should be addressed. The basis for the decision-making process taking place within those black boxes should be made comprehensible to those affected; however, many companies have been resistant to laying bare the structure of their algorithms because of commercial sensitivities. New regulations are therefore needed to ensure disclosure. It is also important to enable access for interested third parties to review the behaviour of those algorithms.

Some national and local governments have taken the first step towards creating a framework to govern the public use of AI

Some promising steps have been taken to address these issues. For example, the Article 29 Working Party on the Protection of Individuals with regard to the Processing of Personal Data—an advisory body made up of a representative from the data protection authority of each member State of the European Union, the European Data Protection Supervisor and the European Commission—adopted guidelines on automated decision-making and profiling, including the provision that people should have the right to challenge the decisions and that companies should be able to provide users with an explanation for the decisions reached by automated systems. Along similar lines, the New York City Council passed legislation in December 2017 requiring the creation of a task force to review the use of algorithms by New York City agencies in various public policy decisions and to provide recommendations on how information on agency automated decision systems may be shared with the public. This was the first comprehensive algorithmic accountability bill passed in the United States, and represented an important first step towards creating a framework designed to govern the public use of AI and related digital technologies.

Chapter III

Bridging the development divide

Introduction

Frontier technologies can open up opportunities to close the technological divide and accelerate progress towards the SDGs

Major technological innovation has been led largely by several developed countries that are at the forefront of the technological frontier. Recently, however, developing countries, such as China and the Republic of Korea, have—in the areas of artificial intelligence (AI), autonomous vehicles, biotechnology, the Internet of Things, renewable energy technologies (RETs) and 3D printing—managed to push their way to the technological frontier. In the post-Second World War era, a dozen developing countries were able to advance into the category of high-income countries, several of which developed and strengthened national technological and innovation capacities to become key players in the development of new technologies. Bridging the technological divide has been a key development strategy for many of these countries. In fact, technological advances instil in many developing countries the great hope of bridging the development divide and catching up with developed countries.

The present chapter focuses on less developed countries, including the least developed countries (LDCs), landlocked developing countries (LLDCs) and small island developing States (SIDS)—referred to collectively as countries in special situations—and the challenges they face in taking advantage of existing technologies and managing the adoption of frontier technologies, as discussed in chapters I and II. In particular, renewable energy technologies, biotechnology and digital technology such as AI and crowd-based technologies can open up opportunities for these countries to close the existing technological divide, and to accelerate progress towards the Sustainable Development Goals (SDGs).

Many of these countries are yet to fully absorb the technologies of previous industrial revolutions, and there are significant technological divides that represent a barrier to the development and adoption of the new technologies. For example, more than 1 billion people are yet to have access to electricity and an additional 2.5 billion are described as "under-electrified", i.e., they are in a situation where connections are weak and power outages are common (*The Economist*, 2015). Many people in these countries depend on rain-fed agriculture and use bullock power for cultivation. Reliable sources of electricity are a necessary pre-condition for these countries with respect to climbing up the technological ladder and catching up with developed countries. Within these countries, there is often also a technological divide between people living in urban and those in rural areas, between women and men, and between the rich and the poor.

New technologies create new opportunities for many developing countries

New technologies create new opportunities for many developing countries. Renewable energy technologies and efficient energy storage systems can widen the scope for technological "leapfrogging". With the right infrastructures and institutional frameworks, biotechnologies can greatly improve health and nutrition. As discussed in earlier chapters, the use of AI can support a more efficient production of goods and services in both the public and private sectors. Crowd-based firms such as Airbnb and Uber—taking advantage of breakthroughs in digital technology and algorithms—have benefited both service providers and users through more efficient information flows. To help overcome many of the shortcomings associated with existing technological divides, new technologies can create opportunities for less developed countries if they have the necessary digital infrastructure and applications that are appropriate for smaller markets and different consumption patterns.

There is also the possibility that existing technological backwardness will further widen the technological divides because people in many developing countries may be less prepared to adopt and take advantage of new technologies. The widespread automation and reshoring of many manufacturing jobs, for example, may deepen unemployment and underemployment crises in many developing countries, putting millions of jobs at risk of becoming automated (McKinsey Global Institute, 2017b). The use of robots may erode the low labour cost "advantage" of many developing countries, stifling their industrialization and export and import potentials (Shum and others, 2016).

The next section examines the challenges faced by countries and regions marked by existing technological divides, and the barriers that those divides erect against the development and adoption of frontier technologies. The latter part of the chapter discusses the opportunities and challenges presented by these new technologies to less technologically advanced developing countries and proposes key strategies for seizing the opportunities and overcoming the challenges.

The 2030 Agenda for Sustainable Development makes a commitment to leave no one behind. This means that no country or country group should be left behind, as technological advances create new opportunities for economic growth and prosperity. Technologies—both existing and frontier technologies—present the best hope for bridging the development divide and achieving broad-based sustainable development outcomes in developing countries. Considerable policy intervention will be needed at national, regional and global levels to make sure that the new technologies do not widen the technological divide and leave many developing countries further behind.

Frontier technologies: a bridge too far?

A great technological and developmental divide prevents possible leapfrogging and deriving the benefits of frontier technologies

Many low-income developing countries are yet to take full advantage of technological advances of the past two centuries. Electricity is still beyond the reach of billions of poor people; modern agriculture—entailing the use of fertilizer, pesticides and mechanical power—has not reached millions of farmers in sub-Saharan Africa and South Asia; and clean water and safe sanitation are still luxuries. These are manifestations of a great technological and developmental divide which persists between developed and low-income developing countries.

Closing these development gaps is not only an imperative under the 2030 Agenda for Sustainable Development, but also an absolute prerequisite for many developing countries to exploit the promises of many frontier technologies and bridge the technological divide that limits their growth potentials. Lack of access to electricity, inadequate health and sanitation facilities, dysfunctional education systems, under-developed physical and digital infrastructures prevent the possibility of leapfrogging and taking full advantage of frontier technologies.

The section discusses why the development and adoption of basic technologies remain incomplete within specific regions and countries, focusing on institutional, economic and cultural barriers. It will also discuss how these entrench developmental gaps, which limit the opportunities for harnessing frontier technologies.

Access to electricity: the bedrock of sustainable development

Achieving universal access to modern energy has become a foundational development goal. It is also reflected in SDG 7, which is to "[e]nsure access to affordable, reliable, sustainable and modern energy for all". Electricity—the form of modern energy as envisaged in the 2030 Agenda—is a catalyst for the achievement of many other SDGs, given its positive correlation with improved education and health, gender equality, economic growth and other sustainable development outcomes.

Access to modern electricity is correlated with improved education and health, gender equality and economic growth

Lack of electricity stands in the way of safer and healthier cooking and heating, and hinders access to powered health centres and refrigerated medicines, light needed for study at night, and the power needed to run a business. Electricity is also a prerequisite for the use of computers, access to the Internet and enjoyment of the benefits of frontier technologies such as 3D printing, AI and various applications of biotechnology.

There has been notable progress in ensuring access to electricity in the new millennium. Over 100 million people per year have gained access to electricity since 2012 compared with an average of about 60 million per year in the period from 2000 to 2012. Despite this progress, 1.1 billion people were living without electricity in 2014, of whom 600 million lived in Africa. The proportion of people in sub-Saharan Africa with access to electricity was only 37 per cent.

In addition to low rates of access to electricity, the energy consumption per person in South Asia and sub-Saharan Africa remains very low. A typical refrigerator used in a developed-country household consumes about 500 kilowatt-hours (kWh) of electricity per year, which is greater than annual per capita energy consumption in sub-Saharan Africa. Further, per capita electric power consumption in sub-Saharan Africa has been stagnant since 1990 (see figure III.1 below), exposing a growing divide in energy consumption between developed and developing countries.

While supply-side factors generally explain the low access to electricity, new experimental research reveals demand-side constraints. Lee, Miguel and Wolfram (2016) estimated

Figure III.1

Annual electric power consumption per capita (kWh), developed countries, South Asia and sub-Saharan Africa, 1990–2014

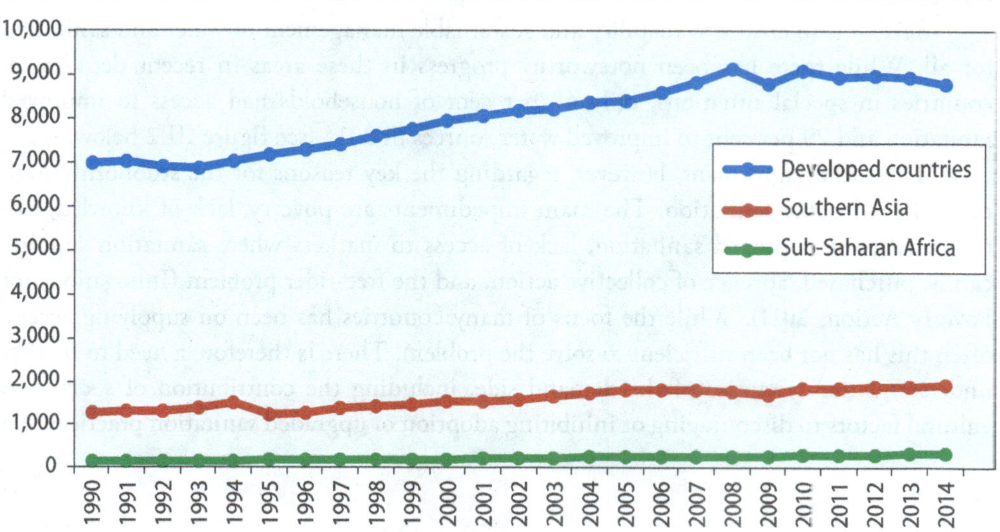

Source: World Bank, World Development Indicators.

that consumer surplus from grid connections was far less than the total connection cost at all coverage levels. That is, many people are still not able or willing to pay for electricity.

Political economy processes have often led some Governments to prioritize supply-side considerations, instead of focusing on increasing affordability and willingness to pay for electricity. The lack of accountability mechanisms has often allowed electricity connections for certain interest groups, while ignoring the population groups needing electricity the most.

Remote areas can "leapfrog" the traditional electric connections and opt for off-grid solutions

The lack of electricity infrastructure in many remote areas presents an opportunity to introduce new types of electricity service. Remote areas could "leapfrog" the traditional electric connections and opt for off-grid solutions. Solar panels—a frontier renewable energy technology—are increasingly viable alternatives for millions in rural populations who cannot afford traditional electric connections. Technological advances and falling costs largely explain the growing demand for solar panels. New innovations integrating mobile money payments with home solar systems, such as the M-KOPA Solar in Kenya, have made it easier for households to adopt alternative energy solutions.

Utilization of solar power is clearly the most cost-efficient strategy for rapid electrification in sub-Saharan Africa (Aubin, 2018). The absence of traditional electrical infrastructure—an apparent sign of backwardness—is in fact an advantage for many developing countries to bypass on-grid electrification and adopt environmentally sustainable renewable enegy technology.

Water and sanitation: a prerequisite for human well-being

Access to clean water and hygienic sanitation is critical for good health and for the survival and development of children

Access to clean water and hygienic sanitation is critical for good health in general and for the survival and development of children in particular. The lack of adequate basic sanitation facilities has serious implications for all dimensions of sustainable development. It results in sickness among children, stunting of their growth and diminishment of their cognitive abilities, all of which contribute to reduced productivity and income later in life. It is hard to imagine how the members of a population can be productive—continuously upgrading skills and taking advantage of many technological breakthroughs—without protecting their health through access to clean water and sanitation systems. In short, the lack of good sanitation affects public health, which in turn affects the ability of people to move up the technology ladder.

SDG 6 is to ensure availability and sustainable management of water and sanitation for all. While there has been noteworthy progress in these areas in recent decades, in countries in special situations, only 48 per cent of households had access to improved sanitation and 79 per cent to improved water sources in 2014 (see figure III.2 below).

The main impediments to access to adequate sanitation are poverty, lack of knowledge of its benefits, lack of access to sanitation supplies, absence of collective action, and the free-rider problem

There is disagreement, however, regarding the key reasons for the stubbornly high rates of inadequate sanitation. The main impediments are poverty, lack of knowledge of the benefits of improved sanitation, lack of access to markets where sanitation supplies can be purchased, absence of collective action, and the free-rider problem (Innovations for Poverty Action, 2011). While the focus of many countries has been on supplying access, often this has not been sufficient to solve the problem. There is therefore a need to further understand the dynamics of the demand side, including the contribution of social and cultural factors to discouraging or inhibiting adoption of upgraded sanitation practices. An

Figure III.2

Access to improved sanitation and water sources, developed countries and countries in special situations, 1990–2015

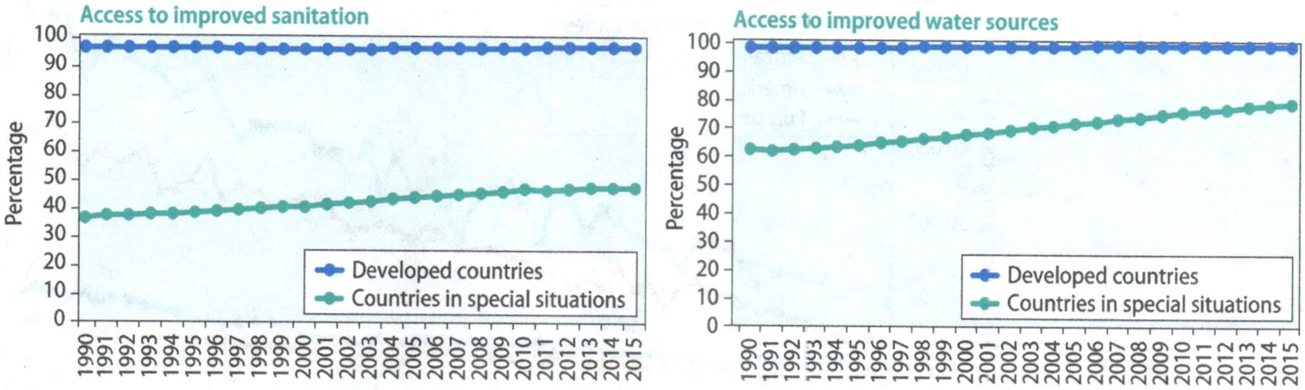

Source: World Bank, World Development Indicators.

integrated approach bringing demand- and supply-side interventions together can increase the possibility of increased adoption of sanitation technologies. New technology—in particular digital technology, ranging from mobile devices to social media—can play an important role in this respect.

Low agricultural productivity: stumbling block to structural transformation

Low agricultural productivity limits the scope and pace of the structural transformation of many developing countries

The 2030 Agenda recognizes the importance of technology for enhancing agricultural productive capacity in developing countries, in particular the LDCs among them (see target 2.a). Broadly, target 2.3 of the SDGs is to double agricultural productivity. Both macroeconomic and microeconomic data suggest that differences in labour productivity between countries are larger in the agricultural sector than in other sectors, which is significant, as 56 per cent of people in LDCs work in the agricultural sector. Moreover, low productivity in the agricultural sector has impacts that extend beyond the agricultural sector, with regard, for example, to food security and improved nutrition of children. Low productivity prevents households and countries from accumulating assets, diversifying their economies and making use of new technologies to move into higher value added sectors. In short, low agricultural productivity limits the scope and pace of the structural transformation of many developing countries.

Since the early 1960s, the green revolution has facilitated the rapid transfer and adoption of new technologies in the agricultural sector, including use of fertilizer and pesticides, irrigation technology, mechanization of farms and new, high-yielding seeds. This enabled the shift in some developing regions from traditional to more modern agricultural methods. However, adoption of these technologies, such as fertilizer, were uneven across regions and countries. A sizeable number of countries missed out on the green revolution, and in consequence lagged in agricultural productivity and yields. The yields of sub-Saharan Africa and the LDCs have been stagnant since the 1960s and have risen—and only very slowly—since the late 1990s (see figure III.3).

Figure III.3

Total cereal yield, Africa, Americas, Europe and least developed countries, 1961–2016

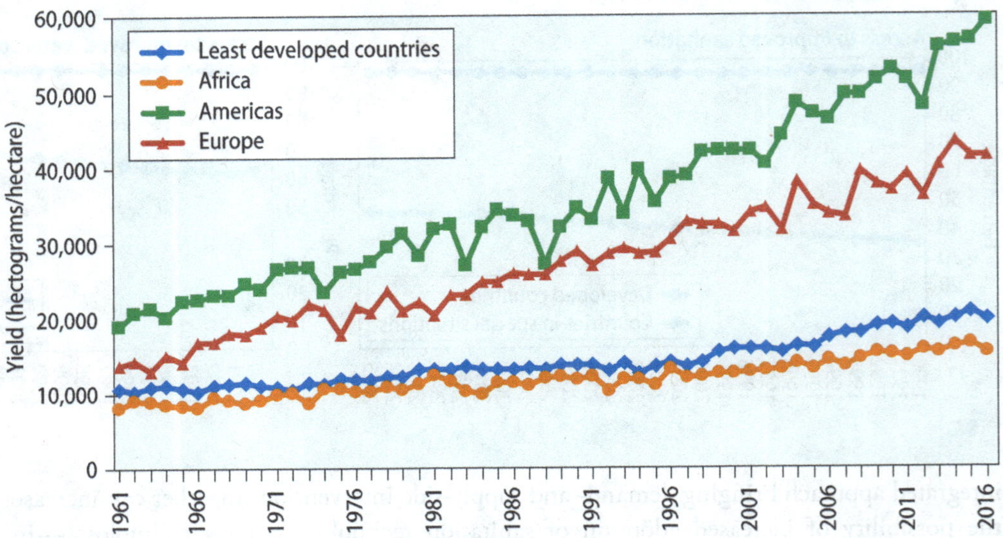

Source: FAOSTAT.

As a consequence of their failure to adopt new technologies, LDCs, including many countries in sub-Saharan Africa, have relied almost exclusively on expanding the area of land under cultivation in order to increase agricultural output, exacerbating deforestation and environmental sustainability. While the land area reserved for cereal production has more than doubled since 1961, yields have increased by only 80 per cent. This is in sharp contrast with South Asia, where land use for cereal production has increased by less than 20 per cent since 1961 but cereal yields have more than tripled (see figure III.4).

Studies have demonstrated that farmers often fail to perceive the potential gains to be reaped from new technology (Henna, Mullainathan and Schwartzstein, 2014). On the other hand, during the green revolution in India, social networks played a significant role in driving the adoption of various high-yield seeds (Munshi, 2004). Along the same lines, in Ghana, farmers who grow pineapple calibrate their use of fertilizer, observing and learning from the practices of others in their network (Conley and Udry, 2010). In many cases, raising awareness among peer farmers has proved more effective than programmes that focus only on information by extension agents from the government (BenYishay and Mobarak, 2014). In this respect, digital social media platforms can potentially further amplify the learning effect by sharing information and creating awareness of new farming techniques and technologies.

Policymaking needs to balance productivity enhancing objectives against their potential impact on labour demand since agriculture is the major source of livelihood and employment

New technologies can play a critically important role in improving agricultural productivity while at the same time reducing or maintaining land area used for agricultural purposes. Drones have the potential to scout crops and to reduce the hard work involved in seed planting and fertilization. Automated irrigation systems can enhance precision and reduce water use and manual labour. The gene-editing of seeds, although controversial, can increase resilience to disease, floods and drought (to be discussed further in the section on catching up with frontier technologies). At the same time, policymaking will need to balance such productivity-enhancing objectives against their potential impact on labour demand and livelihoods, as agriculture is the major source of livelihoods and employment in many developing countries.

Figure III.4
Size of increase in cereal yield relative to increase in land area reserved for production, various regions and least developed countries, 1961–2014

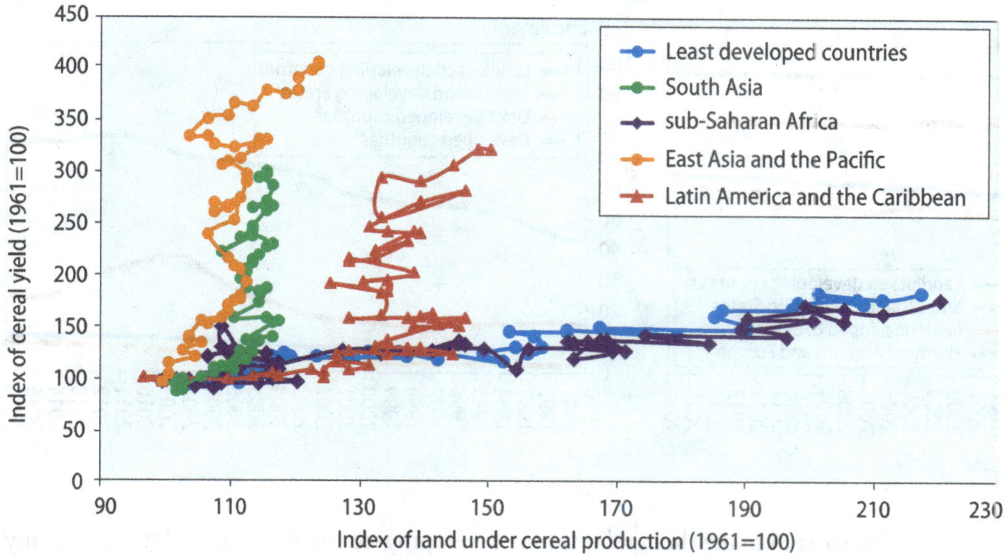

Source: UN/DESA, based on data from https://ourworldindata.org/grapher/change-of-cereal-yield-vs-land-used.

Education: the ladder to future prosperity

SDG 4 is to ensure inclusive and equitable quality education and promote lifelong learning opportunities for all. In recent decades, there have been remarkable improvements in school enrolment rates, which have boosted youth literacy rates. For example, there has been remarkable progress in countries in special situations, especially in the LDCs, where adult literacy rates grew from 45 per cent in 1990 to 58 per cent in 2016. Nonetheless, the gap in the gross enrolment ratio for tertiary education with respect to developed countries has remained wide. For example, SIDS, the best performers among the countries in special situations, averaged only 24 per cent in 2016 compared with developed countries which have experienced steady growth since 1990 (see figure III.5).

Although there has been remarkable progress at the primary education, the gap in secondary and tertiary education has remained wide in countries in special situations compared with developed countries

Similarly, despite considerable gains in school enrolment and literacy over the past decades, the lack of trained teachers and the poor condition of schools are undermining prospects for a high-quality education. In LDCs, only 58 per cent of primary education teachers and 68 per cent of secondary education teachers have the required training. In addition to the lack of qualified teachers, schools often lack basic infrastructure. In sub-Saharan Africa, for example, only about one quarter of schools have electricity and less than half have access to basic drinking water (United Nations, 2017c).

In addition to literacy and numeracy, digital literacy is obviously an essential skill in the digital era. This explains why SDG target 4.4 focuses on substantially increasing "the number of youth and adults who have relevant skills, including technical and vocational skills, for employment, decent jobs and entrepreneurship". Less technologically advanced developing countries will need to improve their secondary and tertiary enrolment rates to increase the opportunities of their population for decent work in a knowledge-driven digital economy.

Reaping the benefits of technological innovation and strengthening domestic capabilities for research require improvement in the quality of schooling

Low-quality education limits opportunities to both adopt technologies and develop domestic capacities for research, which is essential for replicating and improvising new

Figure III.5

Adult literacy rate, population 15+ years, both sexes; and gross enrolment ratio for tertiary education, both sexes, 1990–2016

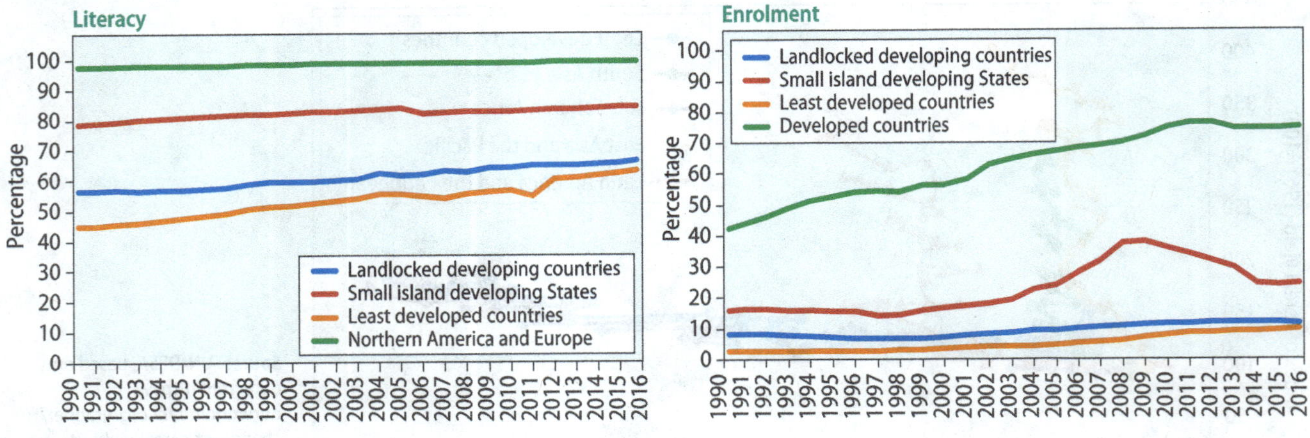

Source: UIS.Stat.

technologies, so as to make them relevant for developing-country contexts. Although many countries have been able to catch up in terms of the number of years of schooling, their capabilities in adopting new technologies and initiating a catch-up process remain limited. Reaping the benefits of technological innovation and strengthening domestic capabilities for research in these countries thus require improvement in the quality of schooling—which remains a challenge that must be surmounted (see discussion in chap. IV).

Evidence related to skill-based technological change in developing countries (see, for example, Berman and Machin, 2000; and Conte and Vivarelli, 2011) stresses the importance of equipping students with the necessary engineering and scientific skills. Massive open online courses (MOOCs) can be helpful in transmitting knowledge in general and facilitating acquisition of new skills. These courses have the advantage of being scalable and customizable to the demands of individual students (Brynjolfsson and McAfee, 2011). For example, one such online course, on AI, offered at Stanford University (Palo Alto, California) in 2010, attracted more than 58,000 students worldwide. Lectures have been broadcast online and student progress is tracked through an automated grading system. This approach enables students around the world to follow a state-of-the-art course on AI at a very low cost, while also enabling the instructors to increase their productivity (Haider, 2018).

MOOCs could potentially help to further develop human capital and promote lifelong learning opportunities. However, if full advantage is to be taken of this technology for all, a basic educational and technological infrastructure must first be put in place. Challenges to be confronted in this regard include underdeveloped information and communications technologies (ICT) infrastructure, the high cost of broadband Internet connections, limits to the availability and capacity of instructors to deliver online lectures, and the limited exposure of students to online learning platforms. Access to broadband Internet connections is still very limited in many developing countries. Many of those countries are struggling to provide electricity connections in rural areas, which makes providing educational opportunities entailing the use of new technologies quite challenging. In many countries in sub-Saharan Africa, the proportion of schools with access to computers and the Internet for pedagogic purposes is below 40 per cent (United Nations, 2017c).

Mobile phones and the Internet: connections to the future

Increased mobile coverage has contributed to a steady increase in the number of Internet users

The 2030 Agenda for Sustainable Development recognizes explicitly the potential of ICT to facilitate global interconnectedness and to accelerate human development. In the last decade, mobile cellular services have spread at a rapid pace. While fixed-broadband services remain inaccessible across large sections of the developing world, increased mobile coverage has contributed to a steady increase in the number of Internet users in all regions.

Access to mobile cellular phones has increased rapidly in both developed countries and countries in special situations, although a wide digital divide remains. In developed countries, the number of mobile cellular subscriptions per 100 people was 121 in 2016, compared with 78 per 100 people in countries in special situations. In the same year, in developed countries, 84 per cent of the population used the Internet, compared with 26 per cent in countries in special situations (see figure III.6 below). And while fixed-broadband penetration reached 30 per cent in developed countries, only 0.9 per cent had similar access in countries in special situations.

Effective use of the Internet is a function of digital literacy

While the Internet has reached many countries quickly, the intensity of use is lower in less technologically advanced developing countries, owing partly to a large within-country digital divide in many of those countries. For example, there are important gaps in access to Internet between men and women, urban and rural areas, and the young and old (see figure III.7). One explanation for the between- and within-country divides is that effective use of the Internet is a function of literacy. Hence, closing the digital divide points to the need to focus on basic and secondary education and digital literacy.

The mobile revolution has given hope to many poor and vulnerable countries that they, too, can become dynamic and innovative players in the digital economy. Mobile phones have connected people not only with other people but also with a realm of undreamt possibilities. For example, in countries of sub-Saharan Africa, M-Pesa has been an inspirational example of what could be accomplished in certain sectors. Further, mobile phones have also contributed to improving the efficiency of agricultural markets (Aker and Fafchamps, 2015), boosting educational outcomes (Aker, Ksoll and Lybbert, 2012) and

Figure III.6

Access to the Internet and usage of mobile cellular phones, developed countries and countries in special situations, 1990–2016

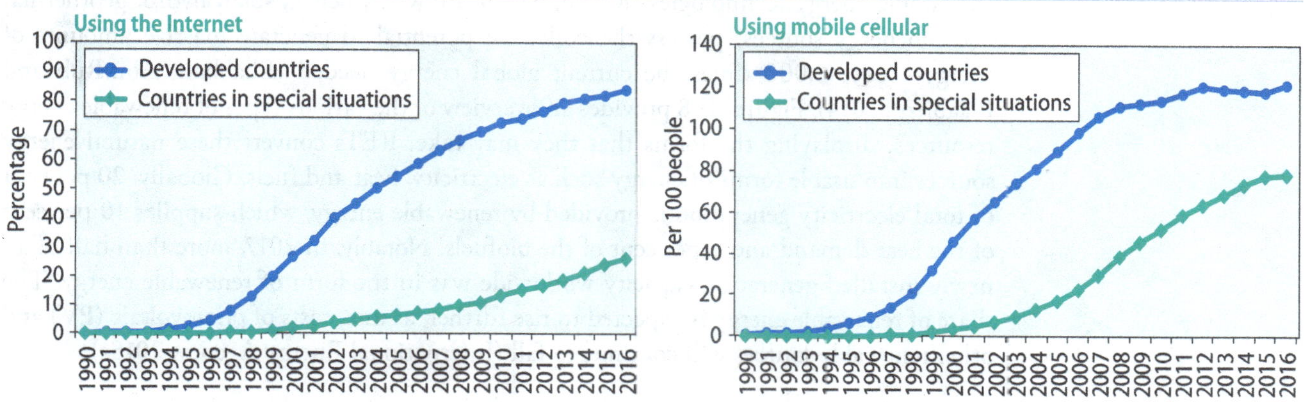

Source: World Bank, World Develoment Indicators.

Figure III.7
Individuals with access to Internet in Africa, by demographic group, 2016
Percentage

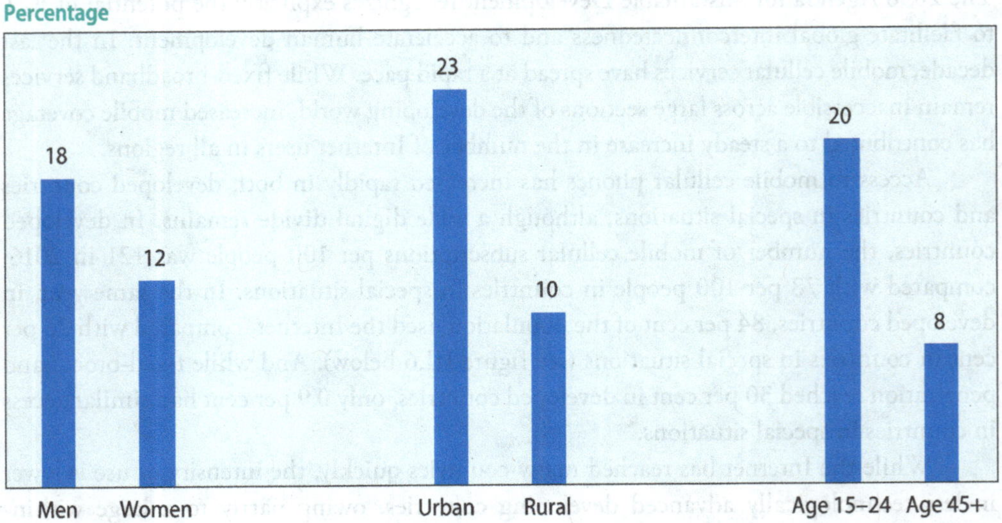

Source: World Bank (2016).

even reducing poverty (Suri and Jack, 2016). However, while mobile phones have spread rapidly, investment in complementary infrastructure such as electricity and cellular stations has not occurred at the same speed. As a result, people in many of these countries still must traverse long distances to charge their phone or receive a signal. Moreover, while the mobile revolution offers useful services for consumers, it has not succeeded in creating a larger number of formal jobs, establishing basic infrastructure for economic development or for attracting other related technologies (Schwab and Davis, 2018). The majority of developing countries must overcome the persistent digital divide if they are to tap the potential of many frontier technologies and step into a sustainable future.

Catching up with frontier technologies

Renewable energy technologies: the best hope for achieving environmental sustainability

Renewable energy technologies (RETs), which use wind, ocean, solar, hydro, geothermal and bioenergy sources, possess the collective potential to generate massive amounts of energy—over 3,000 times the current global energy needed (Ellabban, Abu-Rub and Blaabjerg, 2014). Figure III.8 provides an overview of the various types of renewable energy resources, displaying the forms that they may take. RETs convert these natural energy sources into usable forms of energy such as electricity, heat and fuels. Globally, 20 per cent of total electricity generation is provided by renewable energy, which supplies 10 per cent of the heat demand and 2 per cent of the biofuels. Notably, in 2017, more than half of all newly installed generating capacity worldwide was in the form of renewable energy. The share of renewable energy is expected to rise further, as unit costs of photovoltaic (PV) and other renewable sources will continue to fall (International Energy Agency, 2018a).

Figure III.8
Overview of renewable energy technologies

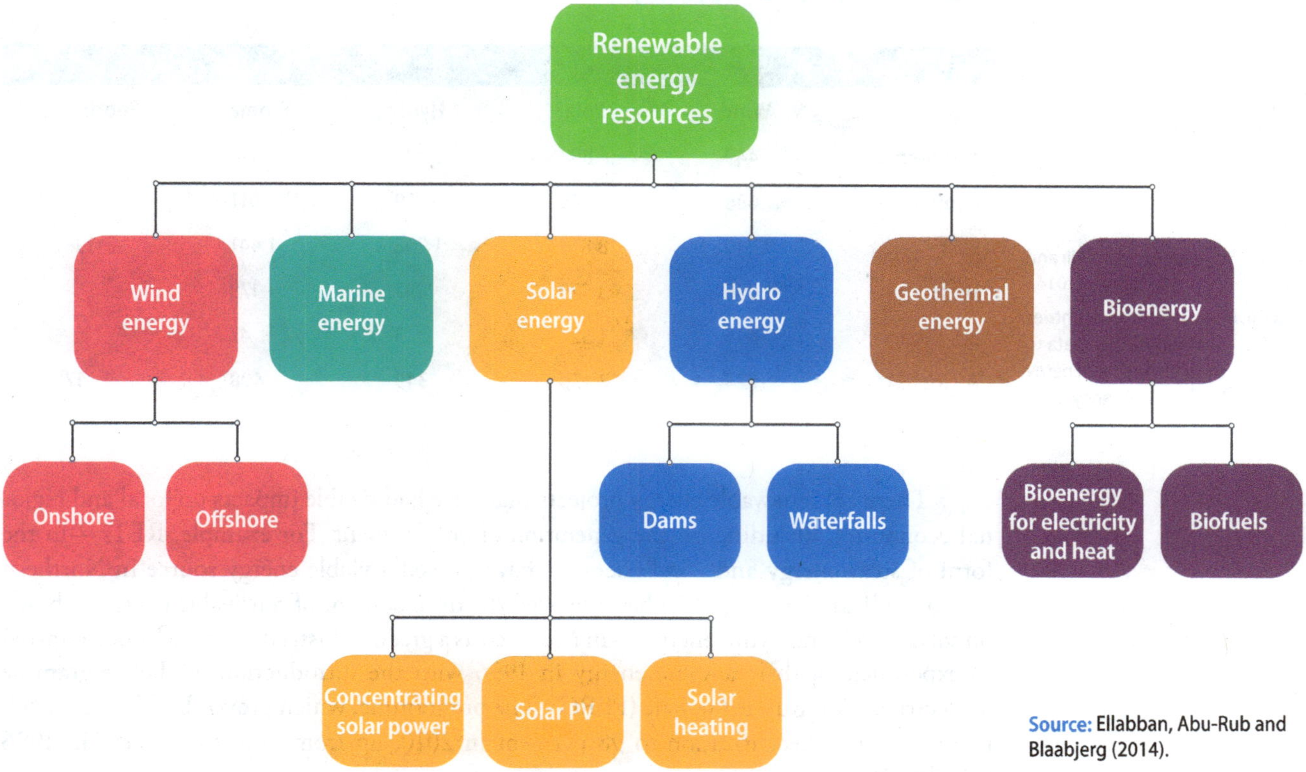

Source: Ellabban, Abu-Rub and Blaabjerg (2014).

Development and adoption of renewable energy technologies

Use of RETs enables reduction of GHG emissions, improvement of watersheds, access to clean energy and green employment opportunities

In general, the use of RETs enables the reduction of greenhouse gas (GHG) emissions, the improvement of watersheds, access to clean energy and green employment opportunities. Shifting to renewable resource-based power generation also maximizes the beneficial impact of electric vehicles on the environment. The use of RETs can foster sustainable development through (a) appropriate resource management, (b) economic sustainability through infrastructure and service development for provision of affordable renewable energy to rural populations, (c) social sustainability by improving the welfare of the poor and supporting women's income generating capacities and (d) financial sustainability by ensuring programme implementation of RETs in the short and medium term (Bugaje, 2006).

Renewable resources are yet to be fully exploited in sub-Saharan countries. Currently, renewable power generation capacity is 28 gigawatts (GWh) compared with a total power generation capacity of more than 145 GWh.[1] Hydropower accounts for more than 90 per cent of total renewable energy capacity in Africa. Data for 27 African countries that report to the International Energy Agency (IEA) indicate that wind is abundant in West and East Africa, hydro and biomass are abundant in Central Africa, and solar energy is available in all regions. Each source of renewable energy can potentially supply the total African electricity demand; solar energy, for example, could provide more than 2,000 per cent of the total electricity for final consumption in 27 African countries (see table III.1).

1 One gigawatt-hour (GWh)=1 billion (10^9) watts/hours which can supply energy to a medium-sized city.

Table III.1

Electricity generation potential from renewable energy as a percentage of total final consumption of electricity

	Wind	Solar	Hydro	Biomass	Geothermal
Northern	449	898	35	114	-
Central	688	5 245	6 059	9 011	-
East	3 240	8 875	1 298	1 441	198
West	1 096	3 520	292	178	-
Southern	416	1 527	13	47	-
Africa IEA[a]	**724**	**2 136**	**349**	**498**	**17**

Source: Mandelli and others (2014).
a Covering 27 African countries that report their data to the International Energy Agency (IEA).

There are renewable energy projects that have had sizable impacts on local and regional economies, including on the generation of employment. For example, RETs—in the form of solar energy and wind energy—have proved a viable energy source in Northern Africa. Vidican Auktor (2017) has reviewed the development of renewable energy—based on solar, wind, and hydro energy—in Morocco as a green industrial policy. Morocco started to experiment with renewable energy in 1996 with the introduction of the Programme d'Électrification Rurale Globale (PERG). The programme, which proved highly successful, increased rural electrification to 98 per cent in 2010, up from only 15 per cent in 1996 (Haider, 2018).

The employment impact of PERG was also significant, with about 13,000 direct and indirect jobs having been created by the Programme by 2006. The positive experience of renewable energy in Morocco also led to the launch of the National Renewable Energy and Efficiency Plan in 2008 with the aim of harmonizing different renewable energy strategies (ibid.).

There is potential for further development of RETs in Caribbean countries based on the abundance of renewable energy resources

RETs also contribute to energy generation in a few Caribbean countries such as Grenada (photovoltaic), Barbados (solar water heating), Jamaica (wind) and Suriname (wind). The use of clean energy has been cost-effective in the face of volatile oil markets and has promoted reliance on local resources, reduced GHG emissions and generated green jobs. There is also potential for further development of RETs in the region, based on their abundance of renewable energy resources (Shirley and Kammen, 2013). For example, under the National Energy Policy of Grenada, it is projected that 20 per cent of energy consumption in the stationary power and transportation sectors will be met with renewable energy by 2020; waste to energy from biomass and municipal solid waste hold great potential, although infrastructure for these systems is not yet in place. Distributed generation in the form of solar PV and solar water heating already have applications for the water treatment and distribution and ecotourism sectors. Policies that currently encourage distributed solar technologies would also increase the resilience of the Grenada grids to storms and other disasters (United Nations, 2012).

Broadly, although the primary energy supply for power generation and final consumption in many SIDS (mostly for transportation and industry) is based on imported oil, a few countries have sizable shares of renewable energy sources in total electricity generation (hydropower in most cases), including Fiji (54 per cent), Belize (53 per cent), Suriname (46 per cent), Dominica (40 per cent) and Papua New Guinea (39 per cent). Tokelau (a Non-Self-Governing Territory administered by New Zealand) has become 100 per cent solar PV (Timilsina and Shah, 2016).

A study of a wide group of political jurisdictions (34) in the Caribbean was conducted on the role of institutional factors (entrepreneurship, local champions, electricity utility, informal institutions and international agencies) in the adoption and development of RETs. It was found that informal elements, such as historical legacy, cultural norms and degree of stakeholder interactions can be as important as formal institutions and policy structures (e.g., tax schemes, economic incentives and subsidies) in promoting the adoption and development of those technologies (Ince, Vredenburg and Liu, 2016).

In Viet Nam, where nearly 2 million households live in sparsely settled, remote rural areas, stand-alone household-size RETs, such as solar PV and wind generators, have been proposed as offering a good solution to the problem of the high cost of grid extension. As decentralized RETs can be located closer to demand, distribution and transmission costs and energy and capacity losses would be reduced. RETs can also create local employment since installation, operation and maintenance would be conducted mainly in rural areas (Nguyen, 2007). Further, a study by Sen and Bhattacharyya (2014), centred on Palari, a remote village in the State of Chhattisgarh (India), suggests that a hybrid combination of RETs at an off-grid location (e.g., wind turbines, solar PV systems, biodiesel generators and small-scale hydropower) could generate electricity and serve as a cost-effective alternative to conventional grid extension.

In the Philippines, a pilot project has been developed to allow rural communities to access affordable solar energy and ICT. For example, the Leapfrogging Autonomous Micro-Technopolis in Boxes (LAMTIB) initiative, for which the Renewable Energy Corporation (REC) SolarBox is the driving technology, is a pilot development project designed to enable rural communities in off-grid areas to access affordable solar energy and ICT (Aunemo, 2015). The project, which is in its initial stages of implementation aims at strengthening connectivity, food security, education, health care and small-scale business. Via satellite, the local community can gain access to information and means of communication, including remote control engineering of the solar panel installations. The project also includes a process for cultivating larvae for use in a sea farm located in the Santa Cruz barangay.[2] Immediate access to the larvae, whose production and monitoring are made possible by solar electricity from the SolarBox, eliminates long travel distances, thereby increasing their survival rate. Another goal of the project is to raise awareness through use of online education systems run by solar electricity. Local communities are also provided with medical expertise and a telemedicine system, operated by the Philippine Red Cross. The sea farm in Santa Cruz has begun to generate economic activity in the community by sourcing untapped raw materials locally and integrating them with various new activities so as to facilitate sustainable growth. Local businesses are expected to expand through the use of solar energy and Internet connectivity, as a means of gaining key information on production and markets.

2 A barangay is the smallest administrative division in the Philippines, constituting the most local level of government.

Recent developments in battery technologies have made RETs in off-grid locations more viable options for many communities in Asia and beyond

Recent developments in battery technologies have made RETs in off-grid locations more viable options for many communities in Asia and beyond. New energy storage technology is crucial in RET-based mini- and off-grid systems as the means of handling moment-to-moment fluctuations in production or consumption (Eller and Gauntlett, 2017). In the case of mini-grids: battery systems are installed for backup to ensure a stable flow of power; and both solar PV systems and batteries are built independently from the centralized grid (IEA, 2018a). Mini-grids with energy storage systems are a cost-effective and time-saving option for isolated communities as regards meeting SDG 7, which is to ensure "access to affordable, reliable, sustainable and modern energy for all".

As storing energy is particularly important for intermittent power plants, such as renewable electricity sources, it can play a significant role in meeting the need for low-carbon electricity in many developing countries. Among several types of batteries for stationary storage, the lithium-ion battery is considered most promising, as the capacity of lithium-ion battery storage has been improving and its costs declining, owing to the development of electrical vehicles (EVs) (see chap. II). This battery is becoming a popular option for battery-based renewable systems (Diouf and Pode, 2015).

In this context, EVs in many countries have become the quintessential symbol of rapid growth in the renewable energy industry, including in the use of RETs. While they provide opportunities for clean energy transportation, their continued development presents challenges in connection, for example, with their energy storage capacity. Renewable energy policies have been directed not only towards reduction of carbon dioxide emissions but also towards the creation of local environmental and health benefits; facilitation of energy access, particularly in rural areas; advancement of energy security goals through diversification of the portfolio of energy technologies and resources; and improvement of social and economic development through employment opportunities (Ellabban, Abu-Rub and Blaabjerg, 2014). Table III.2 illustrates the likely positive impacts that the deployment of RETs may exert on three dimensions of sustainable development, i.e., social development, environmental protection and economic development.

Challenges and strategies

Fossil fuels could continue to be the primary source of energy in many developing countries if policy incentives and long-term commitment are not in place

Although the use of renewable energy resources is rising, fossil fuels still account for 80 per cent of the world's energy supply. It is likely that fossil fuels could continue to be the primary source of energy in many developing countries if policy incentives and long-term commitment are not in place.

The share of electricity generation based on RETs is nearly 20 per cent in LDCs, landlocked developing countries and small island developing States as a whole, which indicates that the potential of renewable energy use is still untapped. While hydropower and bioenergy are major sources of energy worldwide, other sources, although technically feasible and commercially available, cover only a fraction of their potential markets (ibid.).

Deployment of RETs is confronting various socio-economic, institutional, technical and environmental challenges. Economic barriers persist when the cost of a given RET is above the cost of competing alternatives; market-related and technical barriers are also important determinants of the cost and use of RETs. Economic, market and technical barriers contribute to higher capital costs and prevent the development and adoption of RETs. The significance of barriers differs for each technology and market, while affordability and willingness to adopt change as a technology matures along the path towards commercialization.

Table III.2
Positive impacts of RETs on sustainable development

Input	Outcome		
	Social	**Environmental**	**Economic**
Social	Local ownership and decision-making	Improvement of environment-friendly behaviour	Building of community assets
	Community building	Higher quality of life	Regional development
			Improved income diversification and distribution
			Employment
Environmental		Reduction of GHG emissions	Renewable energy industry
			Higher-quality growth
Economic			Enhancement of shareholder income and community income

Source: UN/DESA.

A comprehensive study of Caribbean countries has demonstrated that the development of a renewable energy industry progressed when the incumbent electric utility wielded less influence in setting policies for the development of RETs. This reflects a classic conflict of interests, the case where incumbent utilities often have little incentive to welcome a new source of energy, which would replace traditional sources. It is not surprising, then, that utility companies typically promote business models that do not support renewable technologies. On the other hand, the involvement of the electric utility is often essential to facilitating and sustaining the renewable energy sector since it has acquired local experience (Ince, Vredenburg and Liu, 2016) and amassed the capital investments required for renewable energy projects.

Small island developing States face major barriers to the development and use of RETs

Small island developing States, including those in the Caribbean, face four major barriers to the development and use of RETs: an inadequate energy information network and lack of awareness of the benefits of renewable energy technologies; poor financing mechanisms through which to implement renewable energy projects, including regional loan structures and technical assistance for banks; weak or non-existent regulatory frameworks to enable renewable energy development; and inadequate technical capacity in the renewable energy field (Wiesser, 2004).

Broadly speaking, energy policies and planning guidelines in developing countries are important to ensure that there is a proper evaluation of RET potential—one that is not impacted by the vested interests of public utilities or electricity boards which may prioritize traditional high-carbon energy technologies (ibid.).

Deployment of RETs for electrification in rural areas entails high upfront equipment costs, high costs for transmission and distribution, a high dependence on external resources and institutional support

In remote rural areas, deployment of RETs for electrification often entails high upfront equipment costs, high costs for transmission and distribution, a high dependence on external resources and institutional support. Economic barriers include a high initial capital cost, failure to estimate future risks related to fossil fuel, and lack of pricing policies that include the economic costs of environmental damage, as well as the lack of an appropriate level of subsidies for incentivizing RET use at household levels. Legal and regulatory barriers include legal frameworks that discourage investment in RETs and excessive requirements for small power producers. The lack both of access to credit for consumers and investors and of the technical, geographical and commercial capacities needed by market participants to take economic decisions (Urmee, Harries and Schlapfer, 2009) also inhibits the potential of RET deployment and use.

In their study of Malawi (with regard to efficient stoves and efficient tobacco barns), Rwanda (with regard to household and institutional biogas) and the United Republic of Tanzania (with regard to solar energy, domestic biogas, efficient stoves and efficient ovens), Barry, Steyn and Brent (2011) pinpointed four main types of factors that should be taken into account for the selection of a particular RET:

(a) Technology factors, including maintenance and support over the life cycle of the technology and transfer of knowledge and skills to relevant people;

(b) Site selection factors, including identification of a local champion to enable continuation after implementation, adoption by the community and identification of suitable sites for pilot studies;

(c) Potential income generation and costs, including initial installation costs; and,

(d) Management and technological capacities.

In the countries under study, these factors often became barriers to the adoption and development of RETs owing to an insufficient number of skilled personnel, weak institutional capacities to implement effective environmental policies, lack of knowledge of the advantages and opportunities presented by RETs, lack of the training and knowledge transfer needed to support the maintenance of the technology, and lack of community education programmes designed to reduce user reluctance to accept the technology. At the same time, international cooperation can make a significant difference in these areas through support of actions by countries to strengthen institutional and innovation capacities across sectors.

A study by Ahlborg and Hammar (2014) on Mozambique and the United Republic of Tanzania indicates that the use of hydropower for off-grid electrification in remote rural areas can be a good complement of and forerunner to the national grid, while at the same time underlining the barriers to implementation. For example, opposition to the exploitation of protected areas, as well as seasonal droughts and high planning costs for small-scale hydro, reduce the use of hydropower. Moreover, interest in wind power is low due to expected high costs and energy fluctuations. Solar PV is used in both countries but not on a wide scale because it is both expensive and unsuitable for productive use due to low capacity.

Policies for making renewable energy technologies the main energy source

The challenges associated with RET development and deployment underscore the need to develop well-designed strategies along three main axes: (a) increasing complementary investments in sectors beyond energy generation so as to maximize social, environmental and economic impacts of RETs; (b) strengthening a nation's institutional framework to facilitate the deployment of RETs and; (c) designing national and sectoral policies aimed at integrating the renewable energy sector into the framework of a comprehensive national energy plan that is within the scope of a national development strategy.

There is a clear need for the deployment of RETs to be integrated with, and complemented by, investments in other sectors, such as infrastructure, social services, local finance, education and rural development. The government needs to invest in its administrative capacity to engage in systematic and timely communication with local communities so as to facilitate the use of RETs, provide subsidies to reduce capital costs and facilitate market development. The chosen RET must reflect the priorities of local populations, taking into account their capacity and willingness to pay. There is also a clear need for more effective communication and awareness building regarding the costs associated with the use of RETs. Renewable energy projects should demonstrate how RETs can improve livelihoods through, for example, job creation in rural communities.

The deployment of RETs needs to be integrated with, and complemented by, investments in infrastructure, social services, local finance, education and rural development

There should also be concerted efforts at local levels to expand access to credit and financing opportunities in order to facilitate the development and adoption of RETs. Governments should consider lowering import tariffs and taxes for imported components of RETs, as well as support greater investment in research and development (R&D) to render RETs more commercially viable for poorer segments of the population. National innovation systems can play an important role in identifying and developing specific RETs, while at the same time taking into account country- and region-specific opportunities and challenges.

For SIDS in particular, any public incentive would have to be attractive enough to make renewable energy sources competitive against other sources of energy in the small-sized markets of these countries. Fiscal incentives such as feed-in tariffs, tax incentives and production subsidies may be needed for the effective adoption and development of RETs.

Government participation in, and support for, developing necessary institutional frameworks will remain critical for the adoption and development of RETs. In this sense, the 2030 Agenda for Sustainable Development and the Paris Agreement adopted under the United Nations Framework Convention on Climate Change[3] are key institutional pillars of the process of bringing together all nations for the purpose of ensuring that economic, social and technological progress occurs in harmony with nature. There also needs to be clear and unequivocal policy signals, prioritizing renewables within the energy policy and the national energy matrix. Government interventions are also needed to establish standards and codes of practice and to integrate renewable energy development with environmental policies and energy efficiency. Building national capacities for RET, including the training of personnel, will remain key for facilitating further development and use of renewable energy.

The reform and strengthening of institutional frameworks is needed to enable adoption and development of new technologies to become a flexible, collaborative and integrative enterprise at the local, national and international levels. Adequate cross-sectoral and international collaboration could ensure proper cooperation between the energy sector and other sectors such as agriculture, environment and forestry.

Strengthening of institutional frameworks is needed for a flexible, collaborative and integrative development of new technologies at the local, national and international levels

There is also strong evidence that the countries that have successfully promoted RETs combined their long-term development strategies with concrete policies and measures designed to support their aspirations, including effective management and the setting up of government structures for the implementation of renewable energy projects. National

3 See Adoption of the Paris Agreement in United Nations Framework Convention on Climate Change (2015).

development strategies should prioritize RETs and incorporate specific incentives—including subsidies for R&D—to encourage private sector participation in development, generation and transmission of renewable energy.

Biotechnologies: eradicating hunger and achieving good health are within reach

Advances in biotechnology, precision farming and production ecology can unlock the capacity to carry out structural transformation and bridge the development divide with developed countries

Agriculture faces global challenges which include meeting the growing demand for food, reducing poverty and malnutrition, and achieving environmental sustainability. However, the yield growth rates reached with conventional plant breeding and agronomic practices have on average declined as a result of soil erosion and low productivity. As discussed above, stunted agricultural labour productivity in many developing countries, particularly in sub-Saharan Africa, makes structural transformation of their economies a daunting challenge. Advances in biotechnology, precision farming and production ecology offer hope for a significant boosting of crop yields and agricultural productivity, with the potential for unlocking the capacity to carry out structural transformation and bridge the development divide with developed countries. This will remain critical for achieving many SDGs, including eradication of extreme poverty and hunger.

Biotechnologies can improve living standards in countries in special situations, increasing food output and nutritional quality and improving the health status of their population. Genetic bio-fortification of food crops can be economically and biologically effective in reducing micronutrient deficiencies and alleviate malnutrition through, for example, the nutritional enhancement of vitamin A-fortified rice (FAO, 2011). Maize can also be an appropriate crop for bio-fortification, since many people, e.g., in sub-Saharan Africa, consume maize at most of their meals. Recombinant protein targeting of seeds and the use of high-volume food-processing technologies (e.g., freeze-drying) can reduce the need for a "cold chain" between the point of production and the point of delivery (Ma and others, 2005). However, adoption of new crop varieties and related agricultural technologies often face cultural barriers in traditional agrarian societies, with lack of knowledge and awareness of their benefits and costs. Effecting bio-fortification of crops may therefore require not only extension services for seed distribution, but also mass awareness campaigns for farmers and community members, focused on informing how new crop varieties will improve their health and well-being. That genetic modification of crops holds out hope for eradicating hunger doesn't mean that poor farmers shouldn't be fully informed of both the benefits and the risks so that they can make an informed decision.

The tool of gene adaptation for development of insect-resistent crop varieties can be utilized by smallholders to reduce their exposure to the risks of pest damage and yield loss, without being required to introduce chemicals. Growth of insect-resistant cotton in a number of developing countries attests the successful application of this technology in generating higher productivity and higher farmer incomes, while ensuring equity and sustainability (Raney, 2006). Transgenic crop alternatives are being developed that display resilience to hazards such as drought, freezing, salinity, and soil toxins such as aluminium and heavy metals. Crops bearing those traits require less irrigation and provide more reliable yields (Tonukari and Omotor, 2010). Along similar lines, improved herbicide tolerance of crops can augment the incomes of poor farmers by increasing crop yields and reduce the amount of time needed to clear weeds.

Effective development and adoption of biotechnology in less advanced developing countries can also impact health in a positive way if new products and technology were to become affordable and adjustable to health-care settings, as well as socially and culturally acceptable, while addressing the most pressing health needs. Table III.3 below illustrates a few of the biotechnologies that are potentially important for many developing countries.

Table III.3
Relevant biotechnologies

1	Modified molecular technologies for simple and affordable diagnosis of infectious diseases
2	Recombinant technologies for development of vaccines against infectious diseases
3	Sequencing of pathogen genomes for the purpose of building an understanding of their biology and identifying new antimicrobials
4	Female-controlled protection against sexually transmitted diseases, both with and without contraceptive effect
5	Bioinformatics for identifying drug targets and examining pathogen-host interactions
6	Genetically modified crops with added nutrients for countering specific deficiencies
7	Recombinant technology for making therapeutic products (e.g., insulin, interferons) more affordable
8	Combinatorial chemistry for drug discovery

Source: UN/DESA, based on Daar and others (2007).

Advances in biotechnologies can directly contribute to improving health outcomes for millions of poor people in developing countries

Advances in biotechnologies can also directly contribute to improving health outcomes for millions of poor people in developing countries. They can support a more accurate diagnosis to spur prompt treatment, limit the spread of disease and prevent waste of resources on wrong treatments. Some recombinant vaccines for malaria and hepatitis, imported at a fraction of the cost for standard imported medicines, have been tested in a number of poor countries with promising results. The technology for more efficient drug and vaccine delivery systems is also important because most vaccines are administered by injection, which can increase the risks of contamination and contagion as many blood-borne diseases such as HIV/AIDS and hepatitis B are transmitted through unsanitary injections. Frequent dosing of, for example, powdered and edible vaccines and controlled-release formulations can replace multiple doses; and refrigeration can ensure safety with respect, e.g., to possible environmental contamination, improving access to drugs and vaccines and potentially saving millions of lives. Recombinant therapeutic proteins are also relevant for developing countries, where 60 per cent of all deaths are due to non-communicable diseases—a figure that may grow up to 73 per cent by 2020. Biotechnologies for environmental improvement such as bioremediation can also help transform unhealthy pollutants in the soil or water and improve public health (Daar and others, 2007).

Similarly, plant-derived pharmaceuticals (PDPs) has a huge potential in terms of enabling low-cost drugs and vaccines to be supplied to developing countries. Making use of traditional knowledge on the capacity of some plants to reduce the effects of diseases, laboratory analysis can help identify the plant substances and agents that have healing capacities. Cultivating and experimenting with those agents to produce pharmaceuticals and vaccines present the opportunity to develop a uniquely innovative branch of the pharmaceutical industry. PDPs can help transform the agricultural economies of developing countries and improve the health care and productivity of poor people. There is a great potential for the cost-effective production of molecules that can reduce the spread of infectious diseases, particularly HIV/AIDS. Local and regional production of PDPs can become more feasible when carried out in proximity to populations that need these pharmaceuticals.

Hunger and poverty are rooted in inequality, which would need to be addressed within a comprehensive and integrated approach to poverty reduction

Biotechnologies are not a panacea. The importance of proved health strategies such as health education are central to many health-related challenges, including combating HIV/AIDs and other epidemics. Similarly, improvements in sanitation can reduce the incidence of water-borne diseases, while basic nutritional education can help prevent nutrient deficiencies. Although biotechnologies can potentially help alleviate hunger, one should not forget that hunger and poverty are rooted in inequality, which would need to be addressed within a comprehensive and integrated approach to poverty reduction.

Joint research in epidemiology, nutrition and food toxicology is needed to select the traits and demonstrate the benefits of bio-fortified crops

Before drawing conclusions regarding how the simple availability of biotechnology may improve agricultural productivity and the health of the rural poor, it is important to keep in mind that trickle-down biotechnologies designed for large-scale farming would need to be reproduced and replicated in smaller farm contexts (Jansen and Gupta, 2009). Moreover, although genetic modification of crops can help support the design of foods with specific health protective properties, joint research in epidemiology, nutrition and food toxicology is needed to enable the selection of traits and demonstrate the benefits of bio-fortified crops in less technologically advanced developing countries (Azadi and Ho, 2010).

Mindful that African countries needed to tap the advances in biotechnology, delegates to the Extraordinary Conference of the African Ministerial Council on Science and Technology, held in Cairo in November 2006, analysed and discussed the report of the High-level Panel on Modern Biotechnology, entitled *Freedom to Innovate: Biotechnology in Africa's Development* (Juma and Serageldin, 2007). Its goal was to generate a critical mass of technology expertise in areas of potential growth and take advantage of Africa's rich biodiversity to develop pharmaceutical products. The report called for an African Biotechnology Strategy to promote this vision within 20 years. The initiative has so far collected vital information on medicinal plants and built pilot databases, while strengthening regional links for mutual collaboration on science and technology among universities, research centres and industry. The objective of the Federation of Asian Biotech Associations, another example of partnership between industry and academia, is to boost investment in biotechnology, international trade in biotechnology products, and the outsourcing of services (Gurib-Fakim and Eloff, 2013).

A survey of the recommendations of 232 developing-world experts from 58 countries was conducted to determine how to boost the potentials of biotechnology and improve public health in poor countries (Daar and others, 2007). The survey's results indicated that there is great potential for intersectoral, regional and international collaboration on building capacity as well as encouraging regions to learn from successful models of biotechnology innovation. They called for increased partnership and capacity-building to improve science education and establish support networks to improve dialogue between biotechnology developers and end users. Experts also underscored the importance of biotechnology as an instrument for improving public health as well as a tool for economic development. A few experts indicated the need to identify appropriate entry points for biotechnology products, exploit domestic and regional markets and build capacity to examine legal, social, environmental and ethical impacts of the advances in biotechnologies. African experts also recommended the use of the New Partnership for Africa's Development (NEPAD) as an entry point into the continent's political agenda, while others stated the importance of a national strategy and public policy on genomics for funding and developing biotechnology.

Challenges in development and adoption of bitechnologies

National agricultural research capacities, environmental and food safety regulations, intellectual property rights (IPR) and agricultural input markets are important determinants of the size and distribution of economic benefits of breakthroughs in biotechnology. Many poor countries are still trying to establish biosafety policies for the first-generation transgenic plants (genetically modified organisms), while key infrastructure for their implementation is often inadequate. PDP technology, for example, faces the challenge of inadeqately equipped laboratories. The commercialization of PDPs is also impeded by concerns regarding biosafety and bioethics and by a lack of public awareness. There is also the potential for contamination and environmental risks because, for example, plants suitable for novel protein enhancement are often staple food crops in many developing countries. The absence of regulations designed specifically for the PDP sector creates concern related to contamination of food and environmental risks (Ma and others, 2005; Sabalza, Christou and Capell, 2014).

Medicines developed by multinational companies are often too expensive and many populations in developing countries cannot afford them

Medicines developed by multinational companies are often too expensive and many populations in developing countries cannot afford them. For example, a non-generic AIDS drug cocktail can cost up to $10,000 annually, while a generic version of AIDS drug developed by India costs only $300—which may still be too costly for people in extreme poverty. Further, big pharmaceutical firms have little incentive to invest in products for treating or preventing diseases affecting poor countries because they produce low returns on investments in high-risk and costly biomedical R&D.

Developing countries have an opportunity to bridge the great health divide by making necessary investments in the development and use of indigenous biotechnogies

Along similar lines, vaccines for pandemic diseases such as measles have long been in use in developed countries but many developing countries have gained only limited access to those vaccines because they have become too expensive. In sum, vaccines and microbicides are not profitable products and the low return acts as a disincentive to private investment in biotechnologies in many developing countries (Salicrup and Fedorková, 2006). Developing countries have an opportunity to bridge the great divide in health outcomes by making necessary investments in the development and use of indigenous biotechnologies. However, support for the development of biotechnology therapies and products for endemic diseases requires infrastructure, well-educated and trained professionals, scientific excellence, regulatory infrastructure and sound health-care systems, all of which are often missing in many developing countries. The national health policies of less technologically advanced developing countries need to prioritize the potential of home-grown biotechnologies with sufficient financial, institutional and regulatory support.

Nearly 90 per cent of R&D in biotechnology is conducted in industrialized countries, where most genetically modified crops such as corn, rice and soybean, are planted. There is nevertheless little biotechnology research on crops such as cassava, white maize and millet, which are planted by poor farmers in sub-Saharan countries. Over the last 30 years, only 15 new drugs have been developed for tropical diseases, compared with 179 for cardiovascular diseases alone. It is also the case that the traits introduced in genetically modified crops tend to be geared towards existing farming practices of industrial agriculture rather than the local practices of small-scale farmers in developing countries (Azadi and Ho, 2010).

The strengthening of intellectual property rights in developed countries and large private investment in biotechnology have resulted in the concentration of key biotechnologies within a few firms

Moreover, the strengthening of IPR in developed countries and large private investment in biotechnology have resulted in the concentration of key biotechnologies within a few firms. Similar to biotechnology firms, companies in the food industry are unwilling to invest in research that is important for agriculture in poor countries owing to the limited market potential, fear of IPR-related piracy and the high cost to meet regulatory requirements. The genetic engineering of foods has also generated environmental and safety issues such as the rise of secondary pests, apart from the primary cotton pest, which can usher in unforeseen ecological changes. Indeed, application of insecticides has been as necessary for transgenic cotton (because of the presence of those secondary pests) as for non-transgenic cotton. Many developing countries are also yet to establish appropriate standards and monitoring rules. Further, there are gaps in communication among government regulators, farmers, scientists and multinational companies in respect of identifying the impact of genetically modified crops on biodiversity and food security, the risk of insects' resistance to genetically modified plant toxins and the ecological impact of the dissemination of genetically modified crops (ibid.).

Genetic modification technology and products also tend to be expensive and inaccessible to subsistence farmers in developing countries. Many less technologically advanced developing countries do not have the capacity to undertake the assessments and monitoring necessary to ascertain whether they would benefit from genetically modified crops and would be able to comply with safety regulations. In addition, genetic modification technology typically also requires adequate education and training of farmers, who may be willing to adopt the technique only if they can achieve an understanding of its use and can be convinced of its benefits (ibid.). Indeed, access to biotechnology by poor countries may also be prevented by the lack of research capacity to determine which biotechnologies would be most useful and how to deploy them, should they be adopted and potentially developed.

The domestic supply of skilled personnel generally depends on the level and composition of public and private investments in education. The universities that are able to develop biotechnologies often license them exclusively to private firms, which typically hold the rights to the sub-licensing of those technologies. Sometimes, these firms may not wish to sub-license a biotechnology in countries with a weak IPR regime, or even if they do market it, that biotechnology may be too expensive for the public sector.

The spreading of biotechnology can also be hindered by an ill-conceived regulatory system

The spreading of biotechnology can also be hindered by an ill-conceived regulatory system. If the regulatory process for genetically modified crops is expensive and time consuming, only large multinationals will be able to afford their commercialization. An expensive and unpredictable biosafety regulatory regime can also become a serious constraint on the commercialization of biotechnology developed by public research institutes because they are often less able, compared with entities in the private sector, to finance the ecological, health and agricultural trials needed to meet regulatory requirements (Ruane and Sonnino, 2011).

Strategies for taking advantage of the breakthroughs in biotechnologies

Taking advantage of breakthroughs in biotechnologies would require strengthening of biotechnological improvements in several areas, including infrastructures, innovation capabilities, human capital, development of enabling indigenous institutions and R&D expenditure. Availability of credit and the reduction of its cost are important determinants of whether poor farmers would adopt appropriate biotechnologies.

While it is necessary to increase the number of skilled scientists and public sector research, the generation of biotechnology products will also require creative arrangements for investment in research, including transfer of knowledge and lowering of barriers to the accessing of knowledge related to new products; as well as the development of a regulatory framework for maintaining a high level of safety.

International partnerships, both public and private, can play a significant role in strengthening the capacity for biotechnology innovation in developing countries

International partnerships, both public and private, can play a significant role in strengthening the capacity for biotechnology innovation in developing countries. Development partners will need to augment financial support and exchange of knowledge to foster human capital development and scientific capacity so as to pave the way towards sustained productivity growth and higher living standards. To improve the adoption and development of biotechnology in those countries, international organizations may need to encourage innovation and form collaborative alliances with institutions in many developing countries. Such technology transfer may be important for turning early-stage technologies into useable and commercially viable products. Moreover, adoption of open-source research practices in biotechnology can facilitate the development of treatments for specific diseases. Various patent pooling arrangements for a given technology can overcome the challenge posed by intellectual property fragmentation which prevents access to essential medicines.

Digital technologies: an opportunity for catching up or falling behind?

The present section explores the opportunities and challenges introduced by AI, automation and crowd-based technologies in developing countries. Notwithstanding the rapidity of the rise of these new technologies, their penetration in the economies of many developing countries has also proved equally rapid, providing opportunities for their populations, including consumers, while also posing challenges. The present subsection analyses early trends, possible positive and negative impacts and policy implications.

Automation and artificial intelligence

Automation and AI hold out the promise of new prosperity while also introducing risks of growing unemployment, underemployment and inequality

Advances in automation and AI, as discussed in previous chapters, are complementary and mutually reinforcing. Both sets of frontier technologies hold out the promise of new prosperity while also introducing risks of growing unemployment, underemployment and inequality. Currently, AI applications are developed and adopted mainly in countries at the technological frontier and in a few advanced developing countries. At the same time, the impacts of their potential applications in less technologically advanced developing countries can be wide-ranging and significant.

The actual and potential applications of AI in sectors such as manufacturing, transportation, language learning, health care and public administration can generate the kind of employment which would call for an increasingly more skilled workforce. Yet, with the right kind of investments in skills development, a less developed country can also acquire an edge in AI and machine learning. In fact, devising computer codes and algorithms—paving the way towards machine learning and, ultimately, development of AI capabilities—is relatively less capital-intensive than development of a competititve manufacturing base.

This presents less technologically advanced developing countries with a huge opportunity to invest in their populations—by enhancing educational systems, particularly in the fields of science and technology, and creating training and skills development programmes—and to thereby catch up with countries at the technological frontier.

Less advanced developing countries can also take advantage of productive sectors that are making use of AI and investing their proceeds in less productive sectors

Less advanced developing countries can also take advantage of productive sectors that are making use of AI and investing their proceeds in less productive sectors so as to further improve productive capacities and expand effective demand through multiplier effects. In fact, data coming from sensors, wearables and individuals are already feeding new activities and creating jobs in data collection, tabulation and analysis, which are useful for generating higher value added and improved efficiency in agriculture, manufacturing and public administration (Ghosh, 2016; McKinsey Global Institute, 2017b).

In fact, the few software engineers and other skilled persons available in less advanced developing countries, either living overseas or at home, can serve as innovation leaders in enhancement, automation and absorption of AI in those countries, which can then take advantage of rapid technological change to invest in upgrading their education and health sectors through the use of suitable AI applications (Gurib-Fakim and Eloff, 2013).

A laissez-faire, laissez-passer approach to AI adoption in less advanced developing countries can weaken social cohesion and aggravate political discontent

Nonetheless, automation can also have negative social and economic implications. A laissez- faire, laissez-passer approach to AI adoption in less advanced developing countries—many with less diversified economies, deep technological divides and double-digit unemployment and underemployment rates—can weaken social cohesion and aggravate political discontent, possibly leading to increased domestic and international migration. The rate of vulnerable employment as a share of total employment in sub-Saharan Africa and South Asia has remained above 70 per cent and 65 per cent, respectively, in spite of their decline for the past 10 years (ILO, 2017)[4]. More broadly, the ILOSTAT database reveals long-term high levels of informal employment as a share of total employment for many developing countries.[5]

Automation (through robotization) and fragmentation of production systems (by new ICT and global value chains) can adversely affect countries that employ a significant number of economically active people in the agricultural sector. For example, the share of jobs at risk of being lost to automation and advanced technologies are above 50 per cent for Angola, Bangladesh, Cambodia, Ethiopia, India, Nigeria, the Philippines and Viet Nam (McKinsey Global Institute, 2017b). In addition, a few recent studies have reported that the impact of new technologies on labour markets has led to polarization of jobs—as discussed in chapter II—for countries at different levels of economic development, a trend expected to continue in the near term. For low-income countries, the changes in employment shares have on average been negative for the medium-skilled during 2000–2013 and slightly positive for the low- and high-skilled, while little change is expected during 2013–2021 in all skill categories. Likewise, for lower and upper middle income countries, both actual and expected changes in employment shares are, on average, quite positive for the high-skilled but negative for the medium- and low-skilled (ILO, 2018).

4 Vulnerable employment is defined as the sum of the employment status groups of own-account workers and contributing family workers.

5 The rates of informal employment for the following selected countries are for the period from around 2013 to 2016: Albania (63.5 per cent), Armenia (51 per cent), Bolivia (Plurinational State of) (70 per cent), Colombia (59 per cent), Dominican Republic (47 per cent), Egypt (54 per cent), El Salvador (68 per cent), Guatemala (79 per cent), Honduras (81 per cent), India (82 per cent), Liberia (80 per cent), Madagascar (91 per cent), Mongolia (47 per cent), Pakistan (83 per cent), Paraguay (57 per cent), Peru (60 per cent) and South Africa (46 per cent).

Dormehl (2017) indicates that some chief executive officers (CEOs) of big companies in developing countries are increasingly encouraged to "hire" AI machines, which can be less costly and more productive than workers, who may periodically leave on vacation, get sick or demand higher wages. In urban areas of poor countries, increasing automation through the introduction of driverless cars and less labour-intensive manufacturing and services can also be disruptive owing to fewer income-earning opportunities for blue-collar workers and weaknesses in or lack of social protection systems (Citi GPS and Oxford Martin School, 2017).

The main question is whether less advanced developing countries would be able to create more jobs without massive training and retraining programmes on digital technologies. According to Brynjolfsson (2011), "AI and automation would continue making the economic pie bigger, but there is no economic law that guarantees that everyone, or most people, will benefit". At the same time, the growing ubiquity of AI applications presents less developed countries with the opportunity to invest in their populations by launching online science and technology education courses; enhancing apprenticeship and retraining programmes; and upgrading R&D and innovation systems (Haider, 2018; Tegmark, 2017; Gurib-Fakim and Eloff, 2013).

The main question is whether less advanced developing countries would be able to create more jobs without massive training and retraining programmes on digital technologies

The implementation of protectionist policies for inward-looking growth by frontier countries and reshoring of manufacturing activities can also harm current prospects for growth and development in less technologically advanced developing countries. The "labour-cost advantage" can quickly disappear, further eroding the fragile employment situation in those countries in the foreseeable future. Yet, the potential use of 3D printing, partly enabled by AI technologies, may create both opportunities and challenges in developing countries with labour-cost advantage exports (see box III.1).

Global value chains have exploited the labour-cost advantage—i.e., the sweatshop-type[6] labour conditions and environmental degradation characteristic of countries where labour laws and regulations can more easily be circumvented (Shum and others, 2016). The medium-term objective of achieving the 2030 Agenda for Sustainable Development makes it more imperative to put social development in the driving seat, so that this labour-cost advantage, based on low wages, can no longer be an adjunct of future sustainable development.

Overall, less advanced developing countries would likely take longer than countries at the technological frontier to adjust human capacities and infrastructures so as to truly benefit from AI. For this reason, policymakers in poor countries need to prepare their populations and economies for new industries which would create new occupations and for jobs that value human creativity and social interaction. On the other hand, swift adoption of AI without any concomitant plan on how to redistribute the income generated from highly productive sectors to less productive ones may prove more detrimental than beneficial, at least in the short-term. Full and decent employment should be a medium-term objective based on implementation of new models of education, lifelong learning and regular (re)training programmes.

Less advanced developing countries would take longer than countries at the technological frontier to adjust human capacities and infrastructures so as to truly benefit from AI

6 Sweatshops are characterized typically by low wages, long working hours and unhealthy working conditions, particularly for women, children and migrant workers.

Box III.1

Opportunities and challenges presented by 3D printing

While a number of developed countries use 3D printing in the construction, manufacturing, aeronautics and health sectors, 3D printing would also open opportunities to less advanced developing countries and countries in special situations, in particular. 3D printing can offer opportunities by overcoming infrastructure bottlenecks and lowering the barriers to manufacturing leapfrogging and exports. It can create opportunities for countries without the technical capacities to develop an entire industrial supply chain.

3D printing can therefore economically empower small businesses by providing more people with access to the means of production. It can also reduce the role of needed economies of scale and contribute to reducing the gap between small and large firms. For example, 3D printing technology can enable the manufacture of local equipment such as toys, farming and domestic tools and spare parts, which could directly improve the livelihood and productivity of small firms, creating new jobs and empowerment in terms of their economic outlook.

Challenges

In the immediate short term, 3D printing can depress import demands from developing countries and create more localized 3D printing production hubs near large consumer and highly developed markets (Hallward-Driemeier and Nayyar, 2018, p. 100). As 3D printing further matures, less advanced developing countries, particularly those relying on low-cost mass manufacturing production, could lose a large amount of business to do-it-yourself manufacturers (Bryane, 2013).

To take advantage of the opportunities provided by 3D printing, developing countries would need to overcome existing technological gaps by investing in access to and adoption of affordable, clean and reliable electricity, improving access to high quality health care and education, and investing in science and engineering-related R&D. The success or failure of 3D printing would depend on improvements in infrastructure, in particular in areas related to energy and the Internet.

In the event that the above challenges can be overcome and the cost of adopting 3D printing declines sufficiently, enhanced international cooperation could further facilitate access to and adoption of 3D printing as a means of supporting economic transformation and industrial development.

Source: UN/DESA.

Crowd-based technologies

Crowd-based technologies form the basis of the so-called sharing economy, which resembles a mix of "gift" and "market" economies in its transactions. Sundararajan (2016) argues that these technologies, characterized by an array of on-demand platforms, are transforming a large number of industries, including transportation, hotels, banks and marketplaces.

Crowd-based technologies have already created new occupations and sources of income generation for individuals and families in less developed countries

Crowd-based technologies have already created new occupations and sources of income generation for individuals and families in less developed countries. Airbnb, for example, has made it possible for an empty room in the home of an individual or household to become a source of income—a support in terms of meeting expenses or even saving for the future. At the same time, the price, relative to that for booking a room in a hotel, is generally attractive to the service user. Similarly, Uber, BlaBlacar and other crowd-based businesses are able to entice clients with their offer of relatively trustworthy and more affordable taxi and transportation services relative to regular taxi, bus or train services. As Sundararajan puts it, "digital trust powers the sharing economy".

Taxi drivers, however, are not necessarily shifting to the new platforms completely. Instead, they often juggle both regular taxi and Uber services, making the best use of both, which will depend on time of day and passenger pickup location. In these types of businesses, both the consumer and the service provider can benefit, without a high degree of risk, aside from the investment costs incurred by the service providers in, say, modernizing their home or a room in that home or purchasing a car. Overall, crowd-based businesses are growing and penetrating all kinds of economic activities, functions and sectors, such as banking (e.g., Lending Club), hotels (e.g., Airbnb), retail (e.g., Etsy), transportation (e.g., Uber, Ola (India)), diversified labour (e.g., Handy), personal services (e.g., Munchery), corporate services (e.g., HourlyNerd), car rental (e.g., Getaround) and risk capital intermediaries (e.g., Kickstarter).

Again, according to Sundararajan, a sharing economy underpinned by crowd-based platforms reflects a new way of organizing economic activity, workers and consumers. Through its peer-to-peer commercial exchanges, the sharing economy blurs the line between the personal and the professional. It is therefore more difficult to determine its impact on the economy, government regulation, labour markets and the social fabric.

One of the important challenges presented by crowd-based platforms is how to help workers, drivers and renters avoid low wages or income

One of the important challenges presented by crowd-based platforms is how to help workers, drivers and renters avoid low wages or income. Other challenges are associated with their lack of social protection and inadequate safety conditions. Many developing countries typically have very low levels of social protection or none at all, while their weak labour-market institutions are less able to negotiate adequate working conditions for workers (ILO, 2014). Nonetheless in some countries, there has been support for the functioning of local crowd-based platforms to enable them to compete with transnational platforms. In India, for example, Ola, by virtue of the fact that it has the capacity to service remote areas, is thereby able to compete with Uber for the same clientele, even if Uber offers better prices.

As noted above, the crowd-based share-economy models raise serious issues regarding social protection. For one thing, they blur the line between employer and employee. Serious equity and ethical questions revolve around the subject of responsibilities: how do the platforms, participants and workers in the shared economy and Governments go about contributing their fair share of social protection? It is argued that most of the income generated is funnelled to a few monopoly firms with headquarters in the big cities of developed countries, which compounds the challenges faced by poor countries with respect to how to adequately regulate the sharing economy (Ross, 2017). Crowd-based platforms—matching buyers and sellers of a particular product or service—typically collect a hefty share of the gross revenue, while participants and workers on the platform provide capital and labour services as well (as attested, e.g., by the cost of roads, vehicles or home improvement), but receive a relatively less equitable share of the revenue.

Rapid deployment and growth of crowd-based technologies are raising additional concerns regarding consumer protection and safety

The rapid deployment and growth of these technologies are raising additional concerns related to consumer protection and safety. For example, it is often the case that women feel less safe when renting a room in a home, where privacy and security are not guaranteed, or when employing a car service to travel long distances or to remote areas. And many less advanced developing countries have yet to implement effective safety and security norms designed to protect people from the risks associated with participation in crowd-based platforms.

Another relevant issue being discussed increasingly is how Governments in less advanced developing countries could go about levying taxes on the use of roads, land, electricity and other public services, which serve as a foundation for the development of crowd-based platforms that benefit both transnational firms and consumers. What would be the criteria for measuring the contribution of employers and workers to income generation and using the figures obtained as a basis for fixing tax rates?

Conclusion

The impacts of crowd-based technologies and AI on developing countries are yet to fully materialize and those impacts will vary across countries and depend on the level of development, quality of institutions and policy flexibilities for coping with the effects of these technologies. The Governments of developing countries will need to upgrade their capacities for regulating crowd-based platforms and collecting taxes on the revenues that they earn in these countries, as discussed in chapter V. However, possible strategic options may not apply specifically to all of these countries. These options include, but are not limited to, the provision of a basic income to people unemployed and underemployed, the broadening of social protection floors, and innovative taxation systems designed to distribute more fairly the income generated by firms and high-income earners and thereby help to support innovation as well as the financing of social security.

As discussed, AI and automation can generate significant unemployment and underemployment of the low- and medium-skilled, at least in the short term, in less technologically advanced countries, particularly those with high shares of informal employment. Therefore, expected employment outcomes and policy design should be carefully assessed before further transfer and development of frontier technologies is undertaken.

On the other hand, new technologies have the potential to create new occupations, representing opportunities for decent employment, if appropriate policies are crafted. In this context, Governments in these countries will need to increase their investments in building and upgrading the skills of the workforce and quality digital infrastructure, including in broadband Internet access, in order to suppport a sustainable development framework. First-order investments can be directed towards training and retraining programmes, apprenticeship programmes, and education focused on life-long learning, project-based creativity and peer-based approaches.

Chapter IV
Fostering innovation, diffusion and adoption

Introduction

The previous chapters discussed the importance of new technologies, their introduction in advanced countries, and the slow technological progress in many developing countries that underpins the development divide. The present chapter focuses on how countries can foster innovation and how other countries adapt and adopt these innovations and promote economic growth.

Technological advances during the past three centuries enabled some societies to leap forward, supporting ever larger populations, reducing poverty, increasing longevity and pushing the frontier of knowledge and technology ever forward. Innovation created more efficient firms and workers, which in turn created more innovative economies. This virtuous cycle created more dynamic, competitive and sophisticated economies.

Technological innovations that create more efficient firms and workers are part of a virtuous cycle

However, many countries and communities within them have not had the same experience. As chapters II and III of this *Survey* show, there are large and growing differences between and within countries in terms of the ability to innovate, access and use technologies. Many developing countries are yet to fully utilize the technological breakthroughs of the past and, increasingly, innovation in frontier technologies is concentrated in a few firms and in a few countries. Many developing countries, particularly least developed countries (LDCs) that are falling behind in adopting and using new technologies, can find themselves in a technology and income trap, continuing to produce basic goods and services that do not encourage innovation and enable structural transformation. It in turn results in a growing development gap.

Innovation in frontier technologies is becoming more concentrated, and the firms and countries that fall behind can find themselves facing a widening technology and development gap

In discussing the links between development gaps and technological divides, this chapter will first explain the connection between innovation and economic growth, and the importance of each for sustainable development. Innovation can be understood as a broad-based activity which subsumes both *process* innovation, reflecting the ability of firms and economies to find new ways of producing existing goods and services; and *product* innovation, i.e., the invention of new products and services. Innovation does not always signify a technological breakthrough—a grand-scale, one-of-a-kind invention. Innovation, broadly speaking, also entails improvements and improvisations of processes and products, which can be small-scale, incremental and even imperceptible.

This chapter explains how both process and product innovations are important for growth. Product and process innovations go hand in hand and complement each other. Unfortunately, while relatively large developing countries have been able to innovate and achieve high rates of growth—often adopting and using technologies developed in other countries—this is not the case for many others.

It is argued here that faster innovation, great or small, and closing the technological divide are important requirements for achievement of higher and sustained economic growth and for a more equitable distribution of economic gains. The chapter discusses key elements of the innovation and diffusion processes, which have implications for the technological divide between developed and developing countries and within those countries. It also highlights four factors that could lead to an even wider divide: (a) continued divergence in the ability of firms and countries to innovate and adopt existing technologies; (b) growing market power concentration; (c) increasingly more stringent and restrictive intellectual property rights (IPR) regimes; and (d) possible confinement of technology diffusion to firms of similar technological capacities.

Keeping up with and catching up to the technological frontier are not automatic processes: they depend on how well a country's innovation system is developed and managed

The chapter discusses the role of Governments in closing the technological divide. For countries and firms, keeping up with and catching up to the technological frontier will depend on how well they can develop and manage their national innovation system (NIS)—a system of interconnected institutions whose aim is to create, store and transfer new technologies. A global technological frontier is broadly defined as the vanguard of technological development worldwide, represented by the set of the most cutting-edge innovations available at the global level. On the other hand, a country's own technological frontier is defined by the set of the most advanced technologies which that country's leading firms or research institutes are capable of employing. In empirical studies, the technological frontier is typically proxied by the productivity of the most productive country or firm, given the close links between technology and productivity, which is discussed subsequently.

Governments play an important role, together with the private sector, in the development of national innovation systems

Within most national innovation systems, the private sector will continue to lead the development of cutting-edge technologies and processes. Nevertheless, Governments play a central role in facilitating the system's development, through establishing and maintaining enabling infrastructures and an institutional environment that incentivizes technology innovation and adoption. The international community has an important role to play as well, as economies and technologies are connected across borders. Various internationally agreed instruments, such as the Addis Ababa Action Agenda of the Third International Conference on Financing for Development,[1] set out the commitment of the technologically advanced countries to help other countries access and adopt new technologies.

A tale of two divides: technology and development

The introduction of new technologies is central to an economy's ability to grow. Indeed, investigation into how countries have historically achieved prosperity reveals the emergence of technology as a central actor. It is no surprise, then, that technology and the process of innovation from which it emerges feature as key factors in modern growth theory.

As firms incorporate new technologies into their operations, they also open up a pathway to continuous learning and the accumulation of new capabilities

Technology helps determine a country's productivity, allowing it to extract more value from a given level of resources, including labour, capital and natural resources. Technology creates new economic opportunities and jobs, which includes creating more capable firms and workers, enabling new business models and connecting many firms and individuals to formal marketplaces. More capable firms and workers in turn create more dynamic, competitive and innovative economies. The efforts of firms to incorporate new technologies and techniques open up a pathway to continuous learning and the accumulation of new capabilities, which triggers a process of structural transformation within an economy.

1 General Assembly resolution 69/313, annex.

Technological change and economic growth

The speed of innovation and how it diffuses determine technological progress, consequently influencing productivity and economic growth

A country's ability to achieve and sustain long-term economic growth is determined by its ability to increase productivity through the use of better technology, together with human and physical capital. New technologies release new capabilities in human and physical capital, expanding the possibilities for firms (see box IV.1 for a discussion on the theoretical underpinnings of technology's effects on growth). How quickly innovation occurs and how it spreads throughout an economy determine the path and speed of technological progress, which has implications for productivity and economic growth (Benhabib, Perla and Tonetti, 2017). In a country with lower barriers to innovation diffusion, laggard firms are easily able to adopt new innovations and become competitive. This holds true also at the country level, where countries can grow by pushing the technological frontier or catch up by making use of available foreign knowledge and technology.

History provides us with some examples of this mechanism at work. The period of the first industrial revolution, which extended roughly from the late eighteenth to the early part of the nineteenth century, represented the dawn of what we now consider "modern" economic growth—growth that is driven by technological change. Innovation of processes and technologies led to a growing mastery of the use of energy, relieving the principal limitations to production at that time (Vickers and Ziebarth, 2017).

More recently, economies that have successfully developed their productive structures—such as Japan, the Republic of Korea, Singapore and Taiwan Province of China—did so by following the pattern of industrialization of the previous century. Those economies took advantage of their latecomer status, making use of available technology, process innovations, and their lower factor costs and mass production capacities to export cost-sensitive products.[2]

These examples notwithstanding, early empirical studies did not find evidence that all economies converge to similar levels of per capita income, as predicted by neoclassical growth theory. As of the present moment, economic convergence has been limited mostly to today's developed countries (see for example, Baumol, 1986). The slower growth of initially poorer countries, as revealed in the historical data, supported arguments that the world has in fact experienced income divergence (Pritchett, 1997). More recent studies on the rapid growth of emerging and developing countries (Derviş, 2012; Fukase and Martin, 2017) have added to this understanding. One important finding is that relatively large developing countries, in which firms are taking advantage of lower wages to enter the labour-intensive production stages offshored by developed countries, have been able to reduce the income gap between them and the developed countries. They have also been able to take advantage of global supply chains (Baldwin, 2016).[3]

Accelerating but unequal technological diffusion

One possible explanation for why many countries do not converge despite the theoretical potential is that they may lack the ability to use existing technologies owing to resource

2 This point was first argued by Gerschenkron (1962). More recent discussions on the advantages enjoyed by "latecomer" countries are found in Lee and Mathews (2013) and Lee (2013; 2016).

3 Baldwin (2016) specifically mentions six countries that achieved notable convergence, recently gaining a global share of manufacturing: China, India, Indonesia, Poland, the Republic of Korea and Thailand.

Box IV.1

Technology as a foundation for growth

What drives the increasingly large gaps in income per capita across countries is one of the central puzzles of development economics. Since the mid-twentieth century, economists have developed various theories to describe the drivers of economic growth. Three main theoretical frameworks are recognized in the economics literature: the Harrod-Domar model, the neoclassical model and the theory of endogenous growth. The role of technology for growth, and how technology is accumulated, constitute a central concern under each of these frameworks and how they address this concern is a key differentiator among them.

In their work in the 1940s, Roy Harrod and Evsey Domar attributed the rate of growth directly to the savings rate, which is a behavioural variable, and the incremental capital-output ratio (ICOR), which is a metric related to technology. Within this framework, faster growth requires a higher savings rate, or a lower capital-output ratio. The simplicity of this model was very attractive for countries seeking a clear policy objective. For a given ICOR and a target rate of growth, policymakers simply needed to achieve a certain savings rate. The Harrod-Domar model suffered from instabilities, however, owing to its fixed capital-output ratio specification. Any deviations would result in rising or falling unemployment rates or capacity utilization.

The Solow-Swan growth model ushered in the neoclassical approach, under which technological changes were recognized as the driver of economic growth. In that model, the capital-output ratio is determined by the neoclassical production function. Output depends on capital, labour and technological progress. This framework defines a stable "steady state" where output per labour (adjusted for technology) is constant and depends on the savings rate, population growth and technological progress. Per capita income growth (and the marginal product of labour) depends on technological progress (the level of income per capita depends on the savings rate and population growth). The neoclassical approach led to a consensus that knowledge, which leads to technological innovation, was the driver of long-run economic growth. However, this model does not explain how technological changes occur, and therefore fails to explain the most important determinant of the growth rate.

This problem led to the development of models where technological progress is a function of endogenous factors such as capital, research and development (R&D), spillover effects, the quality of human capital and technology transfers, among others. These models may differ in their specification, but all recognize the important role of innovation in determining long-run economic growth.

A subset of these endogenous growth models, so-called evolutionary-institutional theories, postulate that technological progress is primarily a function of the organization and efficiency of management of R&D resources, starting from the firm level. These models promote the concept of the national innovation system as a means, for countries, of driving technological change. This is particularly important for developing countries that, while resource-constrained, are still attempting to keep up with, and catch up to, more advanced countries.

Hidalgo and Hausmann (2009) build on this framework with their concept of "product space". In their specification, countries grow by expanding production of existing products and by producing entirely new products. That is, countries combine their existing capacities (technology, capital, labour, etc.) in new ways. They also innovate, accumulating new knowledge and capabilities to develop yet more products. In this way, innovation and diffusion advance the multiplicity of knowledge embedded in an economic system, which allows it to produce more sophisticated products and therefore grow and develop.

limitations. This may be a result of a growing concentration of technology creation in a few countries and firms and of insufficient diffusion of technology within countries.[4]

As documented in chapters II and III of this *Survey*, there are large and growing differences between and within countries with respect to their ability to innovate, access and use technologies. Many developing countries are yet to fully utilize the technological breakthroughs of the past. Also, the development of new technologies is increasingly concentrated in a few countries and a few firms.

The technological divide between countries is significant — and particularly acute in the realm of frontier technologies

The technological divide between developed countries and the rest of the world economy, when measured by the numbers of patent applications or research and development (R&D) expenditures, is wide and growing. China, the European Union, Japan and the United States of America, accounting for 32 per cent of the world's population in 2015, collectively account for a far larger global share in scientific publications (67 per cent), R&D spending (78 per cent) and triadic patent applications (88 per cent) (figure IV.1). The technological divide is even more acute in the realm of frontier technologies. Fujii and Managi (2017) report that the United States alone accounted for an overwhelming 75 per cent of global artificial intelligence (AI) patents granted during 2016–2017.

At the same time, the cross-border diffusion of technology has accelerated. Using data on 25 different inventions in the last 200 years, researchers found that new technologies have diffused across countries at a faster pace (Comin and Hobijn, 2010; Comin and Mestieri Ferrer, 2013). More recent technologies, such as cell phones and the Internet, have arrived in developing countries just a few years after they were first invented in developed

Figure IV.1
Share of global for various activities, selected countries and the European Union, 2015

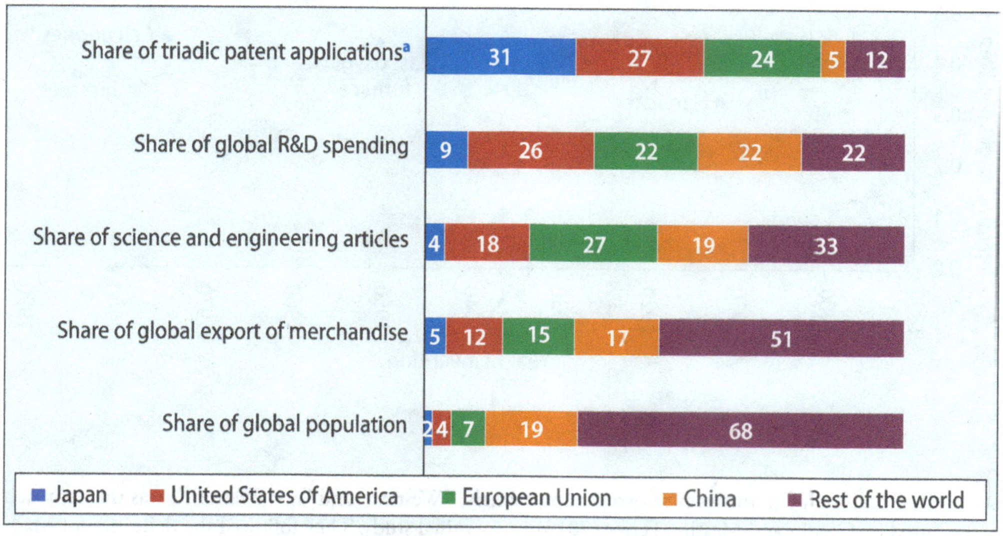

Sources: National Science Board (2016); OECD.Stat; UN/DESA, Population Division (2017); UIS.Stat; and World Trade Organization (2017).

a Triadic patents are a set of patents filed at the three major patent offices (European Patent Office, Japan Patent Office and United States Patent and Trademark Office) to protect the same invention.

4 A closely related challenge is the "digital divide", which is defined as the gap in use of digital technology across communities. For more specific discussions on the characteristics, trends and determinants of the digital divide, see *United Nations E-Government Survey 2014* (United Nations, 2014).

countries. This can likely be attributed to the rapid pace of globalization and the digital revolution, which have taken place in recent decades.

Acceleration of cross-border technology adoption masks the slower pace of technology diffusion within countries

However, the acceleration of technology adoption across countries masks the slower pace of diffusion of these technologies within countries. Developing countries struggle to employ technologies with the same degree of intensity and versatility as developed countries. Even as new technologies have quickly become available to all countries, it takes longer for them to be as pervasive and widely used as in developed countries.

Figure IV.2 displays the differences in the average intensity of use of selected technologies in "non-Western" as compared with "Western" countries.[5] This "intensive margin" measures the differences between the two country groups in terms of the number of users of the technology (e.g., the number of cell phones or computers per capita) and the efficiency with which the technology is used (e.g., tons of Bessemer steel produced with the technology).[6]

Figure IV.2
Intensity of use of selected technologies by "non-Western" relative to "Western" countries, 1890–1990

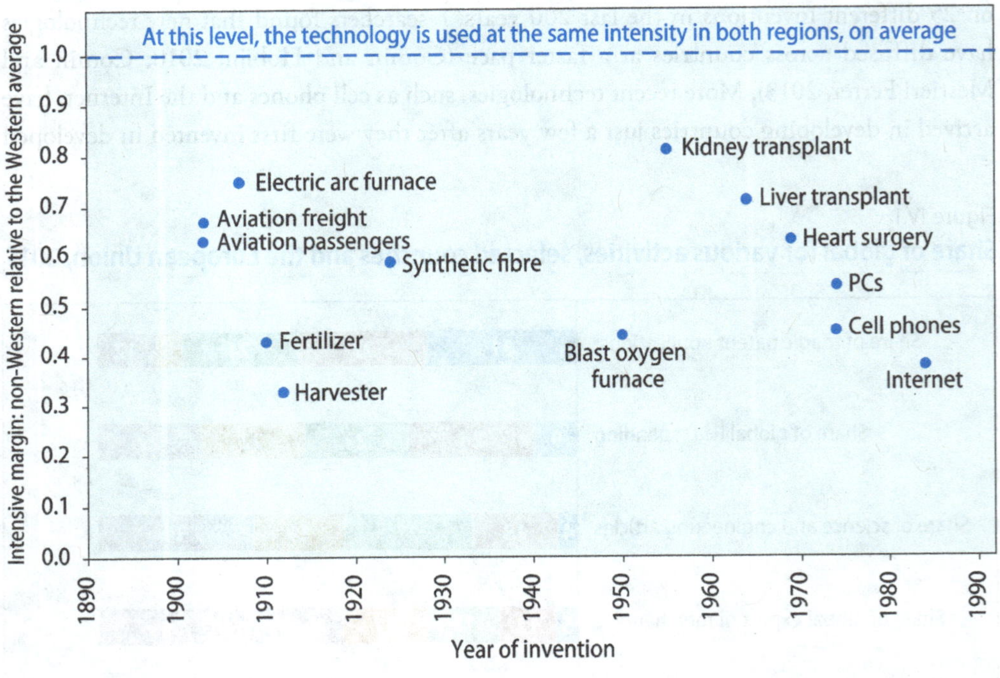

Source: Comin and Mestieri Ferrer (2013).

Note: A value of 1 represents equal intensity between the country groups.

5 The division of countries into two groups, namely, "Western" and "non-Western", was the approach used by Comin and Mestieri Ferrer (2013) in a seminal study. They followed the definition of Maddison (2004). The study categorizes the following countries as Western: Australia, Austria, Belgium, Canada, Denmark, Finland, France, Germany, Italy, Japan, the Netherlands, New Zealand, Norway, Sweden, Switzerland, the United Kingdom of Great Britain and Northern Ireland and the United States of America.

6 The "extensive margin", by contrast, captures the fraction of potential adopters that use the technology (for example, the fraction of farmers that have adopted a new type of hybrid seed).

The difference between the two groups in how intensively each technology is used is significant. For example, the intensity of Internet use in the median non-Western country is approximately one third that in the median Western country.[7] For all technologies, the average level of adoption by the average non-Western country is slightly more than half the average adoption level for Western countries (54 per cent).

Closing the technology divides

If countries are to achieve higher, sustained economic growth and for there to be a more equitable distribution of economic gains, they must fulfil the important requirement of closing the technological divide. All the more so, as new frontier technologies are rapidly changing the make-up of industries and sectors, threatening existing comparative advantages based on traditional factors of production.

Rapid technological change presents opportunities for developing or otherwise latecomer countries...

Fortunately, periods of rapid technological change are times of opportunity for developing or otherwise latecomer countries. Firms that are not saddled with large investments in legacy equipment and obsolete methods of production can explore ways to develop new products with emerging technologies (Lee and Mathews, 2013; Lee, 2016). Countries may not necessarily need a twentieth century industrial base to build a twenty-first century bio-, nano- or information economy. Indeed, a twentieth century industrial base may be a hindrance. It may be easier for a firm without large capital investments to run a new 3D printer to manufacture a specific part rather than master all of the steps required to make that part the traditional way (Hausmann, 2017). Nevertheless, as will be discussed in a later section, the speed of adoption of newly emerging technologies will depend on a wide range of factors. Therefore, it remains difficult to predict the diffusion trajectory of frontier technologies.

...but firms in those countries generally face difficult choices concerning technology investment

In particular, firms in developing countries generally face very difficult choices with respect to investing in technology. Figure IV.3, which portrays this challenge, measures the rate of return to R&D spending according to the distance of countries from the global technological frontier (denoted as zero at the far right along the horizontal axis). For countries that are close to or at the frontier and for countries that are farthest from the frontier (situated at the far left), the returns to R&D spending are small or negative. The largest returns to R&D spending occur in countries that are at a middle distance from the technological frontier. These countries have the capacities and complementary infrastructure required to adopt existing technologies and take advantage of the productivity gains that they yield (Cirera and Maloney, 2017; Goñi and Maloney, 2017).

Countries with intermediate levels of productive capacity and knowledge enjoy an advantage. They can use their existing capacities together with existing and new technologies to expand into many new activities. Countries with high and low levels of productive capacities face more difficulties. Advanced countries are already highly diversified, make most of the existing products and have limited options for copying more advanced products. These countries can progress further only by innovating processes and products that expand their technological frontier. At the other end of the spectrum, countries with few capabilities find it difficult to adopt existing technologies and methods, owing to limitations related to complementary factors, including knowledge, capital, technology and infrastructure.

7 A value of 1 signifies that the technology is used with equal intensity in both groups of countries. A value below 1 signifies that the technology is used relatively less intensively in non-Western countries.

Figure IV.3
Rate of return to R&D according to distance from the technological frontier

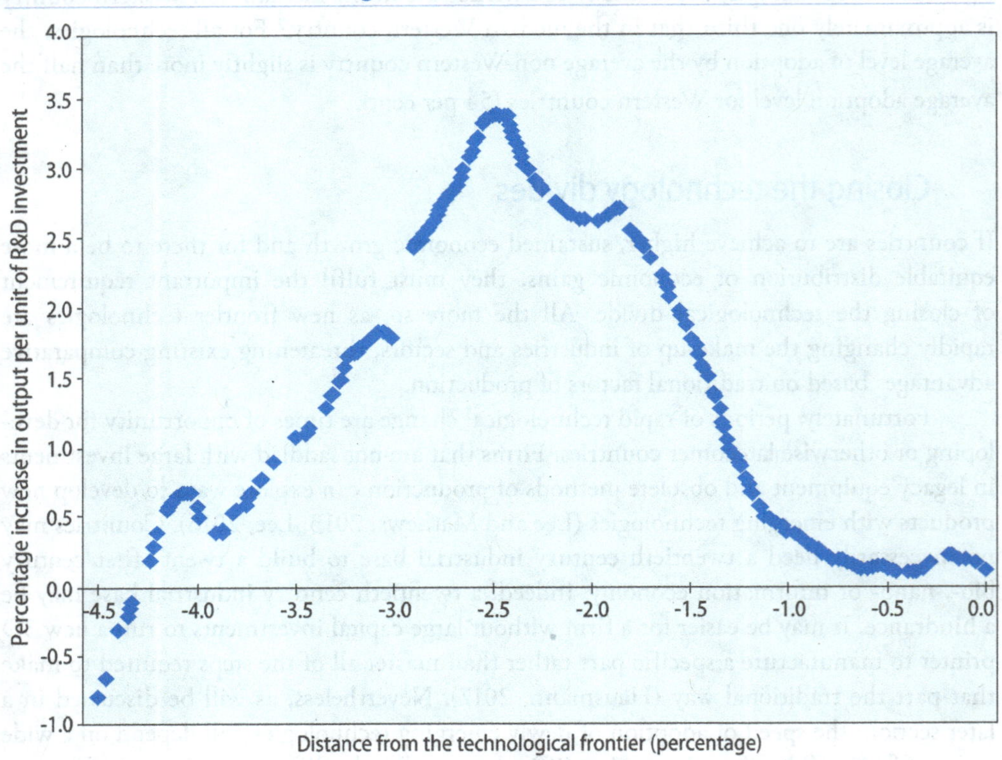

Source: Cirera and Maloney (2017), figure 3.2.

Note: The technological frontier is denoted as zero on the horizontal axis and is measured as the highest GDP per capita (in constant prices) in a given period of time. Each point on the horizontal axis, therefore, measures the distance of a certain country at a certain time from the contemporary technological frontier. The horizontal distance is calculated as the percentage difference between a country's constant GDP per capita and that of the highest constant GDP per capita in the same period.

Without a clear business case to be made for investing in advanced technologies (in terms of capital and human costs as well as expected revenues), firms will find it risky to make the jump into new markets and production techniques. This is made even more difficult by strong IPR rules which help entrench the dominance of a few firms. Another barrier in frontier technologies may be the large concentration of market power in a few large firms, driven by economies of scale, network effects and inadequate antitrust enforcement.

Making existing technologies more accessible and building an innovative economy are difficult policy challenges and there are not many countries that have managed to enable this type of technological upgrading. In recent decades, computer-aided design and manufacturing have allowed some countries to participate in global value chains of increasingly complicated products. This trend might continue, rewarding those that invest in new technologies. In his study of how the Republic of Korea managed to transform its economy, Lee (2013; 2016) demonstrates the power of the successful implementation of such a strategy at the national level, suggesting that the fate of countries at an early stage of development is not determined simply by their comparative advantage and their industrial progress is not dictated by spontaneous market outcomes. Technological upgrading is possible, and Governments can influence this process.

Market-based solutions for technology diffusion need to be supported by a well-functioning national innovation system

Because of the importance of private actors in innovation (see section on the evolving national innovation system below), market-based solutions for technology diffusion need to be supported by a well-functioning NIS, capable, inter alia, of identifying key challenges, directing research agendas, providing funding sources, setting priorities and establishing appropriate IPR regimes. Governments should work with other actors within the innovation systems to address any missing complementarities, such as physical and human capital, whose lack limits innovation and its positive externalities. As shown above, these missing complementarities become more important the farther a country or firm lies from the technological frontier. Regardless of how much a country invests in innovation and technology, if it lacks enough machine, trained workers, appropriate managerial and organization know-how, or complementary infrastructure and institutional arrangements, the returns to that investment will be low (Cirera and Maloney, 2017).

This highlights the importance of understanding the distinctions between leading and lagging national innovation systems. As will be discussed directly below, these two types of systems differ typically in terms of some of their broad features, such as the balance among the roles of different actors, the extent of their reliance on foreign technologies, and their institutional arrangements and complementary infrastructures. They therefore also differ as regards the sets of challenges that they face in their efforts to support technological development.

The evolving national innovation system

At the core of every country's technological endeavours lies its national innovation system (NIS). An NIS is defined as the "set of distinct institutions which jointly and individually contribute to the development and diffusion of new technologies and which provides the framework within which governments form and implement policies to influence the innovation process" (Metcalfe, 1995). As such, "it is a system of interconnected institutions to create, store and transfer the knowledge, skills and artefacts which define new technologies".

At work within an NIS are several key processes: innovation, diffusion, adoption and adaptation. Innovation, which has a broad scope, subsumes both process and product innovations, as already noted. The generation of an initial form of innovation is followed by its diffusion, through which the innovation is broadly disseminated over time among the members of the system. The diffusion process reflects user acceptance of the innovation; and the rate of its adoption by individuals determines the speed of its diffusion at the macro level. Closely related to adoption is adaptation, which refers to the tweaking of the original technology to render it a better fit for local conditions.

It is important to note that these processes are inextricably linked. For example, adoption of a new technology by a large group of users provides useful feedback to the innovators themselves (Jaffe, 2015). Further, broad diffusion keeps laggard firms from falling too far behind the leading firms as regards technological capabilities; and the resulting upward pressure exerted on both frontier and non-frontier firms in terms of their incentives to innovate supports innovation (Benhabib, Perla and Tonetti, 2017).

Linkages among actors in a national innovation system are central to a country's improvements in technology performance

The focus on the NIS is underpinned by the understanding that linkages among actors involved in innovation are central to improvements in technology performance (OECD, 1997). Such linkages are complex and the success of a country's innovation efforts relies on how those actors interact in generating and diffusing innovation. Traditional actors in the NIS include a myriad of private sector firms, universities, research institutes, think tanks, industry associations, advocacy groups, and government agencies and enterprises. They vary in size, engage in activities in different areas of technology and possess varied sets of capabilities.

Figure IV.4
Number of AI patents granted, selected companies, 2010–2016

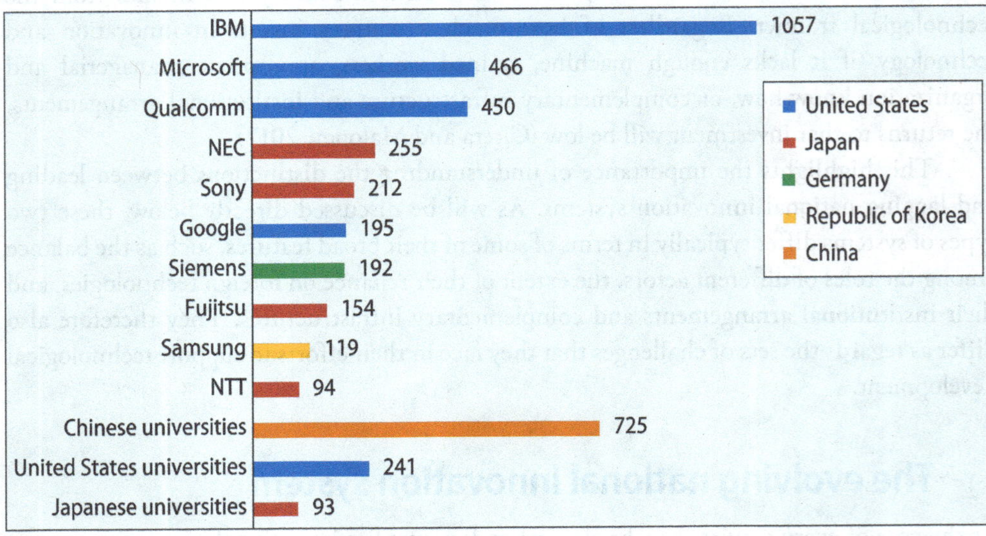

Source: Elaboration of Bruckner, LaFleur and Pitterle (2017), based on data from Fujii and Managi (2017).

Figure IV.5
United States spending on R&D by source, 1953–2015

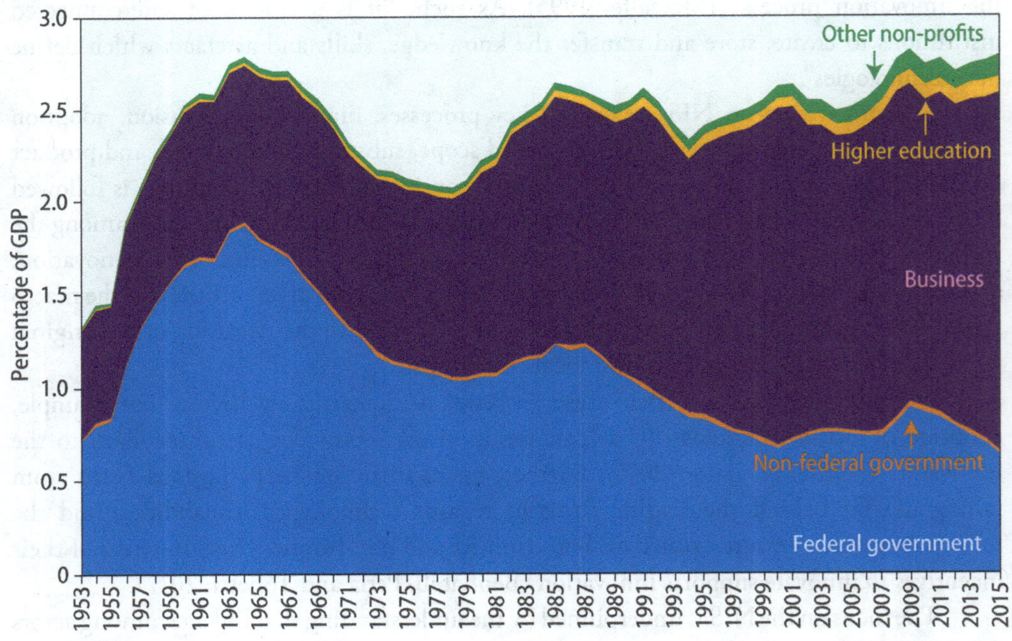

Source: Shambaugh, Nunn and Portman (2017).

In the current technological landscape, it would appear that the private sector has secured a dominant position, as it accounts for many of the advances achieved at the global technological frontier. For example, the latest advancement in AI around the world has been largely led by a small set of large technology companies (see figure IV.4). Moreover, in recent decades, R&D spending by the private sector has outpaced public sector spending, especially in developed countries (see figures IV.5 and IV.6).

Figure IV.6

Percentage of gross domestic expenditure on R&D financed by government: Canada, France, Germany, Japan, Spain and OECD, 1981–2015

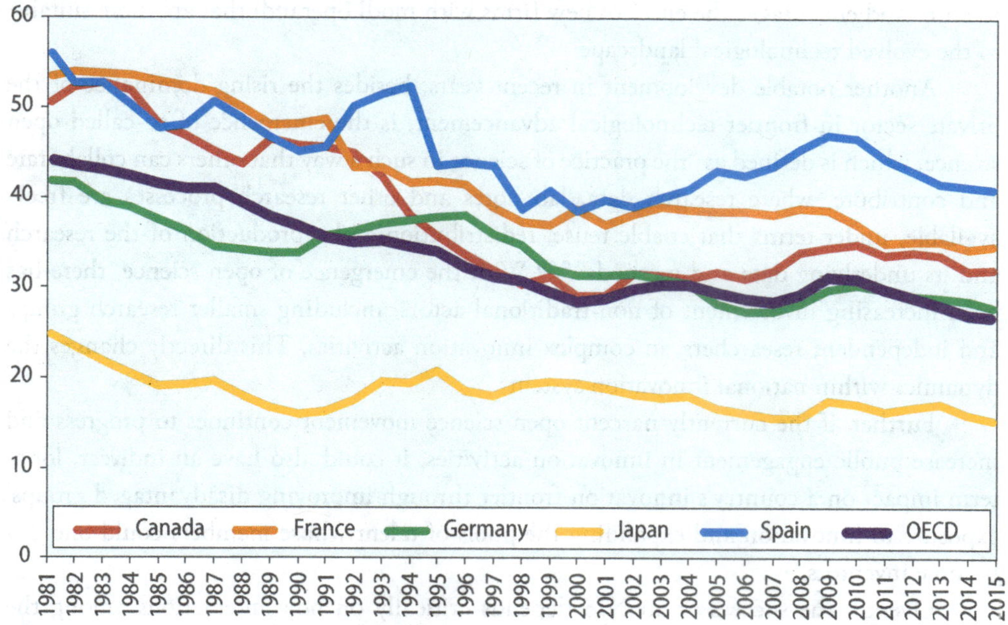

Source: UN/DESA elaboration, based on OECD.Stat:Main Science and Technology Indicators.

The private sector's dominance in the current technological landscape masks Government's catalytic role in fostering innovation

However, the observed dominance of the private sector masks the catalytic role played by government in fostering innovation. Indeed, while one might attribute the success of the Apple iPhone or the Google search engine to the ingenuity of these private companies, Mazzucato (2011) argues that the emergence of some of these firms' innovative products would not have been possible without government support. For example, many of the key technologies that underpin the iPhone and similar smartphones—such as the Global Positioning System (GPS), the touchscreen display and the voice-activated personal assistant—were funded by the United States Government. As for Google, the creation of its search engine algorithm received government financial support through the United States National Science Foundation.[8] From this perspective, despite the private sector's dominance at the technological frontier, Governments play a catalytic—and indispensable—role in driving innovation. Playing such a role effectively, however, would require Governments to address market failures and shape the direction of future innovation by supporting the development of certain technologies at the initial stages, while acknowledging and mitigating their own limitations in respect of identifying the most promising technologies.

Moreover, the fact that some firms are leading global innovation activities does not mean that all firms are eminently capable of undertaking R&D. This is particularly true in developing countries where many firms do not have adequate resources to conduct in-house R&D and therefore face the prospect of highly uncertain returns should they engage in efforts to innovate (see figure IV.3; and Lee, 2013).

In addition, even firms that can engage in R&D do not always act to maximize their innovation potential. Instead of consistently carrying out optimal actions as they continue to gain access to new information, firms may follow certain culturally and historically

8 See "On the Origins of Google" at https://www.nsf.gov/discoveries/disc_summ.jsp?cntn_id=100660.

conditioned routines to enable them to manage that information, which could also limit their innovation efforts (Nelson and Winter, 2009). This highlights the importance of maintaining healthy market competition, as discussed in chapter V, which reduces barriers to entry and encourages the entry of new firms with modi operandi that are more suitable to the evolved technological landscape.

Another notable development in recent years, besides the rising dominance of the private sector in frontier technological advancement, is the emergence of so-called open science, which is defined as "the practice of science in such a way that others can collaborate and contribute, where research data, lab notes and other research processes are freely available, under terms that enable reuse, redistribution and reproduction of the research and its underlying data and methods".[9,10] With the emergence of open science, there has been increasing involvement of non-traditional actors, including smaller research groups and independent researchers, in complex innovation activities. This directly changes the dynamics within national innovation systems.

Further, if the currently nascent open science movement continues to progress and increase public engagement in innovation activities, it could also have an indirect, long-term impact on a country's innovation frontier through improving disadvantaged groups' exposure to innovation and expanding the pools of talent whose members could one day become inventors.[11]

Overall, the success of an NIS depends critically on how interactions among the expanding set of actors and rapid, non-linear technological changes are managed. A key consideration in the context of this national effort is how government policies can guide and incentivize national innovation systems based on a country's specific circumstances, as discussed below.

Supporting a balanced and dynamic national innovation system

National innovation systems across the world typically differ in terms of three key systemic features: (a) balance among the various roles of different actors in supporting innovation; (b) balance between basic and applied research and experimental development; and (c) balance between indigenous innovation and adoption of foreign technology.

9 The definition has been formulated by FOSTER Plus (Fostering the practical implementation of Open Science in Horizon 2020 and beyond), which is a European Union-funded project, conducted by 11 partners across six countries. The project's primary aim is to contribute to a real and lasting shift in the behaviour of European researchers to ensure that open science becomes the norm.

10 For further discussions on open science, see UNESCO (2015) and Royal Society (2012).

11 Analysing data on 1.2 million United States inventors from patent records linked to tax records, Bell and others (2017) found that lack of exposure to innovation can help explain why children from below median income families are 10 times less likely to become inventors than those from families at the top 1 per cent income level, and why there are similarly large gaps among racial and gender groups. Exposure to innovation is defined as contact with someone who engages in innovation activities, for example, through one's family or neighbours. Bell and others (2017) measure such exposure by the patent rate among workers in one's commuting zone, i.e., the average number of patents issued per year to individuals in a given commuting zone between 1980 and 1990 divided by the commuting zone's population between the ages of 15 and 64 in the 1990 Census.

Figure IV.7

Balancing key systemic features of a national innovation system

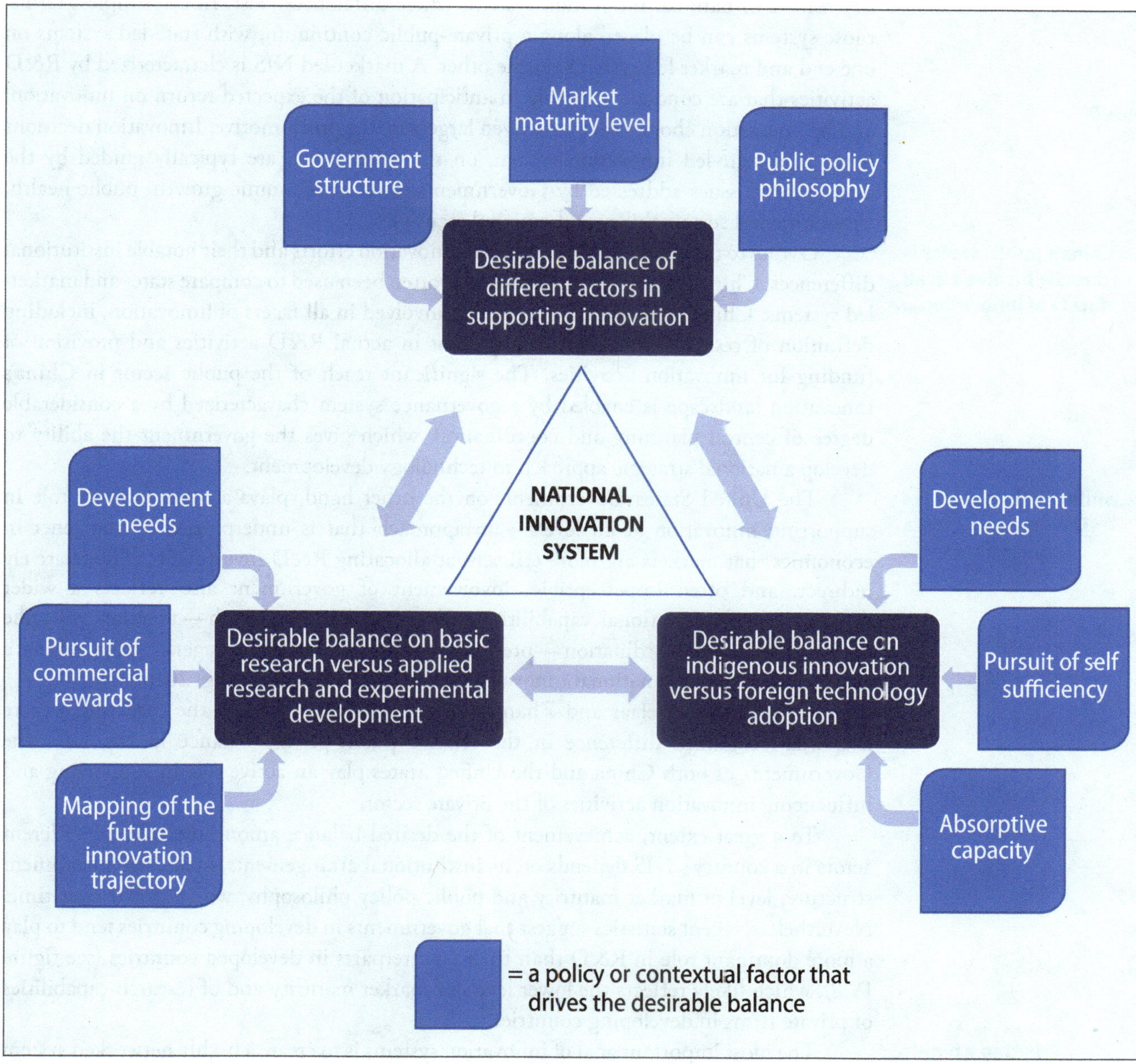

Source: UN/DESA.

Striking desired balances on each of the three key systemic features of a national innovation system is central to bridging the technological divide

A country's capacity to strike the desired balances determines the functioning of its NIS, which in turn determines—especially in the case of a country at a distance from the technological frontier—whether it will be able to bridge the technological divide and achieve sustainable development. Through their awareness of country-specific development and institutional contexts which evolve over time, policymakers play a key role in guiding the innovation systems towards the desirable balance on each of the three fronts (see figure IV.7).

Balancing the roles of different actors in innovation

The nature of the relative balance among different actors in supporting innovation is one key feature of national innovation systems where differences exist. In the simplest terms, those systems can be placed along a private-public continuum, with state-led systems on one end and market-led systems on the other. A market-led NIS is characterized by R&D activities that are conducted mainly in anticipation of the expected return on innovation; and by innovation choices that are driven largely by the profit motive. Innovation decisions made in a state-led innovation system, on the other hand, are typically guided by the development issues addressed by Governments, such as economic growth, public health, environmental sustainability and national security.

China's public sector is directly involved in all facets of innovation...

Owing to their leading roles in global innovation efforts and their notable institutional differences, China and the United States have often been used to compare state- and market-led systems. China's public sector is directly involved in all facets of innovation, including definition of research objectives, engagement in actual R&D activities and provision of funding for innovation activities. The significant reach of the public sector in China's innovation landscape is enabled by a governance system characterized by a considerable degree of central planning and coordination, which gives the government the ability to develop a national strategic approach to technology development.

...while the United States Government plays a more indirect role

The United States Government, on the other hand, plays a more indirect role in supporting innovation at all levels—an approach that is underpinned by the tenet in economics that markets are more efficient at allocating R&D investments. The relatively indirect, and often imperceptible, involvement of government also reflects a wider distribution of institutional capabilities and responsibilities, which—together with the need for extensive coordination—prevents any single government agency from taking a leading role in driving national innovation policy (Melaas and Zhang, 2016).

Nevertheless, Melaas and Zhang (2016) argue that, even in the case where there is a well-recognized difference in the relative public-private balance in the NIS, the Governments of both China and the United States play an active role in supporting and influencing innovation activities of the private sector.

To a great extent, achievement of the desired balance among the roles of different actors in a country's NIS depends on its institutional arrangements, including government structure, level of market maturity and public policy philosophy, which evolve over time. Nevertheless, recent statistics suggest that governments in developing countries tend to play a more dominant role in R&D than their counterparts in developed countries (see figure IV.8), which likely reflects the lower levels of market maturity and of research capabilities of private firms in developing countries.

Creating a highly networked system of actors which facilitates knowledge flow and harnesses their collective innovation potential is most important

The most important goal of innovation systems is to create a highly networked system of actors which facilitates knowledge flow and harnesses the country's collective innovation potential. Mazzucato (2011) uses the experience of Japan in the 1970s and 1980s, compared with the contemporaneous experience of the Soviet Union, to demonstrate the importance of such linkages. Japan's Ministry of International Trade and Industry pushed for policies that centred on coordinating intra-industrial change, intersectoral linkages, inter-company linkages and the private-public balance. Further, in Japan, new knowledge flowed among ministries of science, academia and industry within a framework that was horizontally structured; in the Soviet Union, by contrast, business enterprises were not able to commercialize the knowledge developed by the State. The strong networks among key actors in its innovation system helped to sustain Japan in its quest to reach the global technological frontier.

Figure IV.8

Examples of cross-country variation in the three key systemic features of national innovation systems, 2008–2014 average

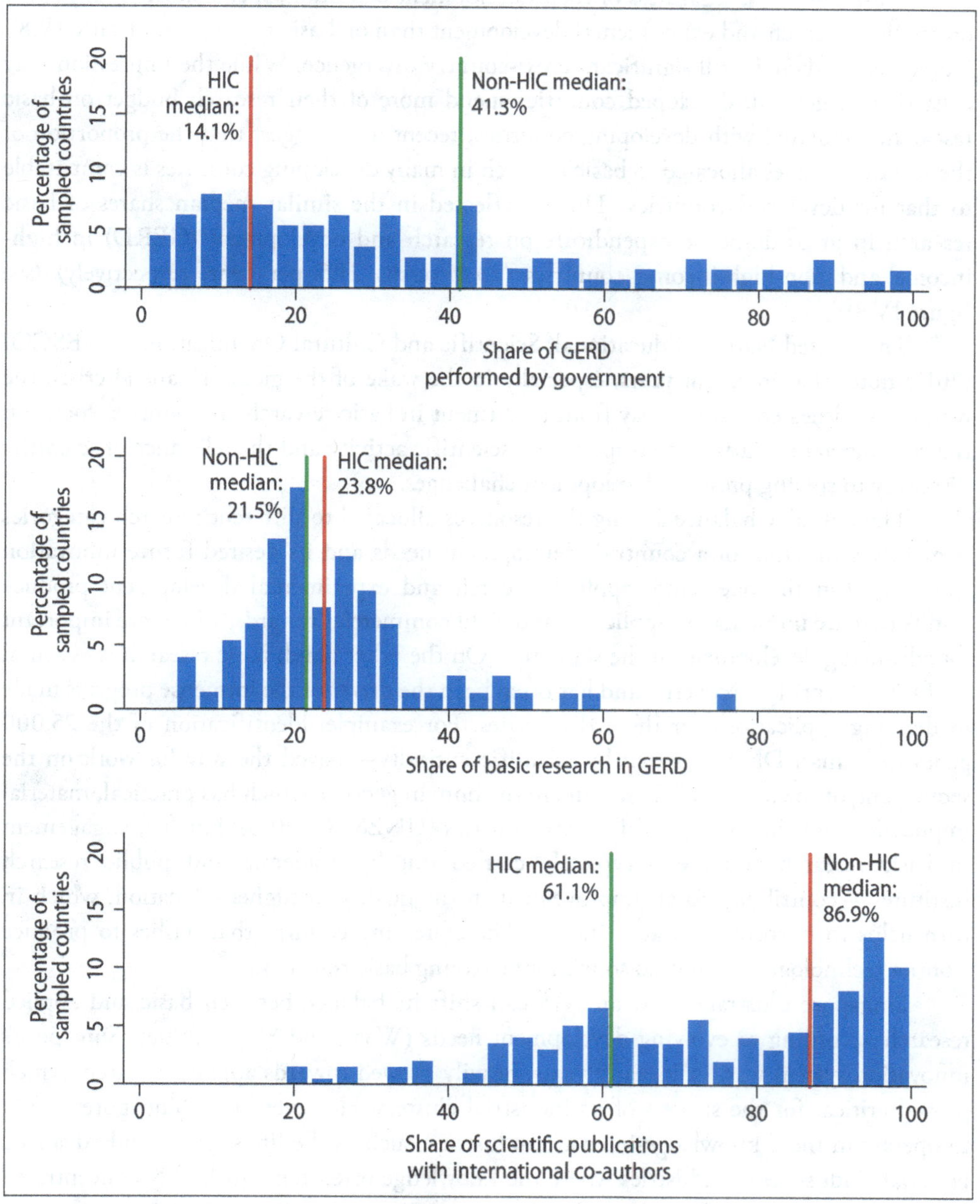

Source: UN/DESA, based on data from UIS.Stat and UNESCO (2015).

Abbreviations: GERD, gross domestic expenditure on research and development; HIC, high-income country.

Note: The figures are histograms, with each bar indicating the percentage of sampled countries that fall into the range of values where the bar is positioned. Sample size for share of GERD performed by government, for share of basic research in GERD, and for share of scientific publications with international co-authors are 111, 74, and 195 countries, respectively.

Balancing basic and applied research and experimental development

Another systemic feature of national innovation systems with respect to which there are divergences is the relative weight placed on basic and applied research and experimental development. The category of basic research is driven largely by a commitment to scientific enquiry and the desire to expand the knowledge frontier, without explicit consideration of the commercial value of the results of that research. The goal of applied research, on the other hand, is to find solutions to practical problems which, typically, improve development conditions. Experimental development entails systematic work, drawing from existing knowledge that is directed towards producing new products and services or improving existing ones.

Most countries, regardless of their development condition, spend substantially more on applied research and experimental development than on basic research (see figure IV.8). Nevertheless, there is still significant cross-country divergence. While the impression may exist that in general, developed countries spend more of their research budget on basic research, compared with developing countries, recent data suggest that the proportion of the research budget allocated to basic research in many developing countries is comparable to that for developed countries. This is reflected in the similar median shares of basic research in gross domestic expenditure on research and development (GERD) in high-income and non-high-income countries (23.8 versus 21.5 per cent, respectively) (see figure IV.8).

The United Nations Educational, Scientific and Cultural Organization (UNESCO) (2015) notes that in recent years, especially in the wake of the global financial crisis, the world has witnessed a shift away from investment in basic research, as countries focus on the commercial rewards to be reaped from scientific activity and the relevance of scientific discovery to solving pressing development challenges.

The desired balance among resource allocations to different research categories depends largely on a country's development needs and its desired innovation trajectory

The desirable balance among the resources allocated to different research categories is mainly a function of a country's development needs and its desired future innovation trajectory. On the one hand, applied research and experimental development produce results that are immediately applicable and yield commercial rewards, which are important for advancing development in the short run. On the other hand, basic research is essential for future scientific discoveries and has often been the driver of the immense progress made in deriving applications for those discoveries. For example, identification of the 25,000 genes in human DNA—driven by scientific curiosity—paved the way for work on the sequencing of the nucleotide base pairs in the human genome which has practical, material implications for the treatment of genetic diseases (UNESCO, 2015). Further, engagement in basic research activities—typically carried out by academia and public research institutes—contributes to an improvement in the quality of higher education, which in turn helps to nurture innovation talent. Therefore, any country that wishes to produce frontier technologies cannot do so without enabling basic research.

Singapore illustrates how an NIS can shift its balance between basic and applied research according to evolving development needs (Wong and Singh, 2008). Singapore's innovation system was, in its early years, heavily skewed towards applied research, which proved critical for the success of its industrial clusters. However, once Singapore sought to operate in more knowledge-intensive industries, such as the life sciences and advanced materials industries—industries where the knowledge often remains highly concentrated in regional innovation clusters in advanced economies—the Government began to put a stronger emphasis on basic research. It was hoped that such a shift would allow the country to acquire more durable competitive advantages.

Balancing indigenous innovation and adoption of foreign technologies

National innovation systems also differ in terms of the relative emphasis that they place on indigenous innovation versus foreign technology adoption. This reflects specifically how much a country relies on foreign support in advancing its own technological development, through, for example, importing foreign technologies or collaborating with foreign researchers. Knowledge obtained through interactions with foreign partners can be products of basic research, applied research or experimental development.

Developing countries tend generally to rely more on foreign technology adoption for technological development, given that innovation is costly, risky and path-dependent (Fu, Pietrobelli and Soete, 2011). Developing countries' stronger reliance on foreign technological knowledge is also reflected in their typically higher share of scientific publications with international co-authors (see figure IV.8).

A country's absorptive capacity and actual development needs are equally important in determining its desirable level of reliance on foreign technologies

However, empirical findings regarding countries' gains from international knowledge transfer offer a mixed picture.[12] The inappropriateness of foreign technology in local contexts is a key reason why the evidence is not always uniform. The results suggest that a country's indigenous innovation is at least as important as foreign technology adoption, as it fosters development of absorptive capacity by improving human capital and encouraging R&D activities.[13] This leads to an important observation: To what extent a country should rely on foreign technologies depends as much on its absorptive capacity as on actual development needs.

The experiences of China and India—both populous developing countries and major originators of international patent applications—provide contrasting examples of how this balance can be pursued. While India has emphasized promotion of foreign technology adoption in specific sectors such as information and communications technologies (ICT), China, generally, has been relatively more active in its efforts to enhance the capacity of the domestic science and technology sectors (Crescenzi and Rodríguez-Pose, 2017). Still, despite this difference in overall emphasis, the remarkable growth of the solar photovoltatic (PV) industry in both countries illustrates the importance of the proper use of mixing and sequencing mechanisms of indigenous innovation and international technology transfer (Fu and Zhang, 2011).[14]

Interdependence of the three systemic features

The three key systemic features of a national innovation system are often interdependent and mutually reinforcing

Striking desirable balances on all three fronts is further complicated by the fact that these features are often interdependent and mutually reinforcing. Efforts by policymakers to guide a country's NIS towards a certain mix on one front could be undermined by efforts on the other two fronts, if they are incompatible. For example, a country that seeks to move towards an indigenous innovation-oriented innovation system would need to engage in commensurate efforts towards promoting basic research, if it hopes to move towards the global technological frontier. This also means that universities and public research

12 See Görg and Strobl (2001), Blomström and Kokko (1998), and Meyer (2004) for excellent surveys of the literature on spillovers from foreign direct investment.

13 Here, absorptive capacity is defined as "a set of organizational routines and processes by which firms acquire, assimilate, transform, and exploit knowledge to produce a dynamic organizational capability" (Zahra and George, 2002).

14 Most leading solar PV companies in both countries complement their international technology transfer by increasing investment in indigenous R&D activities, which has helped to facilitate foreign technology adoption and indigenous technological capability development. Once basic technological capabilities were established, these firms went on to engage in more active technology acquisition and creation through both indigenous innovation and international R&D collaboration. Their successful experience demonstrates the importance of employing the right combination of international technology transfer and indigenous innovation.

institutes, typically the primary undertakers of basic research, would need to achieve greater prominence in the national innovation landscape.[15] Commensurate investments in the education system, beginning with the primary and secondary education levels, would also be required.

On the other hand, a country that seeks to focus on foreign technology adoption should ensure that firms—especially those operating in trade sectors and/or with some foreign ownership—play a more important role, given that international technology transfer occurs largely through trade and foreign direct investment (FDI). At the same time, institutions that facilitate active technology diffusion need to assume a stronger role in the innovation system as well.[16] A stronger emphasis on foreign technology adoption would also likely entail a stronger national focus on applied research and experimental development relative to basic research.

The current technological landscape is marked by rapid changes and convergence of different areas of technology

Last, the current technological landscape is marked by rapid changes and convergence of different areas of technology. As noted by Schwab (2016), the current rapid technological change is characterized by "a fusion of technologies that is blurring the lines between the physical, digital, and biological spheres". The rapid pace and complexity of technological advancement will determine the desirable country-specific balance among these factors.

As technologies have become increasingly complex and the uncertainties associated with their development and adoption have increased considerably, stronger government support is required to help firms and research institutes weather related risks. To compete in this technological landscape, firms will need to access new technologies from both within and outside their traditional competency networks. Countries—especially developing ones—will perceive that their need to maintain an effective channel for introducing technologies from overseas is greater than ever.

A survey conducted by Larsen, Ahlqvist and Friðriksson (2009) on Nordic firms has shown that even those in advanced national innovation systems experience difficulties in identifying new partners from outside their traditional networks and subsequently in achieving convergence of different technologies. The survey highlights the importance of stronger involvement of mediating organizations, such as universities, science parks and sector organizations, which can help firms reduce their search costs.

Macroeconomic determinants of the efficacy of a national innovation system

Enabling regulatory frameworks and complementary infrastructures are crucial in generating incentives for innovation

Any efficiently functioning NIS, regardless of its broad systemic features, requires an enabling environment which provides sufficient incentives for innovation. Several macroeconomic factors are particularly crucial in influencing such incentives and driving the efficacy of a nation's innovation process.

15 Switzerland, a world-class leader in innovation which spends a high proportion of its research budget (30 per cent) on basic research, has illustrated the advantage of establishing a clear division of labour between the public and private sectors, with the public sector playing the leading role in non-oriented basic research and the private sector focusing on translation of scientific breakthroughs into competitive products (UNESCO, 2015).

16 Elaboration of the role of those institutions will be found in a subsequent discussion on the challenges faced by NIS in their efforts to catch up and keep up.

One key factor is market competition. For every technology market, there is a market-specific optimal level of competition for incentivizing innovation.[17] On the one hand, firms may not be sufficiently incentivized to innovate if there is little competition. On the other, too much competition could discourage firms from innovating, as intense competition reduces the expected profits resulting from innovation. Lower profit also reduces the room for firms' investment in R&D activities.

An appropriate level of antitrust regulation must be in place to ensure that there is a level playing field for technology developers and to promote market entry. Intellectual property regulation is another important part of the overall regulatory framework, as it determines the trajectory of national innovation endeavours. Too little intellectual property protection, without alternative mechanisms to compensate innovators, can discourage innovation. On the other hand, overly stringent intellectual property protection can also hamper innovation, as it constrains knowledge flow. Further, regulation—for example, on consumer protection and privacy—is central in ensuring that the direction of technology development will improve social welfare and that such improvements will be shared equitably across the population.

Another key component of the NIS is complementary infrastructures (whose importance has been detailed in chapter III), which include technical facilities, legal and business services, and telecommunication and transportation infrastructure.

Innovators face different financing needs and interact with different financial intermediaries at various stages of product development

From a broader perspective, infrastructure also includes the all-important financial infrastructure, encompassing payment systems, insurance services, credit information bureaux and collateral registries. These infrastructures are crucial to the effective operation of the various financial intermediaries that can support innovation. Depending on the stage of their product development, entities engaged in innovative activities would experience different financing needs and would therefore need to interact with different financial intermediaries (United Nations, Economic Commission for Europe, 2009).

At the early stages of product development, when there is a high risk of failure, innovative entities need access to forms of financing that do not entail guaranteed repayment. These include merit-based awards and infusion of external equity which allows investors to monitor the functioning of the business and exercise significant control over it in order to manage the downside risk of their investment. Whereas merit-based awards are often provided by public agencies, external equity typically involves angel investors, seed funds and venture capital funds. More recently, crowdfunding has also emerged as an alternative financing source for early-stage innovative activities (Agrawal, Catalini and Goldfarb, 2014).

However, traditional financial intermediaries such as bank lenders and stock markets become more important as the innovative activities move into the later development stages and require additional financial resources.

Challenges faced by national innovation systems in keeping up and catching up

Successful national innovation systems are typically characterized by a strong knowledge base, a well-functioning market system and developed institutions and infrastructures

17 Market competition is typically measured by market share, price-cost margin or the Herfindahl concentration index.

which support innovation activities. However, concerted effort is still required to maintain the competitiveness of those systems for at least two reasons. First, the market institutions and infrastructures can deteriorate. Second, as the global technological landscape evolves rapidly, leading national innovation systems could find themselves hindered by what has now become legacy infrastructures and institutions (although they had previously served the systems well).

For example, legacy information technology (IT) infrastructure which cannot process a large amount of unstructured data with high speed could hamper considerably the development of AI technologies. Further, as will be elaborated in chapter V, the rise of big data and algorithms are significantly changing the nature of competition dynamics, which poses regulatory challenges. Within this context, the key challenge for the leading national innovation systems in adapting to the evolving technological landscape is therefore to continue investing in the latest infrastructures and refining institutional arrangements.

Laggard national innovation systems face a more pressing need to account for every factor that influences physical, human and knowledge capital accumulation

National innovation systems that are far away from the global technological frontier, on the other hand, are facing a different set of challenges in their effort to catch up with the technological leaders. Cirera and Maloney (2017) argue that the scope of the national innovation systems that must be taken into account by policymakers in developing countries is much larger than the scope of those in advanced economies. In developing countries, the need is more pressing to account for every factor that influences the accumulation of physical, human and knowledge capital and the institutions and markets that support such accumulation, including education systems, financial markets and trade agreements.

In reality, many developing countries still have weak institutional structures for supporting innovation. Their innovation systems tend to be highly fragmented, with a large number of small enterprises, an often overcrowded public sector support system which fails to provide sufficient technological support services and infrastructures, and a limited research community which is not well connected to development realities (Aubert, 2005).

At the same time, many developing countries—which typically experience faster economic development—require higher adaptability of their innovation systems (Varblane, Dyker and Tamm, 2007). Furthermore, FDI in developing countries is playing a more important role than in the developed countries, which means that the globalization process is exerting a stronger influence on the development of innovation systems in developing countries. Improving institutional and infrastructure quality of laggard NIS is therefore imperative.

Countries also need to ensure that the development of high-tech industries does not occur at the expense of support to medium- and low-tech industries, which typically account for a much larger share of employment and output (Varblane, Dyker and Tamm, 2007). Rather, development of high-tech industries must be complementary to that of the medium- and low-tech group. Indeed, technological advances achieved in the high-tech industries should enhance the competitiveness of medium- and low-tech industries.[18] Conversely, the application of advanced technologies in medium- and low-tech industries can provide feedback to the high-tech industries and further technological development.

A key effort required for the support of industries at the early stages of innovation is the building up of firms' managerial and organizational capabilities, which are crucial for effective management of innovative activities (Cirera and Maloney, 2017). Firms in

18 The wood and paper industry in Finland—a small open economy—offers an example of how international competitiveness can be achieved through use of high-tech technologies in different segments of mature medium- and low-tech industries (Viitamo, 2003).

developing countries typically lag behind those in developed countries in the acquisition of such capabilities, which cover, inter alia, the capacity to take a long-term view, project evaluation skills, and a human resources policy designed to assure the presence of staff for R&D projects.

It is equally important for laggard national innovation systems to develop a model for active management of technology diffusion. Successful experiences of economies of East Asia in earlier phases of technological development—when they lacked resources and advantages other than temporary cost advantages—have demonstrated the importance of development of a network of institutions for technology diffusion and organizational management (Mathews, 2001).

It is crucial for laggard national innovation systems to develop a model for active management of technology diffusion

Institutions such as public sector laboratories, developmental consortia and well-established national firms were tasked with accelerating the private sector's technology uptake. They identified the technological knowledge and related resources that were most readily available for leveraging by firms in support of industrial development. This was important, as firms tend to be myopically focused on the search for knowledge and solutions within their existing competency neighbourhood (Fagerberg and Godinho, 2006). The support provided by these institutions meant that firms could channel their energies into transforming innovations into technological capabilities and competitive products.

Drivers of diffusion in an interconnected technology landscape

Previous discussions on the innovation systems of East Asian economies have demonstrated that diffusion plays a central role in advancing a country's technological development. Diffusion is also crucial for the materialization of broad development impacts of new technologies, both those generated domestically and those generated beyond borders.

Diffusion is arguably more important than innovation in closing the technology gap between and within countries. From an allocative efficiency perspective, one could argue that innovation gaps of a certain magnitude between and within countries are acceptable or even desirable, considering that countries, firms and individuals vary in terms of their innate innovative capacity. What truly matters when it comes to ensuring equitable sharing of benefits ushered in by frontier technologies is that these technologies, once created, be accessible to and adoptable by the broader population.

Cross-border technology diffusion: international trade and investment and a global IPR regime

Effective cross-border technology diffusion is central to closing the between-country technological divide, as discussed in chapter III. The existing literature generally focuses on international trade and FDI as two key international technology transfer channels.

International trade is a key technology diffusion channel from both the exporter and the importer perspectives. On the one hand, firms can acquire new technologies that are embedded in intermediate goods and capital equipment via importing from foreign firms. On the other hand, firms could also learn by exporting, through interactions with their overseas customers, although this transmission channel appears to be a weak one (Keller, 2004). As regards the key channel of FDI, the strength and speed of technology transfer

International trade and foreign direct investment are two key channels for international technology transfer

depend on the ownership structure of the firms that receive such investment and the extent of interaction between the receiving firms and the rest of the domestic economy.

International technology cooperation is a complementary channel

International technology cooperation is yet another technology transfer channel. Recent establishment of the Technology Bank, first proposed in paragraph 52 (l. Joint actions) of the Programme of Action for the Least Developed Countries for the Decade 2011–2020;[19] and the launching of the Technology Facilitation Mechanism, in the 2030 Agenda for Sustainable Development[20] under Sustainable Development Goal 17.6, are among the international community's latest efforts to strengthen international cooperation on science, technology and innovation. Facilitation of technology transfer is a key objective under both mechanisms (United Nations, 2017c).

The efficacy of international technology transfer is influenced by the global IPR regime and trade and investment agreements

The efficacy of these international technology transfer channels is influenced by several factors, notably the global IPR regime and the complex web of multilateral, plurilateral and bilateral trade and investment agreements. In practice, multilateral, plurilateral and bilateral trade and investment agreements often have specific IPR components, making them important components of the global IPR regime.

While IPR are crucial in ensuring that innovators can properly benefit from their creation, they are also capable of creating obstacles to legitimate trade, thereby weakening a key international technology transfer channel (Kamperman Sanders, 2018).

Only a harmonized level of IPR protection could ensure a level playing field in international trade. Gaps in the scope of IPR protection and enforcement would lead to trade distortions and disrupt international technology transfer. As for the role of IPR in attracting FDI and facilitating technology transfer, empirical evidence has presented a mixed picture, as the relationship between IPR and FDI in developing countries appears to vary by industry, the level of economic development and the policy environment of the host country, and the mix of natural resources and human capital.

Overall, existing studies on international technology transfer have suggested that human capital levels, the historical path of technology adoption, institutions and policies, geographical proximity of countries, and aggregate demand for new technology are key factors in explaining cross-country differences in technology adoption (Comin and Mestieri Ferrer, 2014).

While higher levels of human capital are generally associated with higher levels of technology adoption, it is important to note that this trend varies across different technologies. For example, Comin and Hobijn (2004) found secondary school enrolment has a strong positive association with adoption of mass communication technologies, but not with adoption of other technologies—such as those used in textile and steel industries—that are less skill-intensive.

Past trends in technology adoption have been revealed to be another important determinant of technology adoption. Comin and Hobijn (2010) found that the observed persistence in technology adoption—i.e., the notable positive association between adoption of old technologies and subsequent adoption of new ones—is most likely driven by the accumulation of sector-specific technological knowledge. Such knowledge, generated by firms through their adoption and use of technologies across time, enables new technologies that are used in their specific industries to be adopted more easily.

19 *Report of the Fourth United Nations Conference on the Least Developed Countries, Istanbul, Turkey, 9–13 May 2011* (A/CONF.219/7), chap. II.

20 General Assembly resolution 70/1.

Besides a harmonized and flexible global IPR regime, enabling institutions are also central to faster diffusion of new technologies. Comin and Mestieri Ferrer (2014) argue that without proper institutions to protect technology adopters' rights over their technologies or the income that they generate, firms, households or individuals might be deterred from investing in and adopting new technologies. Moreover, a lack of inclusive institutions may allow political or economic incumbents—whose economic or political rents are threatened by new technologies that broadly reduce transportation and communications costs—to lobby for the creation of barriers that hamper technology diffusion (Acemoglu and Robinson, 2000).

Other studies have found that geographical proximity and the levels of aggregate demand to be notable drivers of technology adoption. With regard to geographical proximity, it is argued that technology tends to be more easily transmitted between firms or individuals in countries that are closer to each other, given that technology adoption requires knowledge which is often derived from interactions with others and that the frequency of those interactions is typically influenced by such proximity (Comin and Mestieri Ferrer, 2014). As for the role of aggregate demand, Comin and Mestieri Ferrer (2010) found that technology adoption is sensitive to movement of business cycles, suggesting that higher aggregate demand is associated with faster technology diffusion.

Determinants of adoption behaviour

The process of devising policies that facilitate technology diffusion can be aided by a sound understanding of what determines technology adoption behaviour

Policies can facilitate technology diffusion if they have been devised with a sound understanding of the determinants of the adoption behaviour of individual firms, households and individuals. This accords with the view of Shankar and Foster (2016) who, in their capacity as Behavioural Science Advisers to the United Nations, emphasized the cruciality of understanding people's behaviours in achieving the 2030 Agenda.[21]

The existing economic literature generally supports the view that the process of technology diffusion is the cumulative result of a series of individual calculations which weigh the net benefits of adopting a new technology, subject to limited information, uncertainty and financial constraints, against those of using existing alternatives.

In seeking to explain levels of demand for new technologies that are lower than the levels that standard cost-benefit analysis alone would predict, contributors to the more recent literature have examined the role of intra-household or intra-firm externality in decision-making (Miller and Mobarak, 2013; Atkin and others, 2017). This refers to the inability of the member of a firm or household who has control over purchasing decisions to take into account potential benefits and costs accruing to other members in the same household or firm from use of a certain product.

Another set of contributors to the emerging literature use insights derived from behaviourial economics to explain technology adoption behaviours. These insights reveal that people's behaviour is shaped by habits, inclinations and frequent disjunctions between intentions and actions (Brown, Zelenska and Mobarak, 2013). Moreover, heuristics, or information-processing rules that reflect a departure from full rationality—associated with, e.g., loss aversion, mental accounting, present-biased preferences and low self-control—

21 Increasing emphasis on such human behaviour-centred approaches can also be seen in a number of countries and international organizations that launched initiatives seeking to leverage behavioural insights to address policy challenges (see, for example, Behavioural Insights Team (2016) and World Bank (2015)).

also help to explain why it may be difficult for firms and households to invest in potentially profitable technologies.[22]

Thaler (1999) presents evidence demonstrating that loss aversion—i.e., a greater sensitivity to losses than to gains—plays an important role in individuals' financial decision-making. Such an aversion could reduce technology adoption below levels supported by rational cost-benefit analyses. He also argues that mental accounting—a set of cognitive operations used by individuals to mentally organize and evaluate financial activities—influences financial decisions in ways that violate the economic principle of fungibility. For those individuals who engage in mental accounting, money that has been reserved for or "saved" in one mental account cannot be easily transferred to another such account. This suggests that individuals may be more incentivized to save enough for investment in technology adoption if they have in mind a highly specific technology in which to invest (i.e., if they have opened a dedicated mental account), whereas individuals may be under-incentivized if they have only a vague intention of saving for future adoption of some yet-to-be identified technology.

In addition, the tendency of individuals to value current over future consumption (which illustrates a present-biased preference), or their inability to always act rationally in their own best interest (which illustrates the low self-control problem), makes it more difficult for them to invest in the adoption of welfare-improving technologies.

Rising importance of social and economic networks in technology diffusion

One subject that in recent years has received increasing attention in the economics literature is the role of social and economic networks (e.g., networks of firms and households) in technology diffusion. The interest in such networks, reflecting the economic, social and cultural constructs of a society, is motivated primarily by two factors.

The first is "technology externality" (also commonly referred as "network effect"). The term means that the value of a new technology is influenced by the extent to which it is adopted by others, either because the technology is used to facilitate interaction with others (e.g., the telephone, email or social media platforms) or because the provision of supporting facilities for the technology depends on the size of the user community. The second factor is the pervasive role of social and economic networks in influencing the spread and assessment of technology information, particularly through social learning (Wolf, Just and Zilberman, 2001; BenYishay and Mobarak, 2015).

Growing interconnectedness of technology decisions and increasing complexity of technology have made the role of networks in technology diffusion more salient

It can be argued that the current technological landscape has made examination of technology diffusion from a network perspective more relevant than ever. In particular, there are three developments that could currently justify a stronger emphasis on the role of networks in technology diffusion. First, the rise of social media and the Internet of Things has led to the growing interconnectedness of the technology-related decisions of firms, households and individuals and the impacts of those decisions. People are now increasingly aware of and influenced by other people's decisions, including their choice of technology.

Second, the increasing complexity of technology has been accompanied by the explosion of availability of technological information in the public domain. As a result of

22 For detailed discussions on these heuristics, see Thaler and Sunstein (2008).

this phenomenon, firms, households and individuals have been encouraged to rely even more on their networks to obtain, verify and process information on new technologies. Indeed, empirical evidence has shown that the pursuit of social learning is more evident within the context of the adoption of complex technologies (Liverpool-Tasie and Winter-Nelson, 2012; Oster and Thornton, 2012).

Third, there is an unevenness in technology diffusion which makes the study of diffusion patterns and their driving factors a critical task. The technology diffusion literature has traditionally focused on linking differences in technology adoption behaviour to the heterogeneous characteristics and preferences of firms, households and individuals. For example, the existence of the technological divide across countries is often attributed to differences in their innovative and absorptive capacities.

While capacity differences are certainly a key factor in this regard, it may not fully explain differences as related to technology adoption. The analytical work of Bala and Goyal (2001), for example, demonstrates that in a setting where agents are divided into different groups with more direct information links among agents within the same group as compared with links across different groups, technologies with different pay-offs can be adopted by agents in the long run even if they all have the same preferences and start off with the same beliefs.

This suggests that in an environment where there are different communities within a population, it is possible for one group to adopt a superior technology while another group converges towards adoption of an inferior one, even if the two groups are similar in terms of, e.g., educational levels and initial technological capacity. This can occur when all agents have incomplete information on new technologies and must learn about them from observing the technology choices of others. It can lead to cycles of social reinforcement which eventually push the group towards long-term adoption of a particular technology even if that technology does not represent the best option. These results explain the role that formal and informal networks play in technology diffusion, within the context of between- and within-country differences.

Policy challenges for bridging the technological divide

Previous sections discussed key features of, and enabling factors associated with, technology innovation and diffusion processes. Differentiated progress in the development of these processes leads to differentiated access to and adoption of technologies, resulting in the technological divide.

Continuing challenges: divergence of innovative and absorptive capacity

Continued divergences in innovative and absorptive capacities could further widen the technological divide

The continued divergences in innovative and absorptive capacities could contribute to a further widening of the technological divide. This is clearly displayed by the significant divergences across firms worldwide in terms of managerial capabilities, which are a critical facet of firms' overall innovative and absorptive capacity (see figure IV.9). Such divergences reflect the significant discrepancy in a number of underlying drivers, including human capital, complementary infrastructures, institutional quality and financial access (see, for examples, figures IV.10, IV.11 and IV.12 and the discussions in chap. III).

Figure IV.9
Distribution of firm-level managerial capabilities, high-income and non-high-income countries, 2004–2015

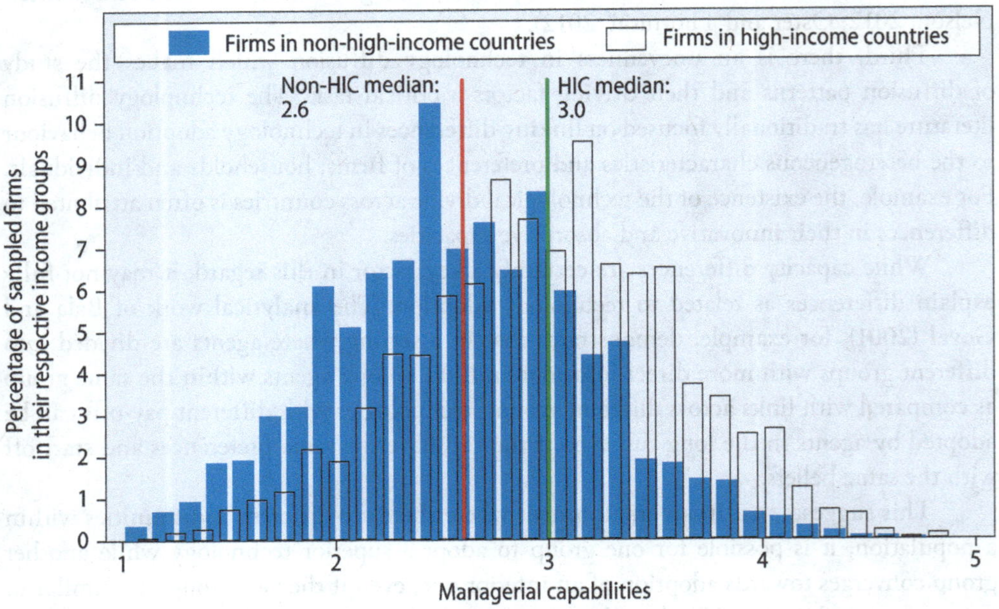

Source: UN/DESA, based on World Management Survey.
Abbreviations: HIC, high-income country.
Note: Managerial capabilities are scored from 1 to 5, with 5 representing the highest level. For further information on the World Management Survey, see Bloom and Van Reenen (2007). This sample includes 6,760 firms within high-income countries and 4,942 firms within non-high-income countries. Data on these firms were collected for various years over the period 2004-2015. The difference in the respective medians of the two country groups was found to be statistically significant, after a comparison of the Bonett-Price 99 per cent confidence intervals for the two medians.

Figure IV.10
Inequality in tertiary education levels, high-, low- and middle-income countries, 2011–2015 average

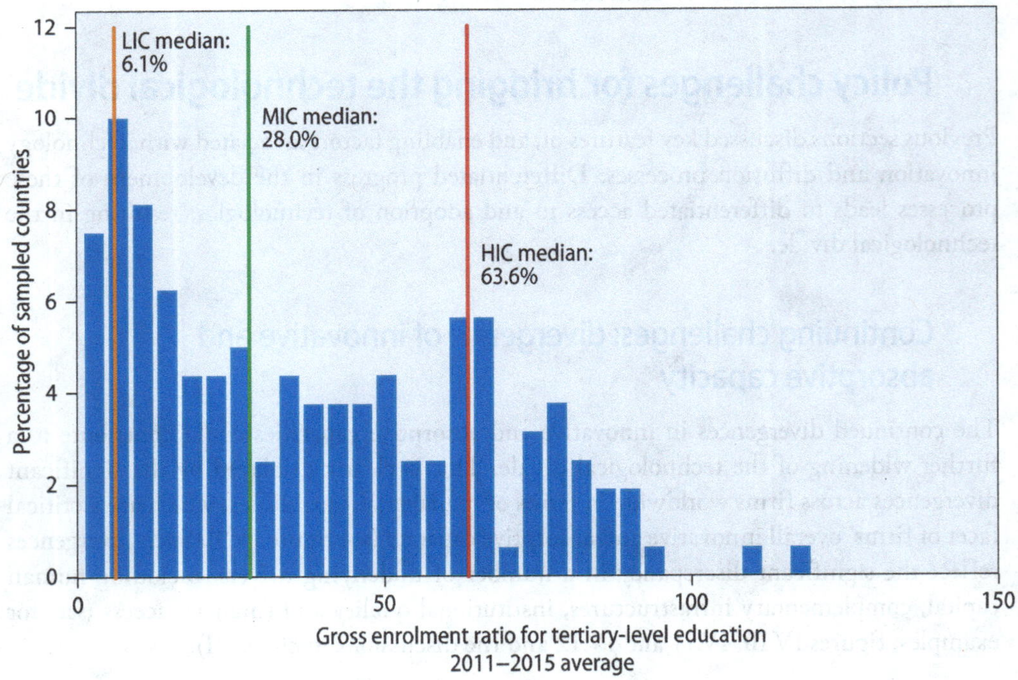

Source: UN/DESA, based on World Development Indicators.
Abbreviations: HIC, high-income country; LIC, low-income country; MIC, middle-income country.
Note: The figure is based on a sample of 160 countries.

Figure IV.11

Differences in perceptions of regulatory quality, high-, low- and middle-income countries, 2016

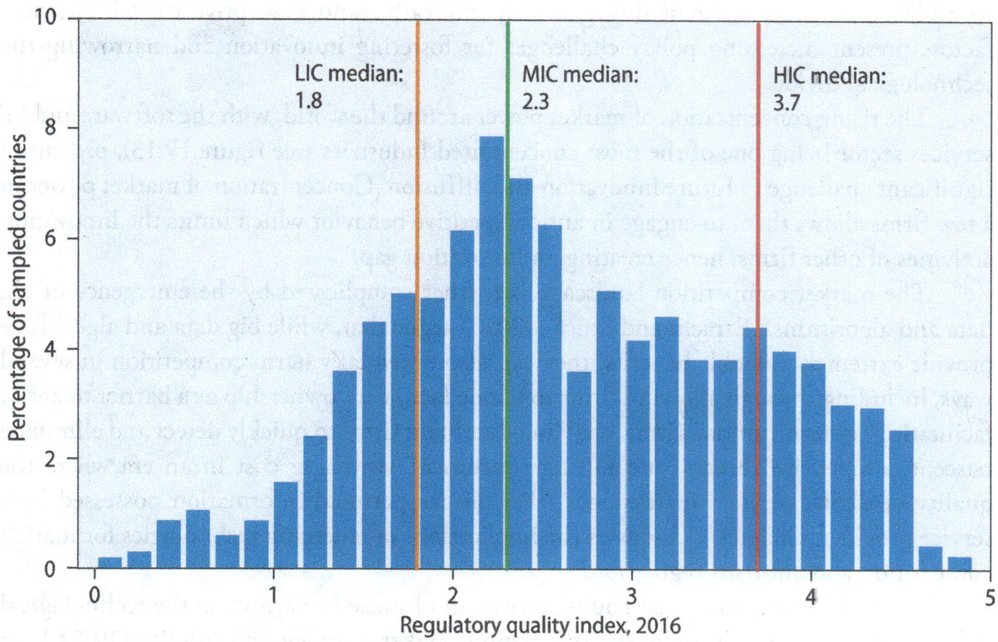

Source: UN/DESA, based on Worldwide Governance Indicators.

Abbreviations: HIC, high-income country; LIC, low-income country; MIC, middle-income country.

Note: The figure is based on a sample of 204 economies. The regulatory quality index captures perceptions of Governments' ability to formulate and implement sound policies and regulations which promote private sector development. The original regulatory quality estimates were rescaled, so that the values range from 0 to 5, with 5 denoting the highest regulatory quality. For further information on the World Governance Indicators, see Kaufmann, Kraay and Mastruzzi (2011).

Figure IV.12

Inequality in financial access, high-, low- and middle-income countries, 2014

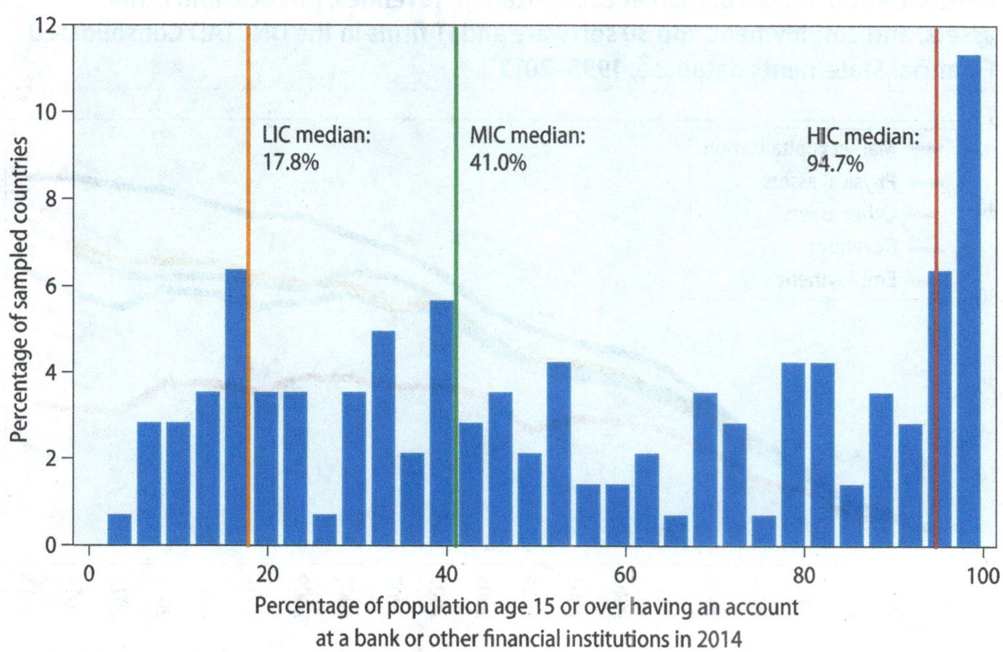

Source: UN/DESA, based on data from Global Findex database.

Abbreviations: HIC, high-income country; LIC, low-income country; MIC, middle-income country.

Note: The figure is based on a sample of 159 countries.

Emerging challenges: market concentration, the IPR regime and networks

Rising market concentration, stringent IPR regimes and the rising salience of networks in technology diffusion pose challenges for narrowing the technological divide

In addition to the consistent divergence in innovative and absorptive capacities, three factors present increasing policy challenges for fostering innovation and narrowing the technological divide.

The rising concentration of market power around the world, with the software and IT services sector being one of the most concentrated industries (see figure IV.13), presents a significant challenge to future innovation and diffusion. Concentration of market power in a few firms allows them to engage in anticompetitive behavior which limits the innovation activities of other firms, hence creating an innovation gap.

The market competition landscape is further complicated by the emergence of big data and algorithms. Ezrachi and Stucke (2016) argue that, while big data and algorithms provide extremely valuable benefits, they can also potentially harm competition in several ways, including through allowing firms to use de facto data ownership as a barrier to entry, facilitating collusion among firms, enabling dominant firms to quickly detect and eliminate nascent competitive threats, and raising consumers' switching cost in an era where the quality of digital services increasingly relies on the personal information possessed by a service provider. Chapter V discusses the implications of emerging technologies for market competition and antitrust regulation.

Another development that could serve as an obstacle to narrowing the technological divide is the increasingly stringent IPR regime. Baker, Jayadev and Stiglitz (2017) have argued that the current regime is not well aligned with the needs of developing countries and that it serves corporate interests in developed countries disproportionately.[23]

Figure IV.13

Concentration indices of market capitalization, revenues, physical and other assets, and employment, top 30 software and IT firms in the UNCTAD Consolidated Financial Statements database, 1995–2015

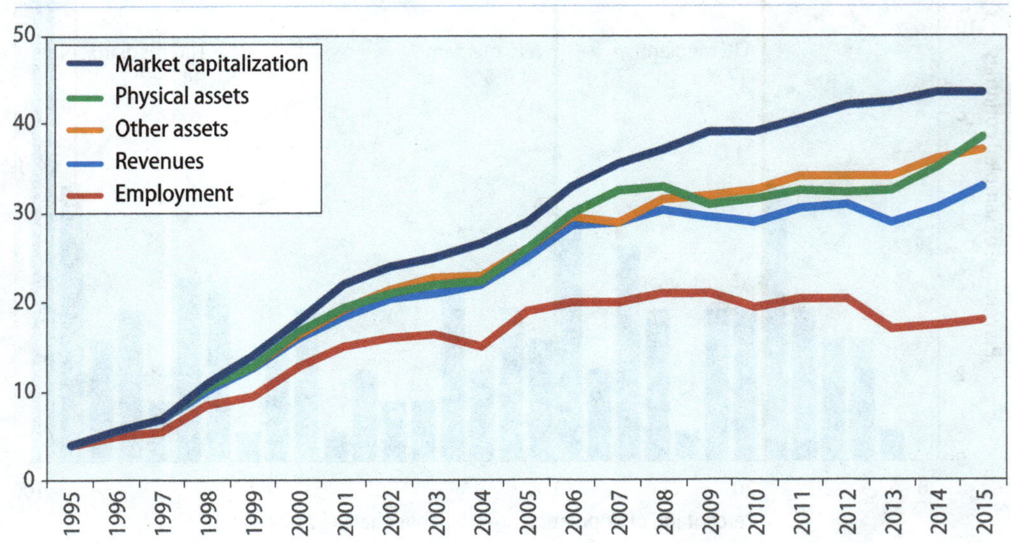

Source: UNCTAD (2017), box figure 6.B2.1.
Note: Concentration indices here measure the top 30 firms' observed share in the specified variables relative to their hypothetical equal share, assuming equal distribution of the specified variable among firms. An increase in the indices indicates an increase in market concentration.

23 Those authors highlight the fact that pharmaceutical patent protection is extended for global pharmaceutical companies at the expense of the health of the poor.

Moreover, multiple studies indicate that there is no conclusive evidence—especially for countries that lie at a distance from the technological frontier—that greater IPR protection has a strong positive influence on domestic technological development (Odagiri and others, 2010; Dosi, Marengo and Pasquali, 2007).

In fact, aggressive IPR measures may have impeded technology transfer in many developing countries, as they pose significant restrictions on knowledge flow. Indeed, some trade agreements even contain restrictions on so-called investment measures (including prohibitions on imposing technology transfer or domestic content requirements (United Nations, 2011, p. 182)), which limit the scope of international trade with respect to facilitating technology transfer. Such measures could also encroach on countries' policy space for conducting industrial policies, subsequently affecting their innovation efforts. Chapter V discusses how to improve the flexibilities of the global IPR regime.

Yet another development that poses challenges for bridging the technological divide is the rising salience of social and economic networks in technology diffusion and innovation. While theoretical and empirical studies found that knowledge could potentially spread across networks quickly, given the short average social distance between individuals, households and firms (Jackson, Rogers and Zenou, 2017), such a rapid transmission of knowledge does not always occur or translate into broad adoption of new technologies.

One key reason is that firms, households or individuals with similar characteristics—e.g., income and technological capacity levels—behave in clusters. This means that technology information flows and technology externalities would be confined largely within these clusters, which could lead to differences in technology adoption behaviour between groups. It could also slow the spread of technology information across groups and lead to underinvestment in technology owing to complementarities in behaviours. For example, a firm will be less likely to invest in a new technology if its partnering firms are not doing the same.

Furthermore, from a dynamic perspective, social and economic structures are constantly changing and the interaction between technology diffusion and network formation could lead to a second-round effect which would further worsen the technological divide.

Clustering of interactions within networks of firms with similar technological capacity could lead to larger technological divides

A potential risk is that diffusion of new technologies will occur largely within clusters of firms with high technological capacity. This could lead to an even faster improvement in these firms' technological capability, which in turn would make them even more inclined to interact with each other. Meanwhile, firms with low technological capacity would be excluded from participation in this dynamic and could risk losing the opportunity to reach the technological frontier owing to the lack of interactions with frontier firms. Under this scenario, small initial differences in technological capacity could potentially lead to large technological divides in the long run.

Role of Governments in bridging the technological divide

A country's innovation system must be developed in line with its development circumstances and national technology aspirations

Within the context of these continuing and emerging policy challenges, the importance of the role of Governments in bridging the technological divide cannot be overstated.

In principle, a Government needs to develop its NIS in line with its development circumstances and national technology aspirations. The process of advancing the NIS should also be informed by the ambitions of the 2030 Agenda for Sustainable Development and other global and regional initiatives, such as the Paris Agreement adopted under the

United Nations Framework Convention on Climate Change[24] and the Sendai Framework for Disaster Risk Reduction 2015–2030.[25] Policies need to steer the system towards striking appropriate balances, as discussed earlier. Further, policymakers need to be guided by their continuous assessment of ever evolving development and institutional contexts to ensure that the system proceeds in the right direction.

Innovative and absorptive capability gaps need to be narrowed in bridging the technological divide

Specifically, Governments, especially in developing countries, should aim at achieving the following goals in their efforts to bridge the technological divide. First, innovative and absorptive capability gaps need to be narrowed. A key component of this effort would be to improve overall human capital, with targeted support directed towards disadvantaged groups. Policy actions to improve the education system should focus on children's early development, with greater exposure to innovation provided for women and disadvantaged youth (Bell and others, 2017), and on incentivizing workers to invest in skills relevant for the rapidly evolving labour market. To support prospective workers in their efforts to identify the right skills, Governments can work with the private sector and labour unions on developing programmes that provide key information on strategic sectors, including on employment prospects, career pathways and demands for existing and emerging skills.[26]

With a view to improving innovative and absorptive capacities, firms' managerial and organizational capabilities must be continuously improved. Governments can provide support to firms, especially small and medium-sized firms, by facilitating the provision of business advisory and management extension services. This is particularly important, as firms often lack the scale required to assess the value of these services (Cirera and Maloney, 2017) or are unaware of what they themselves lack in terms of managerial and organizational capabilities (Bloom and Van Reenan, 2007). In providing support, Governments could focus on introducing credible mechanisms which would ensure that employees who are in the best position to assess a new technology are sufficiently incentivized to accurately report their assessment (for example, offers of wage contracts conditional on process efficiency) (Atkin and others, 2017).

Technology information must be made widely accessible in supporting innovation and technology diffusion

Second, technology information must be made widely accessible. In supporting innovation, Governments need to play an active role in facilitating transfer of technology information within the NIS. As discussed earlier, the successful experiences of some East Asian economies in the early phases of their technological development highlight the potential of establishing a network of institutions for technology diffusion, which could include public sector laboratories, developmental consortia and large public firms. These institutions would identify available knowledge and other resources useful for technological diffusion and make these resources available to other actors within the NIS.

In supporting technology diffusion, Governments need to actively foster public awareness of new technologies, including through demonstration programmes and a reduction in the costs associated with the search for technology information. Governments should also acquire a better understanding of the structure of existing social and economic networks, which are key information-sharing channels. Governments can develop plans for communicating technology information, including, for example, through identification

24 See Adoption of the Paris Agreement in United Nations Framework Convention on Climate Change (2015).

25 General Assembly resolution 69/283, annex II.

26 Singapore has inaugurated such a practice through its Skills Framework initiative (see www.skillsfuture.sg/skills-framework).

of "champions" of new technologies which are well connected within a given network structure.

Policymakers need to improve financial access and make it more inclusive

Third, financial access needs to be improved and made more inclusive. Governments can work with a range of stakeholders, including academia, the private sector and consumer advocacy groups, in selecting and providing funding for products that have great welfare-enhancing potential but are yet to be commercialized. In particular, Governments might consider setting up innovation funds with a diversified portfolio (United Nations, 2017c). These funds could spread risks across multiple investments, so that gains from successful investment would compensate for losses arising from failures. Governments can also provide tax incentives which encourage innovation, including R&D tax incentives for small and new firms and refundable tax credits that would be applicable when firms have negative tax liabilities (IMF, 2016).

Policymakers also need to ensure the presence of a vibrant venture capital (VC) industry, in view of its vital role in connecting institutional investors with high-potential innovation projects at the early stages of their development cycles. The United Nations Economic Commission for Europe (2009) argues that Governments need to support all four stages of the VC cycle: fundraising, investing, value-adding and exiting. Potential support can range from helping institutional investors better understand venture capital as an institutional investment class to introducing government fund-of-funds programmes which support VC funds during the natural down cycles of fundraising; and from investing in VC funds with conditions that incentivize VC managers to contribute to the success of their investments to creating an environment in which VC investors can sell their ownership stakes at prices that compensate them sufficiently for the risks they take.

Enabling institutional arrangements and complementary infrastructures need to be put in place to support innovation and technology diffusion

Fourth, institutional arrangements and complementary infrastructures which enable both innovation and diffusion need to be put in place. Governments need to address systemic failures—which include market failures, such as unfair market competition, markets' inability to price in positive externality, and asymmetric information—and inadequate or inefficient interactions between NIS actors (United Nations, 2011, p. 132).

A proper IPR regime must be established and maintained to ensure that firms are sufficiently incentivized to innovate, without unnecessarily deterring technology diffusion.[27] Governments also need to play an active role in technology standard-setting efforts, as introduction of standards can help to kick-start penetration of new technologies. A more detailed policy discussion on these institutional issues, including their international dimension, is presented in chapter V.

Technology policy could benefit from the insights generated by the behavioural economics literature

Formulation of these policy actions could benefit from the insights generated by the behavioural economics literature, which emphasizes that economic agents sometimes act in ways that deviate from the rationality assumed under many of the economics models that have informed policymaking processes for decades.

Policymakers must engage in deliberations and make decisions regarding the pace of technology innovation and diffusion, in order to minimize disruptions to social and political stability. At the same time, Governments should remain aware of their own limitations and take a flexible approach towards formulating and implementing policies.

Last but not least, while national policy actions are central to the narrowing of the technological divide, those efforts cannot be fully effective without strong international

27 For example, technical information contained in patent documents need to be made publicly accessible so that innovations can have positive spillover effects on the broader technology community.

collaboration. Accordingly, there should be policy options for closing technology gaps between and within countries, which will be discussed from an international cooperation perspective in chapter V.

Chapter V
International cooperation for managing frontier technologies

Introduction

Previous chapters of the *Survey* have demonstrated that frontier technologies possess a strong transformative potential and that institutions and policies play a crucial role in determining how this potential is realized in each country and community. Policies can—and will—determine the impact of those technologies on the Sustainable Development Goals (SDGs). While national policies remain critical, international cooperation will play an increasingly important role in shaping the impact of frontier technologies in an age of globalization and interconnectedness.

International cooperation will play an increasingly important role in shaping the impact of frontier technologies in an age of globalization and interconnectedness

For example, without international cooperation, the technology divide discussed in chapter IV will not be bridged. Accordingly, the international community should consider options to facilitate technology transfer and foster national innovation capabilities. Moreover, making the knowledge that underpin certain key technologies more freely accessible at the global level may be crucial to ensuring our common future in the planet.

Without effective international cooperation, stringent regulations in one country will create opportunities for regulatory arbitrage among countries. In addition, a race to the bottom can occur if countries use less stringent regulations as a strategy to attract foreign investment and participate in global value chains. A case in point is that of differential rates of corporate international taxation. A concerted international effort will be required to ensure that gains reaped through the new technological breakthroughs are more equitably distributed within and across countries to the benefit of all.

A concerted international effort will ensure that gains derived from new technological breakthroughs are more equitably distributed within and across countries

The rapid pace of technological change, the uncertainty associated with it, and specific characteristics of emerging technologies may render traditional policymaking cycles and processes inadequate. Those characteristics include their speed of diffusion, the way in which they cross jurisdictional, regulatory and disciplinary borders, and their increasingly political profile in terms of how they embed and exhibit human values and bias (Schwab, 2018). As stated by the Secretary-General of the United Nations, it is crucial to avoid the naïve idea that "traditional forms of regulation like the ones we have today will work to address the challenges of the future" (United Nations, 2017a).

Regulatory mechanisms that bring together all stakeholders—including not only Governments, companies and scientists but also the civil society and academia—are needed. These frameworks must foster freedom of innovation, which is absolutely essential for the future of humankind, while at the same time, protecting and upholding human rights, which is critical for maintaining social cohesion, stability and peace.

Frontier technologies require policy processes that are flexible and adaptable (United Nations, 2018b). In technology development, experimentation generates perspective, revealing not only what technologies can do but also what they cannot do; and provides

Frontier technologies require policy processes that are flexible and adaptable…

some idea of when and at what scale a technology is appropriate. A similar approach to policies, institutions and regulation should be fostered.

...capable of incorporating information and emerging knowledge

A more flexible policy process, capable of incorporating information and emerging knowledge, will be needed to scope, assess, implement and monitor policy interventions. Innovation hubs and public policy labs which embody the spirit of experimentation and inclusion already exist in some countries. Such labs are found, for example, in the European Union[1] and in some cities in the United States of America.[2]

The present chapter addresses the issue of market-power concentration while underscoring that bridging the technology divide makes international cooperation imperative. The "winner-take-most" phenomenon has allowed a small number of technology firms to dominate their respective industries at the global level, challenging traditional checks and balances at the national level. International cooperation must therefore address excessive market power in the frontier technology sectors. This chapter also identifies the challenges faced by international taxation in the context of the digital economy and digitalization. Those operating within the current tax framework, designed with the traditional brick-and-mortar economy in mind, find themselves in uncharted territory when attempting to tax income associated with intangible activities and transactions enabled by the Internet and frontier technologies. The chapter also explores broader ethical questions, complementing the discussion presented in chapter II. It highlights a range of initiatives that are being undertaken by nations and jurisdictions worldwide with the aim of creating or updating relevant laws and regulations so as to ensure that they reflect the evolving challenges associated with emerging technologies.

A global dialogue, involving all stakeholders, is needed to identify the risks and opportunities associated with frontier technologies

The chapter concludes with a discussion on the wider role that is being played by the United Nations through support to Member States as they strive to shape new technologies in ways that promote the common good, human dignity and prosperity and protect the environment. While many frontier technologies present immense opportunities for fostering sustainable development, they also pose considerable risks. A global dialogue, involving all stakeholders, is needed to identify those risks and opportunities. The United Nations can serve as an impartial facilitator among Governments, the private sector and civil society organizations for the presentation of objective assessments of the impact of emerging technologies on sustainable development outcomes.

Bridging the technological divide

The technological divide—both between and within countries—poses significant challenges to the achievement of sustainable development, as highlighted in chapter III. Other chapters, chapter IV in particular, have revealed glaring differences in innovative and absorptive capacities among countries, drawing attention to the persistent, and even growing, technology divide among countries. In its resolution 72/242, the General Assembly noted with concern that "important and growing divides with regard to science and technology remain between and within developed and developing countries".

The technological divide is driven by both inadequate access to and suppressed demand for technologies

The technological divide, however, is not driven exclusively by lack of access to emerging technologies. While it is necessary to improve access to new technologies, granting access does not necessarily translate into their widespread adoption and diffusion. New

1 See https://ec.europa.eu/jrc/en/news/policy-labs-innovative-take-public-administrations-better-policies.

2 See www.governing.com/commentary/col-data-policy-labs-states-urgently-need.html.

technologies that are clearly superior to existing alternatives have not always being widely adopted, despite active and continuous interventions from the development community. In this regard, there is increasing awareness of the importance of feed-back linkages between supply and demand in the innovation process, particularly of how feedbacks from users can help to better direct resources and capabilities for innovation to meet societal or market needs (OECD, 2011). Clearly, the factors that suppress demand for welfare-improving technologies need to be addressed.

Support international technology transfer and national innovation

One key challenge for bridging the technology divide is to improve access to technologies. As discussed in chapter IV, many developing countries tend to rely heavily on foreign technology adoption in advancing their national technological development. Developing countries also need to achieve a certain level of indigenous innovation activity in order to build absorptive capacity and, eventually, move closer to the global technological frontier.

The international community has a role to play in supporting both cross-border technology transfer and nations' indigenous innovation efforts

The international community has a role to play in supporting both cross-border technology transfer and nations' indigenous innovation efforts. The following discussion highlights four areas in which international cooperation can be particularly conducive to improving access to technologies. The discussion aims at promoting an international discussion on their potential and our common future, while acknowledging at the same time that some of the proposals may be difficult to achieve.

Improve flexibilities of the global intellectual property rights (IPR) regime

Rigidities in the global IPR regime make technology transfer difficult

The protection of intellectual property rights (IPR) serves to encourage innovation by ensuring that innovators are sufficiently compensated for their efforts.[3] However, rigidities in the global IPR regime make technology transfers difficult. The IPR protections within the World Trade Organization (WTO) framework are not aligned adequately with the needs of developing countries, as they often tilt towards protecting well-established rights, traditionally emanating from developed countries. This view is echoed in the 2011 *Survey* (United Nations, 2011), where it is argued that the world's heavy reliance on private transfer of technology—supported by the current global IPR regime—is not necessarily optimal, as private investment-dependent technological diffusion would be too slow.

The TRIPS Agreement allows WTO member States to retain some important flexibilities in accessing technologies through international channels

The World Trade Organization Agreement on Trade-Related Aspects of Intellectual Property Rights (TRIPS Agreement) has nevertheless allowed WTO member States to retain some important flexibilities in terms of accessing technologies through international channels (Kamperman Sanders, 2018). One example is the latitude provided by the Agreement to countries in interpreting three criteria of patentability, i.e., novelty, involvement of an inventive step, and industrial applicability, taking into account domestic

3 At national levels, protection of IPR involves a range of institutions, including legislative bodies (which design IPR laws), judicial systems (which adjudicate IPR-related disputes), national patent and trademark offices (which administer the patent and trademark systems) and tax and trade authorities (which enforce IPR measures that involve taxation and tariffs). At the international level, the TRIPS Agreement—the most comprehensive multilateral IPR agreement—anchors the global IPR regime, which also consists of a wide range of trade and investment agreements having IPR components. WTO and the World Intellectual Property Organization (WIPO) are two multilateral entities that provide international forums for discussing and making decisions on IPR-related matters.

development objectives.[4] For example, in 2015, the WTO Council for Trade-Related Aspects of Intellectual Property Rights extended—until January 2033—its previous decision on exempting the pharmaceutical products of least developed countries (LDCs) from complying with key provisions of the TRIPS Agreement. Among other things, the exemption allows LDCs to choose whether or not to protect pharmaceutical patents and clinical trial data.[5] Yet another flexibility under the patent system makes it possible for countries to engage in compulsory licensing, i.e., a Government can allow someone else to produce the patented product or process without the consent of the original patent owner. Bond and Saggi (2016) argue that compulsory licensing is perhaps the most important kind of flexibility provided by the TRIPS Agreement.[6] Specifically, article 31 of the Agreement outlines the conditions under which compulsory licensing is allowed, while leaving space for Governments to interpret those conditions.

Lack of access to original test data poses challenges to reproduction of a technology by other firms, even if they have been granted a compulsory license

Even with a compulsory license, countries can still face considerable challenges. A key challenge revolves around the issue of "data exclusivity", through which protection of clinical trial data is granted to the original patent holder (Kamperman Sanders, 2018).[7] In the case of pharmaceutical products, the existence of data exclusivity imposes constraints on non-patent owners' access to clinical trial data, which are costly and time-consuming to generate, but central to establishing the safety and efficacy of generic products.[8] Lack of access to such data therefore poses significant challenges to other firms with respect to reproducing a technology, even if they have been granted a compulsory licence.

The international community would require a multi-pronged flexible approach, granting developing countries sufficient latitude in determining their national patentability standards, maintaining or even expanding patent exemptions for LDCs and other countries far away from the global technological frontier, creating conditions that make compulsory licensing more feasible and effective, and making access to technology data more inclusive.

Ensure national policy space for indigenous innovation

Despite the long-standing stalemate at the Doha Development Round, strengthening multilateralism offers the best option for developing countries with respect to addressing the issue of reduced policy space and exercising their collective power to ensure that trade liberalization fosters sustainable development. In its 2018 report, the Inter-agency Task Force on Financing for Development (IATF) has called on WTO members to show col-

---

4 Countries that have recently changed patentability standards include India (in 2005) and the contracting States of the European Patent Convention (in 2010). Effectively, these practices allow authorities to reduce the number of patents that do not facilitate significant innovation, but rather serve mainly as a hindrance to technology transfer. See Ali and Rajagopal (2017); Beatty (2011).

5 See www.wto.org/english/news_e/news15_e/trip_06nov15_e.htm.

6 The case of the pharmaceutical industry of Bangladesh attests to the potential of compulsory licensing in advancing domestic technological development (Gay, 2018). In effect, room to engage in compulsory licensing—a vital global support measure for the industry—has allowed Bangladesh to pursue an industrial policy that has successfully promoted its pharmaceutical sector through import substitution and, increasingly, export promotion.

7 Typical examples of such data include clinical trial data that are submitted by patent owners in the process of obtaining marketing authorization for pharmaceutical products (ibid.).

8 For example, European Union legislation for medicines grants the originator of an innovation exclusive rights over data regardless of the reasons for the licence and even in emergency situations ('t Hoen, Boulet and Baker, 2017).

lective leadership by reiterating their commitment to open, fair and mutually beneficial trade, which is crucial for supporting technology transfers, economic growth and prosperity (United Nations, 2018a, chap III.D, recommendation 1).

In addition to the global IPR regime, traditional bilateral and regional international trade agreements (RTAs) and international investment agreements (IIAs) have had restrictive effects on domestic policy space and innovation (United Nations, 2011) which extend beyond the scope of WTO. There has been an evolution of the focus of RTAs from tariffs and rules of origin to the removal of impediments and the reduction of costs and risks associated with the operations of international production networks. In this context, RTAs continue to restrict policy space, leading to competitive liberalization in developing countries and to the premature adoption of policies not necessarily compatible with their development needs (Cortez and Arda, 2015, pp. 155–156).

In turn, application of traditional IIAs has often had unintended impacts, such as constraining regulatory space and increasing countries vulnerability to financial penalties levied by arbitration panels set up to settle investor-state disputes, including disputes related to intellectual property rights (Kamperman Sanders, 2018).[9] To align IIAs with the SDGs, countries have embarked on a reform process whose aim is to create a new generation of IIAs (United Nations, 2018a, p. 124). This process encompasses the need to preserve regulatory space, including for industrial policy, and improvements to, or omissions of, investor-state dispute settlement (UNCTAD, 2018, p. 96). Member States are also undertaking efforts to reform outdated IIAs, progressively increasing their coherence with their country's national development strategy. Policy space for supporting innovation should be at the centre of such efforts.

Traditional international investment agreements often constrain countries' regulatory space and increase their vulnerability to financial penalties from investor-State disputes

Harmonize national and international technology standards

Technology standard-setting is a crucial process within the domain of technology innovation and diffusion. For example, the introduction of the Global System for Mobile Communications (GSM) standard, which describes the protocols for second-generation digital cellular networks used by mobile devices, illustrates how standard harmonization has been instrumental in diffusing mobile communication technology (Gruber and Koutroumpis, 2010). A widely accepted standard can also help to close the technology divide by reducing users' adoption cost (Hall, 2006).

The existence of standards can promote innovation by facilitating new products' interoperability and marketability. In practice, standard-setting processes are complex and very often involve competitors who would like to steer the direction of the standard towards their own interest (Burrone, n.d.). As multitude of entities are involved in setting technology standards, it is important that a country has a unified national standards strategy which can help prevent the problem of duplicative efforts and conflicting standards from arising.

A unified national strategy for setting technology standards can help prevent the problem of duplicative efforts and conflicting standards from arising

In setting standards, patent holders are moving away from formal standardization bodies towards flexible standard-setting organizations, where terms of use, the essential

9 Intellectual property is recognized as an investment under bilateral investment treaties, leading to a situation where investors can take national Governments to task over issues of expropriation of property, in breach of fair and equitable treatment (FET) obligations, but also over diminishment of the value of an investment, in breach of legitimate expectations of the investor (ibid., p. 20).

character of patents and royalty rates can be negotiated more freely (Kamperman Sanders, 2018). As standard-setting is increasingly carried out by informal standard-setting organizations led by the private sector, Governments need to strengthen their participation and that of all relevant stakeholders in the processes involved so as to ensure transparency and accountability. It is important to consider that, while standards can exert significant positive impacts, they may also have a negative effect on social welfare by restricting how goods and services are produced. They could also serve as non-tariff barriers, by necessitating excessive testing and even redesigns of products (National Institute of Standards and Technology, 2000).

Global collaboration should aim at establishing internationally accepted principles on developing standards and ensuring consistent interpretation and application of such principles

At the global level, countries should collaborate on establishing internationally accepted principles on developing standards and on ensuring consistent interpretation and application of those principles (United States Standards Strategy Committee, 2016), identifying how technology standards unfairly disadvantage competition and reduce social welfare. There should be a clear international understanding of how standards developed by informal standard-setting organizations can be used in regulation. International cooperation could help to establish a broad acceptance of the use of such standards, reducing the possibility of ending up with conflicting national and regional standards.

Identify and provide technologies as global public goods

Advances in several frontier technologies can help humanity confront many existential threats, including rising sea levels as well as droughts and floods. These challenges make identification and provision of certain emerging technologies as global public goods—i.e., goods that confer quasi-universal benefits on different countries, peoples and generations and whose consumption at the global level is characterized by non-rivalry and non-excludability—an important consideration for the international community.[10]

Provision of an emerging technology as a global public good requires that it be freely accessible globally

Many emerging technologies—notably those that could help to reverse climate change, enhance environmental sustainability or combat pandemics—could be provided as global public goods, by making the knowledge that underpins them more freely accessible at the global level. Provision of such technologies as global public goods would maximize the benefits they produce, supporting our common purpose of ensuring a liveable planet for present and future generations.

An institutional framework is needed to ensure that choices of global public goods reflect stakeholders' aggregated preferences

While the motivation underlying the provision of certain technologies as global public goods is clear, implementation can be complicated. Some have suggested that it should begin with a multi-stakeholder participatory process for the purpose of determining what technologies should be considered global public goods and how they should be produced and distributed (Kaul and others, 2003). An institutional framework would be needed to support this deliberative process. Such a framework should support stakeholders in making choices that are balanced with regard to global public goods—that is to say, sufficiently reflective of aggregation of stakeholders' preferences—and surmounting selected global challenges efficiently, which requires a better understanding of available solutions and of their conditions of implementation (Brousseau, Dedeurwaerdere and Siebenhüner, 2017).

The Intergovernmental Panel on Climate Change (IPCC), for example, whose central objective is to provide climate change assessment and policy options for adaptation and mitigation, could constitute such a framework. It is an organized process that is both global and centralized and, and which at the same time requires considerable coordination among

10 This is the definition provided by Kaul, Grunberg and Stern (1999).

the contributors to its assessment reports who hail from around the world. While the ability of the IPCC assessment reports to identify climate-related challenges is widely acknowledged, their efforts to generate context-specific solutions have generally been less effective.

In practice, the international community faces a major challenge in facilitating flow of technologies and knowledge which can be made functionally excludable by the entities in the private sector that own them (Taylor, 2016), owing perhaps to the significant commercial value that accrues to firms by controlling these technologies or the constraints associated with contractual rights and property claims, e.g., with respect to data sharing. For efficient provision of technologies as global public goods, the aforesaid incentive-related and legal obstacles would need to be addressed.

Efficient provision of technologies as global public goods would need to address incentives and legal obstacles

Overcome constraints on technology adoption

As emphasized at the beginning of this section, technology use is determined jointly by supply- and demand-side factors. While improving access to new technologies is important, their potential benefits clearly cannot be realized if there is no demand for such technologies. Still, there is considerable room for the international community to facilitate both access to and use of relevant new technologies.

One key step is to promote a dual focus by international development projects—on addressing both supply- and demand-side constraints on technology adoption. This would require acquiring a deeper understanding of the domestic formal and informal institutions—including social and cultural norms and structures of social networks—and how they affect technology adoption behaviour, rather than simply imposing new technologies on communities. One mechanism that is addressing demand-side constraints is the newly established Technology Bank, which aims at helping LDCs obtain more complete information on new technologies and how they can be applied within the context of country-specific circumstances.

A dual focus of international development projects—on addressing both supply- and demand-side technology adoption constraints—should be promoted

Foster technological trust

Among the many factors that drive demand for technologies, trust in technology is arguably one of the most important. Building technological trust is particularly important for developing countries, as they tend to experience lower levels of trust in a new technology (see figure V.1). Chakravorti and Chaturvedi (2017) argue that building trust in digital technology would require proper protection of privacy, security and accountability. Ultimately, it is all about protecting fundamental human rights in the digital environment, an issue introduced in chapter II. The expanding scope of harms perpetrated in the digital sphere, which do not respect national borders, calls for multilateral action to proactively define and protect human rights within the digital context (see section on big data below). Developing a definitive global standard on data governance needs to be a crucial component of multilateral efforts, given the pervasiveness of data in the modern technology environment.

Public trust in technologies would also most likely be strengthened if it could be shown that they improve public sector performance. Indeed, digitalization has already contributed to an increase in public sector efficiencies and a reduction of the costs of public finance management. Such gains are accruing from the generation of more and better data, better data management systems and higher-level computer processing power, which can also lead to better policy design (Gupta and others, 2017).

Digitalization has contributed to an increase in public sector efficiencies and a reduction of costs in public finance management

Given that the potential of many of these technologies is still not fully understood, one of the very first steps towards optimizing their use would be to take stock of the ongoing related technology initiatives around the world. The international community can build a database that systematically documents the results of those initiatives, which can then be used to inform future application and regulation of the technology. The establishment of the Technology Facilitation Mechanism platform is an important step in that direction.

Figure V.1
Digital trust surplus/deficit across countries

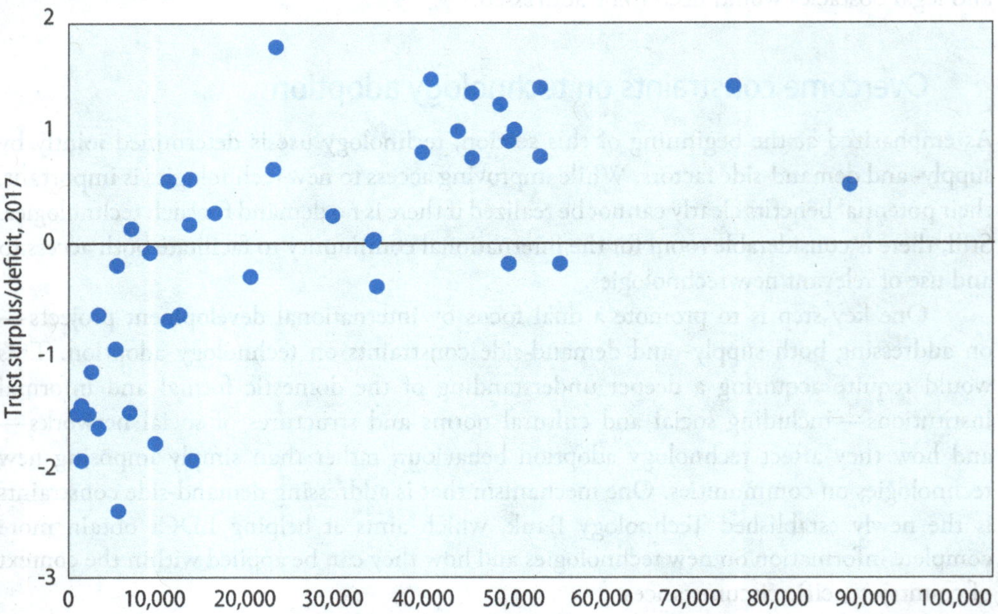

Source: UN/DESA calculation, based on data from Chakravorti and Chaturvedi (2017) and World Bank, World Development Indicators.

Note: Trust surplus/deficit is defined as the gap between users' digital trust environment experience and their tolerance for friction of digital commerce engagement. A higher trust surplus level suggests that users are more patient online and willing to engage with new technologies. Both the level of the digital trust environment experience and that of the tolerance for digital commerce engagement friction are placed along a score scale ranging from 0 to 5, with 5 being the most positive score. As the trust surplus/deficit variable is defined as the difference between the two variables, it runs from -5 to 5, with 5 denoting the highest level of trust surplus. There are 42 countries in the sample.

Addressing the concentration of market power in frontier technologies

An important facet of the technology divide is the gap, among firms, in innovation output and market power. Certain emerging sectoral features—notably the existence of network effects—and global economic integration have contributed to the rise of the "winner-take-most" phenomenon, which allows a small number of firms to dominate their respective industries at the global level and earn growing rents. Firms developing many frontier technologies in the digital domain are increasingly global, controlling an ever-increasing share of their market.

The present section emphasizes the need for international cooperation, given that competition policy has gone global in the last 20 years (OECD, 2014). A rapidly increasing number of competition cases currently have an international dimension, which can be attributed partly to increasing international trade and investment and the growth of global supply chains. This section examines specific developments that have led to the rapid concentration of market power worldwide and particularly in new sectors, including frontier technologies in the digital domain. Specifically, it discusses how the rise of big data and algorithms, and certain shortcomings of the patent system, could pose further challenges to promotion of fair competition.

Increasing market concentration raises concerns

There are concerns that rising market concentration reflects not only leading firms' higher productivity, but also network effects, economies of scale and economies of scope

As discussed in chapter IV, there is a broad trend towards higher market concentration across different industries and, notably, the technology sector around the world. Autor and others (2017) have shown that—in the case of the United States—the rise in market concentration is correlated with a growing number of patents per worker. They also show that that rise in concentration was faster in sectors where labour productivity rose faster. There are, however, deep concerns that such market power concentration also reflects factors other than the superiority of the leading firms' products and services. In fact, the consensus is that many of the world's most dominant technology firms—as early winners in the current technological landscape—have benefited from technology externalities (or network effects), economies of scale and economies of scope (OECD, 2017b). These effects could potentially allow them to remain dominant, without necessarily being more innovative than their competitors.

While the work of Autor and others (2017) suggests that market concentration has not yet produced a notable adverse impact on overall economic productivity, the authors do raise the possibility that firms that initially capture a high market share owing to their superior productivity or innovations later use their dominant position to erect barriers to entry which deters competition. If rising market power concentration is accompanied by a more frequent engagement in anticompetitive behaviours, it could hurt the industry's overall innovation efforts and eventually hamper productivity growth.

There are also growing concerns regarding "regulatory capture", which generally refers to a situation where policymakers or enforcement agencies are in a constant state of "being persuaded" or influenced by powerful firms (Hempling, 2014). The recent ramp-up of major technology companies' spending on lobbying has raised concerns that those firms may acquire unfair advantages through political means.[11]

Big data and algorithms have radically changed market competition

The rise of big data and algorithms, which has become an important feature of the competition landscape, present a new challenge to traditional competition policies. Big data and algorithms transcend national boundaries. They can be designed in one jurisdiction with implications for the rest of the world. This means international cooperation is a must for managing big data algorithms and their potential anti-competitive impact on social welfare within and across national boundaries.

The rise of technology firms that control a key digital platform and wield significant market power creates multiple development concerns

As data and the ability to process them emerge as key competitive factors, Stucke (forthcoming) argues that the rise of technology firms that control a key digital platform and significant market power raises multiple issues, including with respect to (a) degraded

11 For example, Google alone spent more than $17 million in lobbying in the United States in 2017, whereas Facebook spent more than $11.5 million; other tech giants such as Amazon and Apple also set company records in lobbying in 2017 (Brody, 2018).

service quality in the form of lower privacy protection and excessive collection of personal data; (b) possible government overreach, as Governments could seek to gain access to the massive personal data trove possessed by platform companies; (c) wealth transfer from consumers to platform companies, as the latter could extract personal data or creative content without paying for their fair market value; and with access to detailed consumer data and powerful algorithms, firms can also engage in "near perfect" price discrimination and/or "behavioural discrimination" which would allow them to extract more revenues from consumers;[12] (d) deadweight welfare loss, resulting from the forgoing by consumers of the use of new technologies as privacy degrades and technological distrust grows; (e) political issues as platform companies gain considerable ability to affect public debate; and (f) less innovation, as platform companies can use big data and algorithms to engage in anticompetitive behaviours.

Firms could use big data and algorithms to deter market entry, raise consumers' switching cost, unfairly favour their own products and facilitate collusion

Ezrachi and Stucke (2016) argue that there are several transmission channels through which big data and algorithms can flow to hurt competition. First, given the importance of data in the initial training and fine-tuning of algorithms, early incumbents who have amassed a huge quantity of data could wield their data ownership as a barrier to entry, as new entrants would find it costly and/or time consuming to collect the same amount of data accumulated by those incumbents.

Second, firms' accumulation of detailed personal user data could effectively increase consumers' switching cost, especially when it is difficult to transfer personal data across platforms. Google offers a case in point: Through the constellation of products and services that Google provides, ranging from its search engine to its digital personal assistant device, the firm has created a digital ecosystem, rather than a mere assortment of independent products. For any given service within the Google ecosystem, customers will be less inclined to switch to another provider—even if the alternative is superior as a standalone product—since such a move would mean not being able to fully enjoy the positive complementary effect arising from use of other Google services.[13]

Third, and related to previous points, hosting a powerful digital ecosystem could potentially allow a firm to engage in anticompetitive practices by unfairly favouring its own apps over rival apps.

The increasing use of big data and algorithms poses significant challenges to the assessment of anticompetitive behaviours

Fourth, smart algorithms could also help facilitate collusion among firms, as they can be used to monitor behaviours of all firms in the market and stabilize price competition. Under certain market conditions, each algorithm can adopt a strategy that fosters interdependence among operators, entailing, e.g., following price increases by competitors and punishing deviations from the new equilibrium. Another possible means of collusion would be the use of a single algorithm by numerous competitors to establish a hub-and-spoke alignment of prices.

The increasing use of big data and algorithms also pose significant challenges to competition authorities in their efforts to assess anticompetitive behaviours. For example,

12 With access to detailed information on customers' socioeconomic characteristics and purchasing behaviour, firms can establish full consumer profiles, including on their alternative options and reservation prices for different products. This allows firms to engage in "near perfect" price discrimination. Moreover, firms can also engage in "behavioural discrimination", by tailoring their marketing efforts to individual consumers so to maximize the chances that targeted consumers will purchase the advertised products.

13 For example, using a unified Google login allows customers to download all of the apps purchased on one Google device to all other Google devices. This clearly would not be possible if customers utilized devices from different firms.

the increasing use of pricing algorithms which allow firms to establish individualized prices complicates competition authorities' efforts to define relevant markets, which is central to the identification of the types and levels of competition faced by firms.[14]

Moreover, the emergence of big data also affects how authorities assess the implications of mergers for competition, given that combining data—initially collected for different purposes—could potentially allow the new firm created by the merger to gain an insurmountable advantage over other competitors in respect of securing an understanding of customers. As data become increasingly important for competition, regulators need to closely examine mergers that bring large sets of data together.

International cooperation must entail consideration of how to develop preconditions for healthy market competition

It is an imperative that international cooperation entail consideration of appropriate measures to mitigate the negative effects that big data and algorithms may have on competition, including ex post measures that target specific incidences of anticompetitive behavior and ex ante ones that focus on developing the necessary preconditions for healthy market competition. Moreover, for these measures to be truly effective, competition authorities would need to coordinate with other regulators such as privacy and consumer protection officials. Regulators should also consider the distributional effect of different regulatory measures, ensuring that smaller firms will be subject to compliance requirements that are proportionate to the size of their operations and will therefore not be overburdened.

Regulators need to take a broader view of the harms that anticompetitive behaviours can inflict, including a lowering of privacy protection

Specifically, regulators should first consider taking a broader view of the harms that anticompetitive behaviors can inflict. The traditional antitrust focus has been on quantifiable harms such as excessive prices and reduction of consumer welfare. However, firms could also compete on the basis of other features of the products and services they provide, including by lowering privacy protection (Stucke and Grunes, 2016).

Second, in ensuring data that will not be effectively used as a barrier to market entry or as a means of increasing consumers' switching costs, Governments should consider introducing a right to data portability, which would give a data subject the right to receive and transfer his or her personal data that were initially collected by one organization. The General Data Protection Regulation, agreed by the European Parliament and the Council of the European Union (see chap. II and section on appropriate standards and ethical boundaries below), has already included such a right and is expected to foster competition among digital services and interoperability of platforms.

Third, there is the need for a clear international understanding on rendering algorithms more transparent and accountable for their effects (OECD, 2017a). In practice, this would require tackling daunting challenges such as making complex algorithms comprehensible to the public.

Fourth, international cooperation should also entail adoption of rules to govern algorithm design. For example, regulations could be introduced to restrain algorithms from

14 A key traditional analytic tool for defining relevant markets is the Small but Significant and Non-Transitory Increase in Price (SSNIP) test, which essentially determines whether a market—comprising a selected set of products—is relevant in an antitrust investigation through identification of the price elasticity of those products. If a hypothetical small but significant, and permanent rise in prices of these products does not lead to a switch by a sufficient number of customers to alternative products, a market could be considered relevant. While in this case, the ability of competition authorities to accurately observe prices charged by firms is crucial, the prevalence of pricing algorithms that change individualized prices rapidly makes this exercise highly difficult. See OECD (2017a).

adjusting to certain changes in market variables, such as prices charged by other firms—a practice that is essential to sustaining collusion.

Patents are increasing the possibilities for anticompetitive behaviour

Greater patent application backlogs and longer pendency periods increase possibilities for anticompetitive behaviour

Over the past two decades, mirroring rapid technological advancement, there has been a significant increase in the number and complexity of patent applications filed around the world (see figure V.2), resulting in a greater backlog and substantially longer pendency periods (OECD, 2010). Longer pendency periods result in greater uncertainty regarding which inventions are and will be protected by patent rights, which has implications for competition.

Figure V.2
Total patent applications, by income group, 1985–2016

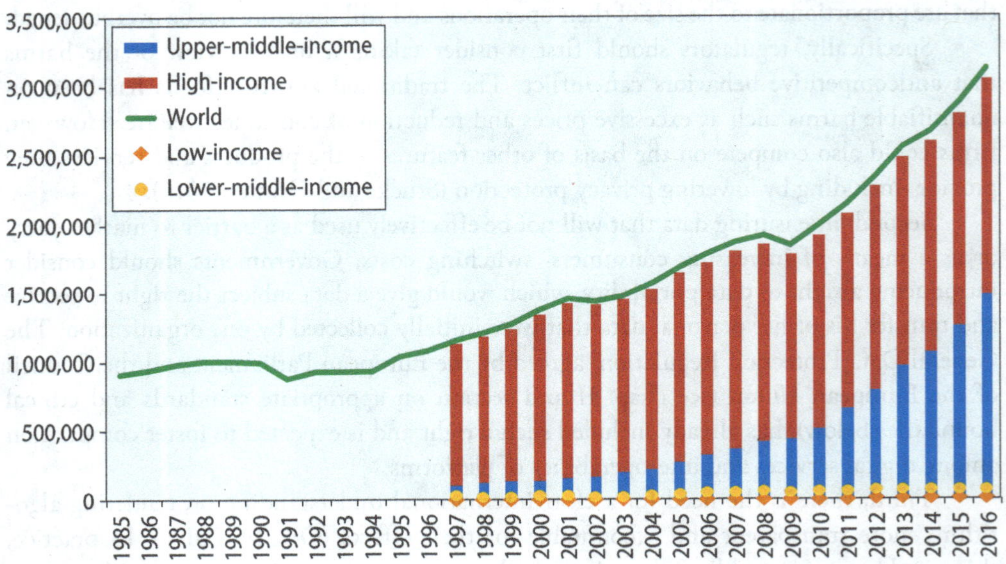

Source: UN/DESA elaboration, based on World Intellectual Property Organization (WIPO) statistics database.

Note: The disaggregated data indicate where, among the income groups, the patent applications were filed. Disaggregated data before the year 1997 are not available.

Firms also have been engaged in the strategic use of the so-called divisional patent application.[15] In essence, a set of divisional patent applications all derive from an earlier, related application, but each of them is examined separately and has a separate publication schedule. The use of such an application allows firms to keep their pending patents hidden from the public for an extended period of time, which also helps them engage in anticompetitive behaviours. A dominant firm, for example, can keep patent applications pending through a divisional patent application until a rival launches a new product. The dominant firm can then make a modification in the patent in an additional filing so that

15 It should be noted that the practice using the divisional patent application is much more common in the United States than in Europe.

the patent, in describing the new product perfectly, will allow the firm to sue its rival for infringement.

Stronger international cooperation is needed now more than ever

Competition law has become a policy concern in an increasing number of countries over the last two decades (OECD, 2014). The number of jurisdictions with competition law enforcement rose from fewer than 20 in 1990 to about 120 in 2014. At the same time, with many firms operating in multiple countries, many competition cases now have an international dimension.[16]

International cooperation among competition authorities is important

The international dimension of competition policies continues to expand. This intensification is a development that naturally calls for greater international cooperation among competition authorities. Such international cooperation is particularly important considering that—owing to factors such as differences in regulatory and judicial philosophies and the set-up of competition authorities—there is a persistent divergence in terms of antitrust enforcement between the European Union and the United States, arguably the two most influential jurisdictions in the area of competition policy.

Importantly, this divergence also extends to their approach to dealing with big data. While authorities in the European Union have openly maintained that big data should be subject to the abuse of dominance provision under article 102 of the Treaty on the Functioning of the European Union, the United States has resisted the idea of treating big data as an "essential facility", which would require that a firm with possession of those data must share them with its competitors (Lugard and Roach, 2017). Given that other jurisdictions often look to the two for guidance concerning antitrust jurisprudence, the divergence could also develop globally.

Blair and Sokol (2013) argue that when different jurisdictions have different levels of regulatory stringency, the most stringent antitrust system may produce the global standard. For example, two firms that operate in multiple jurisdictions would not be able to merge if one national competition authority, applying a tougher standard to the merger, does not approve it, even if it is cleared by all other relevant competition authorities. Therefore, if the antitrust rules are being too rigidly applied in a certain jurisdiction, they could hurt customers both within and outside the jurisdiction.

Without cross-country harmonization of competition law, high capital and technology mobility could discourage full enforcement

A second point is that insufficient cooperation could impact national competition authorities' ability to enforce their national laws. High capital and technology mobility allows firms to engage in regulatory arbitrage with relative ease, which could discourage Governments from fully enforcing their competition laws. This issue is particularly salient for small economies where sales of international firms in those economies account for a small portion of the firms' total revenues, but a significant portion of these economies' output (Gal, 2013). If the competition authorities of such economies are to impose a significant regulatory burden, it would likely drive firms away.

Third, repeated submission of the same information to multiple competition authorities is costly and time consuming for firms and competition authorities (OECD, 2014). With more firms engaging in cross-border economic activities and more countries

16 For example, more than 90 per cent of fines imposed by the United States authorities on cartels have been international; and the number of cartel cases investigated by the European Union involving a non-European Union participant increased by more than 450 per cent during the period 1990–2014.

introducing competition laws, the implications of insufficient cooperation among competition authorities are going to be felt only more acutely in the future.

Considering the need to tackle cross-border competition cases, there needs to be greater harmonization in competition law across countries. Furthermore, there needs to be stronger international cooperation on ensuring competition enforcement, which would require addressing such challenges as differences in legal systems, special procedures for gathering evidence and related limitations, trust issues and the implementation of leniency and immunity programmes (UNCTAD, Trade and Development Board, 2017).

While effective formal cooperation on tackling cross-border competition cases is rare, authorities should still seek informal cooperation

Only a few competition authorities engage in effective formal cooperation. Owing to limitations in resources and enforcement experiences, recent and smaller authorities typically find it difficult to participate in meaningful cooperation with other national competition authorities. Nevertheless, in the absence of formal cooperation, authorities should still seek informal cooperation through regional groupings and other cross-national arrangements. The United Nations Conferences to Review All Aspects of the Set of Multilaterally Agreed Equitable Principles and Rules for the Control of Restrictive Business Practices (the UN Set, which is the only multilateral agreement on competition policy) provide an opportunity for competition authorities around the world to establish contacts and exchange views on competition-related issues. Moreover, the International Competition Network and OECD also provide similar specialized venues which should continue to be utilized.

Digitalization and international tax cooperation

Digitalization is transforming conventional notions of how businesses are structured, how firms interact and how consumers obtain services, information and goods

Governments in both developed and developing countries face growing challenges with respect to collection of adequate revenues to finance sustainable development-related expenditure. The digitalization of the economy is transforming conventional notions regarding how businesses are structured, how firms interact and how consumers obtain services, information and goods (Muro and others, 2017). E-commerce, for example, is transforming global business and opening up international markets, including possibilities for inclusive trade growth in developing countries (United Nations, 2018a).

Digitalization is also posing new challenges for the international tax framework—a system devised almost a century ago at the League of Nations, based on criteria that rely primarily on the physical presence of companies in foreign countries (Falcão, 2018a). Understanding the consequences of digitalization for international taxation is important, as it creates opportunities for multinational enterprises to engage in base erosion and profit shifting (BEPS).[17] Digitalization allows large firms to centralize their functions in certain jurisdictions, often in very low- or no-tax jurisdictions, thus leading to base erosion and profit shifting concerns. The importance of highly mobile intellectual property in the digitalized economies has only exacerbated these risks.

17 Base erosion and profit shifting (BEPS) are tax planning strategies that exploit gaps and mismatches in tax rules in order to artificially shift profits to low- or no-tax locations where there is little or no economic activity. Although some of the schemes used are illegal, most are not. In 2013, OECD and G20 countries adopted the 15-point Action Plan on Base Erosion and Profit Shifting to address BEPS. The full BEPS package was endorsed by the G20 leaders in November 2015, and more than 110 countries and jurisdictions have committed to its implementation, as members of the Inclusive Framework on BEPS, which was established in June 2016.

International tax rules are not ready for the digitalized economy

Technology has allowed companies to do business (i.e., to buy, sell and provide access to services) through Internet and mobile apps, without their needing to be physically present in the country. In the current tax framework, this represents a substantial handicap with respect to the capacity to tax associated income, as a country is allowed to tax only the income that is derived from the activities that occur physically in its jurisdiction.

Physical presence—typically defined as the existence of a permanent establishment for a set period of time[18] for corporations, or a fixed place of business for individuals—is key. Crafted for the brick-and-mortar economy, the current international tax law presumes that if there is not enough substantial activity to justify the establishment of a branch or a subsidiary in the source State, the source State is not entitled to tax (Falcão, 2018b). Under existing rules, digital companies often have no tax liability in jurisdictions where they have users and customers. In this framework, countries in which digital activities are carried out are unable to tax the income generated in their own territories, even though those activities benefit from their consumer base, their infrastructure or their commercial resources. For example, a digital platform providing free or paid services will most likely be taxed only in the country where it is resident, regardless of where the activity occurred or the value was created. Box V.1 illustrates the issue with a recent example.

Under existing rules, digital companies often have no tax liability in jurisdictions where they have users and customers

Box V.1

The Google case: France

The problems faced by national tax systems in their efforts to tackle the impacts of the digital economy are perfectly illustrated in a case decided on 12 June 2017 by the French Administrative Court of Paris. The case concerns the taxation of Google's activities in France, where as in most countries around the world, Google is the market leader in online advertising. French individuals and companies that wish their products to be advertised online sign contracts with Google and Google advertises their brand names in their search engine pages and in other online Google products. Google has a sizable physical presence in France: Google France—a subsidiary company of Google Ireland—employs hundreds of people whose task is to streamline the advertisement activities performed for its French customers. Those customers do not, however, sign formal advertisement agreements with Google France but rather with Google Ireland, which subcontracts Google France to assist in providing tailor-made advertisement services to French customers. The activities performed by Google France are remunerated by Google Ireland at a transfer price of 8 per cent cost-plus, i.e., Google France receives 8 per cent of profits on top of the expenses it incurred in performing its services. The other 92 per cent of the business profits are taxable in Ireland.

France, just like Belgium, Italy and the United Kingdom of Great Britain and Northern Ireland, was rather displeased with the low level of profits attributed to Google France, believing that, in reality, the activities of Google France were much more substantial than what was reflected in the profit margin assigned to Google France in the transfer pricing agreement. The French tax authorities therefore issued a series of corrective tax assessments of the Google group for its activities in France. While respecting the cost-plus arrangement between

(continued)

18 Determined through tests concerning certain agreed thresholds in international tax treaties.

Box V.1 (*continued*)

the two legal entities, they concluded that on top of that, Google France was to be considered to have provided activities for the benefit of Google Ireland that went beyond the inter-company agreement. This being the case, the tax administration in France argued that besides the activities of its subsidiary company, Google Ireland had a "permanent establishment" in France to which part of the profits of the online advertisement business in France had to be attributed.

However, the French Court rejected the claim made by the tax authorities. Even though Google France did carry out important functions of the advertisement business in France, like marketing and sale of online services, it did not have the power to legally bind Google Ireland or to sign contracts in its name, even if many elements showed that Google France's employees were de facto negotiating the contracts and involved in the signings, and even if Google Ireland was merely rubber-stamping the pre-made agreements. Under the current rules, the presence of actual economic activities in France and the creation of value as a result of Google's access to the French consumer market was held not to be sufficient to establish that Google Ireland's activities in France had passed the permanent establishment threshold and that more of the profits of the business were taxable in France.

The appeal by the tax authorities to the Administrative Court of Appeals is currently pending.

Source: France: Tribunal Administratif Paris, 12 June 2017, Judgment No. 1505178/1-1.

The digital economy has raised questions concerning the appropriate characterization of income that results from digital access to goods or services

Taxation of search engines and social media platforms, which not only provide free services to users across borders but also gather data that enable them to sell targeted advertisements and earn revenues without physical presence, poses additional challenges to tax authorities. The digital economy has also raised questions concerning the appropriate characterization of income that accrues from digital access to goods or services. For example, the concept of the traditional sale of goods can now be expanded to include a licence for downloading a digital file and the concept of a manufacturing activity can now be expanded to include digital manufacturing via 3D printing. The utilization of "cloud" transactions raises similar questions, to the extent that the location of the cloud is unclear, undisclosed or scattered through multiple jurisdictions.

Digitalization in the framework of BEPS

Digitalization of business models makes international taxation more challenging because of the difficulty of defining and measuring the value of intangibles and deciding where such value is being generated (United Nations, 2018a). Digitalization also facilitates large firms' centralization of their functions in what are often very low tax or no-tax jurisdictions, raising additional concerns related to base erosion and profit shifting. Action 1 of the Action Plan on BEPS aimed at identifying the main issues related to the taxation of the digital economy, including the application of indirect taxes to its activities.

To ensure efficient and fair allocation of taxing rights across countries, the international tax system might need to undergo fundamental changes

BEPS Action 1 was intended not to establish a forum on revisiting the international tax framework for the digital economy (Falcão, 2018b) but rather to analyse those transactions that gave rise to BEPS-related considerations as a result of the use of a digital interface. However, discussions on the new ways of doing business in light of digitalization have inaugurated a broader debate on the allocation of taxing rights and attribution of income between the residence and source countries. There is also disagreement on how user-generated value should affect taxing rights (United Nations, 2018a).

Some analysts have noted that tax avoidance opportunities associated with the scale of growth in online business may be putting too much pressure on current tax arrangements.

Therefore, it has been suggested that, in order to ensure efficient and fair allocation of taxing rights across countries, the international tax system might need to undergo fundamental changes (United Nations, 2018a). From the perspective of international corporate tax policy, the question how to treat cross-border digital transactions has become highly contentious. Alternative rules for determining permanent establishment (PE) status based on the maintaining of a significant digital presence, as opposed to a significant physical presence, for a certain period of time are being discussed (Falcão, 2018b).

Unilateral measures

Neither the final report on action 1 of the Action Plan on BEPS nor the interim report prepared by the Task Force on the Digital Economy, a subsidiary body of the OECD-housed Inclusive Framework on BEPS (OECD, 2018b), has addressed the possibility of a long-term multilateral resolution to the issue of digitalization in international taxation. The interim report suggests policy considerations for countries wishing to introduce short-term measures for dealing with the effects of digitalization.

Several countries have resorted to equalization levies, diverted profits taxes and withholding taxes on digital transactions to capture income from digital activity

Several countries have resorted to equalization levies, diverted profits taxes, and withholding of taxes on digital transactions to capture income from digital activity. OECD broadly groups unilateral measures into four categories: (a) alternative application of the permanent establishment (PE) thresholds (alternative digital PE definition); (b) withholding taxes; (c) turnover taxes; and (d) specific regimes to deal with large multinational enterprises (MNEs). Table V.1 illustrates how the taxes are categorized.

So far, only India ("significant economic presence concept"), Slovakia ("expanded definition for fixed place of business") and Israel ("significant economic presence test") have proposed rules which aim at diluting the requirement for permanence and physical presence at a specific location to establish nexus for net taxation (OECD, 2018b, p. 135). However, other countries (including Austria, Indonesia, Thailand and Turkey) have announced that they are considering similar rules, or have proposed draft legislation to that effect.

The aim of the measures is to overcome the absence of physical presence in the source country and establish liability to tax based on other factors, such as "digital" or "online" presence, as unilaterally identified by the nation proposing the new legislation. In broad terms, these measures would correspond to the formulation of a "digital permanent establishment" concept applicable only at the national level.

Table V.1
Classification of uncoordinated unilateral measures

Alternative PE thresholds	Withholding taxes	Turnover taxes	Specific regimes for large multinational enterprises
Significant economic presence test (e.g., Israel, India)	Broader royalty definitions	Sectoral taxes, such as for advertisement (e.g., Hungary)	Diverted profits tax (e.g., United Kingdom, Australia)
	Technical service fees		
Virtual service PE (e.g., Saudi Arabia)	Online advertising	Levy on Digital Transactions (e.g., Italy)	Base erosion and anti-abuse tax (e.g.. United States)
		Equalisation levy (e.g., India)	

Source: Falcão (2018a), based on OECD (2018a).

Unilateral measures do not address the core concerns of digitalization

Unilateral measures in international taxation should be viewed as loophole-closing instruments only. While they can tackle tax competition, deter aggressive tax planning and avert the erosion of the tax base at a macrolevel, they generally tend to increase complexity and are unlikely to lead to a more stable tax system. In short, they are only short-term fixes which do not address the core concerns of digitalization.

Moreover, in its latest report, the Inter-agency Task Force on Financing for Development reiterates the affirmation of Heads of State and Government and High Representatives in the Addis Ababa Action Agenda of the Third International Conference on Financing for Development (para. 28)[19] that efforts in international tax cooperation should be universal in approach and scope, while fully taking into account of countries' different needs and capacities (United Nations, 2018a, chap. III.A, recommendation 1).

The need for long-term multilateral solutions

As digitalization expands, international tax systems should be reoriented towards taxing profits at the locations where activity is conducted and value is added

As digitalization expands, international tax systems should be reoriented towards taxing profits at the locations where activity is conducted and value is added. This principle was agreed by Heads of State and Government and High Representatives in the Addis Ababa Action Agenda. The discussion concerning the digitalization of the economy is particularly important now, because of the momentum gathered to revisit international tax rules and to reinstate the origin of wealth principle (OECD, 2018b)[20] and the concept of economic allegiance. A reinstatement would suggest that a taxpayer should be liable to tax in the jurisdiction where it is economically active, because that is the jurisdiction where the taxpayer enjoys the benefits of public infrastructure (BEPS Monitoring Group, 2017) and public goods (Schön, 2018).

Importantly, this may be the first time that the source versus residence split would not be synonymous with a split between developing and developed countries, or between industrialized and emerging economies, since all countries have an interest in averting the erosion of their respective tax bases and capturing a new revenue source (Falcão, 2018b) The prevalence of digitalized markets is occurring at a time when countries are rethinking their tax policies and reforming corporate income tax principles; there is therefore potential momentum for re-discussing the concepts introduced in the 1920s by the League of Nations.

There are different views on how to adapt international tax rules to the digitalization of the economy. Some experts doubt the desirability—or even the possibility—of ring-fencing digital companies for the purpose of designing special tax treatment. However, in recent policy debates, other experts have raised the prospect of adopting tax rules that would be restricted to specific business lines (United Nations, 2018a).

The challenge is how to align taxable profits with real economic activities and value creation in a digital economy

The challenge is how to align taxable profits with real economic activities and value creation in a digital economy. The objective is not to tax companies that are incidentally doing business in a foreign country, but rather to tax those that are undertaking substantial

19 General Assembly resolution 69/313, annex.

20 The origin of wealth principle was enunciated in a 1923 report commissioned by the League of Nations. In that report, the economists took a view that the place where the income is produced should be assigned a preponderant share of the tax revenue because that place should be considered the place of origin. See Report on Double Taxation submitted to the Financial Committee: Economic and Financial Commission Report by the Experts on Double Taxation—Document No. E.F.S.73.F.19 (5 April 1923). Available at http://adc.library.usyd.edu.au/view?docId=split/law/xml-main-texts/brulegi-source-bibl-1.xml;chunk.id=item-1;toc.depth=1;toc.id=item-1;database=;collection=;brand=default.

economic activity while engaging with the consumer market, making use of the country's local infrastructure, developing an interactive relationship with customers, or gathering data that can add value to the business.

The Committee of Experts on International Cooperation in Tax Matters has shown leadership on the taxation of cross-border services provision in international tax cooperation (Falcão, 2018b). The Committee of Experts has also established a subcommittee to consider necessary revisions to the United Nations Model Double Taxation Convention between Developed and Developing Countries as well as to provide revised guidance within the context of the digital economy (United Nations, 2018a). The Task Force on the Digital Economy is expected to present a final report by 2020. Any changes made to the provisions of either the United Nations or OECD model conventions as a result of this work will not automatically change the existing base of over 3,000 tax treaties or domestic practices unless Member States take action to incorporate them (United Nations, 2018a).

Current discussions and agreements on effective tax coordination at OECD and in the Committee of Experts can play an important role

Current discussions and agreements on effective tax coordination at OECD and in the Committee of Experts can play an important role in ensuring that global benefits accruing from new technologies are effectively harnessed to ensure progress towards achieving sustainable development in all countries. Currents debates in academia and not-for profit organizations can provide these discussions with food for thought.[21]

Developing countries may be especially hard hit by the complexities and revenue risks arising from digitalization as a result of constraints on human resources and limited access to technological resources. Strengthening national capacities to tax large technology firms, particularly in developing countries, could enable countries to fund national initiatives aimed at facilitating adoption and diffusion of relevant technologies. Strengthened national capacities—to analyse the increasing and accelerating flow of information and the calls for greater provision of such information would also be required.

Setting the appropriate standards and ethical boundaries

There is an opportunity to shape new technologies in ways that promote the common good

The rapid evolution of emerging and frontier technologies has created a unique opportunity to support the achievement of the SDGs. There exists a window of opportunity to shape new technologies in ways that promote the common good, prosperity and human dignity and protect the environment. A common message in the 2018 *Survey* is that technology is not an exogenous force. Instead, it can and should be guided by societal needs and policy prerogatives.

Thus far, it is the more advanced economies that have served as the sphere for many of the prominent ethics-related discussions on, and existing efforts to respond to the chal-

21 The BEPS Monitoring Group, which is an active contributor to the work of the United Nations and OECD, has contributed a public opinion on the criteria that it deems most suitable for the characterization of nexus and substantiality within the context of digitalization. The Tax Justice Network, the Independent Commission for the Reform of International Corporate Taxation (ICRICT) and the BEPS Monitoring Group are long-term supporters of formulary apportionment in substitution for traditional transfer pricing rules. Formulary apportionment rules would attribute to each country its appropriate share of profits from a transaction, based on a previously agreed mathematical formula that derives profit allocation from engagement in activity in a source State. The rationale is that multinational entities should be treated as a single economic group, which should not be separated into its constitutive branches.

lenges posed by, emerging technologies. However, the outcomes of many of these discussions and efforts are likely to affect all countries. Indeed, as the reach of the Internet and the importance of digital society continue to expand worldwide, these ethical discussions will be particularly crucial for the developing world (LaPointe, 2018).

Challenges for governance of emerging technologies

Governance of emerging technologies encompasses the laws, regulations and other rules to which they are subject. The questions how these rules are established and maintained, who is involved in the process of governance and how governance is executed have myriad ethical implications. The examples presented in this section complement the discussion presented in Chapter II.

Privacy and data governance

GDPR is an example of a regulation that increases privacy and data protections for citizens of the European Union

As discussed in chapter II, the General Data Protection Regulation (GDPR), which was agreed by the European Parliament and the Council of the European Union in April 2016, attests to the significant dimensions of technology governance. This sweeping regulation contains an array of increased privacy and data protections for European Union citizens, including breach notification and the introduction of the right to access, to be forgotten (through erasure of personal data) and to data portability (EUGDPR, n.d.). While the views are mixed on the possible societal and ethical implications of the GDPR, supporters of the regulation, such as the United States-based consumer advocacy group Consumer Action, argue that the GDPR will have a positive impact on consumer protection even beyond the EU (Susswein, 2018).

An extended—and heated—debate has been unfolding in the United States over the issue of network neutrality (familiarly referred to as "net neutrality"), and how the United States Government should regulate Internet service providers (LaPointe, 2018, p7). Supporters of net neutrality have argued that it is critical for free and open speech, whereas its critics have argued that it will put a damper on Internet innovation and investment (Knowledge@Wharton, 2017). The emotions stirred up by the issue of net neutrality prove just how significant the ability to codify or disrupt power dynamics through the rules governing emerging technologies is perceived to be.

Cybersecurity

There are significant challenges for Governments and law enforcement agencies in assuring a level of safety and security for citizens and entities with respect to cybercrimes

In the digital realm, there are significant challenges for Governments and law enforcement agencies in assuring a level of safety and security for citizens and entities with respect to cyber-crimes that is equivalent to that for other types of crime (Police Executive Research Forum, 2014). Cybercrimes are increasing worldwide, with developing countries facing particular challenges in combating both international and domestic attacks (Kshetri. 2010).

Ransomware attacks are a form of cyberattack which have been perpetrated successfully by hackers around the globe. In a ransomware attack, a hacker takes control of an individual's or an organization's computer system and data and prevents the victim from regaining access to and control over that data until a ransom is paid. In 2017, over 75,000 ransomware attacks occurred in 99 countries using the "WannaCry" ransomware (Larson, 2017). Government entities from across the globe have been attacked with ransomware as well. In 2018, the city of Atlanta, Georgia (United States) was held hostage by a ransomware strike for over a week, causing massive disruptions of government processes and services (Newman, 2018). Overall, whether they involve accessing private data or using ransomware to hold data hostage, cyberattacks on data and technology can have devastating ethics-related impacts.

Autonomous systems, human augmentation and cloning

Greater international cooperation is needed to prevent regulatory arbitrage

Ensuring the safe and predictable operation of physical autonomous systems is an important challenge (Zgrzebnicki, 2017). The challenge will amplify as these technologies proliferate and interactions between humans and robotic and autonomous systems increase (LaPointe, 2018, p. 16). Disparate legal and regulatory regimes in different jurisdictions and countries can drive the field-testing of such systems to locales with fewer testing restrictions, thereby transferring the risks of this testing to certain populations. Hence, greater international cooperation on the prevention of regulatory arbitrage will be required.

Human augmentation technologies—such as that underpinning the Hybrid Augmented Reality Multimodal Operation Neural Integration Environment (HARMONIE), a semi-autonomous hybrid brain-machine interface developed at Johns Hopkins University (Baltimore, Maryland), which uses a combination of eye tracking, computer vision and brain control to operate robotic upper-limb prosthetics—raise ethical considerations regarding increasingly integrated human-machine augmentation technologies (McMullen and others, 2014). Similarly, the advancing technological ability to clone species raises a host of ethical questions, especially as regards safety.

The United States National Human Genome Research Institute (2017) identifies three different types of cloning: gene cloning, reproductive cloning and therapeutic cloning. Gene cloning produces copies of genes or segments of DNA, while reproductive cloning produces copies of whole animals. Therapeutic cloning, on the other hand, produces embryonic stem cells for experiments aimed at creating tissue replacements for injured or diseased tissues (ibid.). Each type of cloning raises its own set of ethical issues and has its own set of implications. Notwithstanding the occasional spurious claims to the contrary, there is no proof that humans have ever yet been cloned (Ball, 2018). However, the debate over the potential of human cloning was reignited in 2018 after the cloning of two macaque monkeys in China (ibid.).

Unintended environmental impact of digital technologies

While emerging technologies hold promise for sustainable development, they can also create a complex web of negative environmental impacts

While emerging technologies hold promise for the achievement of sustainable development and, in particular, mitigating the environmental impacts of development, they can also create a complex web of negative environmental impacts (LaPointe, 2018). In an increasingly electronic- and digital-driven society, requirements for power as well as the demand for rare earth elements will increase. Rare earth materials and specialized metals are required for the production of many emerging technology devices such as mobile phones, laptops and electrical cars (Graedel and others, 2015). From mining to disposal, these materials can exert severe negative impacts on people.

In 2014, the United Nations University/StEP Initiative (2014) identified electronic waste containing hazardous or toxic substances as "one of the fastest growing waste streams globally". The volume of this waste and its handling and disposal in developing countries are the source of significant environmental and health hazards, particularly among vulnerable populations (Heacock and others, 2016). Increasing global digital inclusion is likely to exacerbate these environmental challenges.

International initiatives for governance of emerging technologies

Complementing various national efforts, international efforts and initiatives are emerging to address the challenges of data protection and privacy, algorithmic accountability, and autonomous systems and AI (LaPointe, 2018).

IEEE Global Initiative for Ethical Considerations in Artificial Intelligence and Autonomous Systems

The IEEE Standards Association launched its standards development initiative in 2016 in order "to move beyond both the fear and the uncritical admiration regarding autonomous and intelligent technologies", as well as align technologies both to foster innovation in the field and to diminish fear in the process (Karachalios, 2017). In addition to creating a recommendation guide entitled *Ethically Aligned Design: A Vision for Prioritizing Human Well-being with Artificial Intelligence and Autonomous Systems, Version 2* (IEEE Global Initiative for Ethical Considerations in Artificial Intelligence and Autonomous Systems, 2018), it has launched a series of standardization project working groups (ibid.; Karachalios, 2017).

Association for Computing Machinery (ACM) US Public Policy Council (USACM) statement on algorithmic transparency and accountability

The initiative adopted the set of seven principles (Association for Computing Machinery (ACM) US Public Policy Council (USACM, 2017)) to support algorithmic decision-making while addressing concerns regarding the inherent barriers to transparency in some algorithms and analytics and any resulting algorithmic bias and potential harmful discrimination. The seven principles comprise awareness, access and redress, accountability, explanation, data provenance, auditability and validation and testing.

Partnership on AI to benefit people and society

The Partnership on AI to benefit people and society (Partnership on AI)[22] was founded by a coalition of major technology companies including Amazon, Apple, DeepMind, Facebook, Google, IBM and Microsoft and now includes more than 50 members from industry, academia and the non-profit sector. The goals of the Partnership on AI include developing and sharing best practices, providing an open and inclusive platform for discussion and engagement, advancing public understanding, and identifying and fostering aspirational efforts within AI for socially beneficial purposes.

Opportunities for international cooperation and the role of the United Nations

There are significant opportunities for international engagement and cooperation on embedding an ethical approach in the design, deployment, implementation and governance of emerging technologies.

22 See www.partnershiponai.org.

Digital rights and data governance

The Internet and the digital economy are fundamentally altering the manner in which people connect across society. Therefore, it is important that the definition of fundamental human rights evolves within the digital context—an issue that is being addressed by the United Nations in various forums. However, with the increased scope of the exposure of individuals to harm in the digital space leveraging multilateral action to proactively define and protect digital human rights has become a matter of urgency.

The definition of fundamental human rights in the digital context is being addressed by the United Nations

With the increasing abundance of digital data and their importance to people and communities, international cooperation would be helpful in developing uniform standards for data governance, which should address data collection, verification, provenance, maintenance, ownership, control and security (LaPointe, 2018). As a patchwork of various laws, regulations, principles and guidelines exists across the globe, multilateral cooperation is necessary for developing a definitive global standard which will guide actions of data professionals and any entities interacting with data. The creation of universal professional ethical standards or a code of conduct for data professionals could be included as a component of the data governance standards development process.

Principles for ethical development of technology

Multilateral cooperation could build on the previous work carried out by standards organizations and coalitions of stakeholders to develop comprehensive and widely accepted principles for the ethical development of technology in the digital era. The United Nations can leverage its convening power to bring Member States and all relevant stakeholders together to adopt a global consensus on legal and ethical standards for guiding research on and development of frontier technologies. Technological advances must include a respect for universally held ethical and human rights standards. The United Nations—given its universal membership and unwavering commitment to human values—is uniquely positioned to facilitate a dialogue among all stakeholders and the development of a global ethical compact for managing the advances in frontier technologies.

The United Nations can leverage its convening power to bring Member States and all relevant stakeholders together to adopt a global consensus on legal and ethical standards for guiding research on and development of frontier technologies

Forging global collective action: the role of the United Nations

While many frontier technologies present immense opportunities for fostering sustainable development, they also pose considerable risks. A global dialogue, involving all stakeholders, is needed to identify those risks and opportunities. The United Nations can serve as an impartial facilitator among Governments, the private sector and civil society organizations for the presentation of objective assessments of the impact of emerging technologies on sustainable development outcomes, including on employment, wages and income distribution.

Existing initiatives

The United Nations is playing a leading role in forging an understanding of emerging technologies and bridging the technology divide

The multi-stakeholder forum on science, technology and innovation for the SDGs is a platform dedicated to forging a common understanding among scientists, policymakers and the private sector and promoting tangible development results. It is playing an increasingly important role in fostering an understanding of emerging technologies and bridging the technology divide. The quinquennial United Nations Conferences to Review All Aspects of the Set of Multilaterally Agreed Equitable Principles and Rules for the Control of Restrictive Business Practices (the UN Set) is an important United Nations initiative designed to facilitate an exchange of views on competition-related issues. The Committee of Experts on International Cooperation in Tax Matters is an important forum for consensus building on international taxation between developed and developing countries.

Both the Commission on Science and Technology for Development and the Technology Bank, which helps the least developed countries navigate the domain of new technologies, address the challenges associated with bridging the technology divide. The World Summit on the Information Society Forum and the Artificial Intelligence for Good Global Summit, both organized by the International Telecommunication Union, constitute other important United Nations initiatives whose aim is to facilitate an understanding of relevant technologies and their sustainable development impact, which includes addressing some of the dimensions of the technology divide.

The United Nations is invested in enhancing capacity development for science, technology and innovation

Several United Nations agencies have also invested considerably in enhancing capacity development for science, technology and innovation. Some of those agencies have developed guidelines and e-learning tools, created new training mechanisms such as academies and virtual institutes, implemented pilot projects in volunteering and capacity-building, and carried out technical assistance initiatives to enhance capacities in the field of technology and innovation (United Nations, 2018a). Table V.2 provides an overview of efforts in this regard up until 2017.

Table V.2

Overview of engagement by United Nations system entities in "frontier" domains

Categories	Subcategories	Number of initiatives
Digital technology initiatives	Artificial intelligence	35
	Nanotechnology and virtual reality	26
	Internet of things	2
	E-government	4
	Digital finance	7
	Cloud computing	3
	General digital technology/data-related issues (data collection)	112
	Transportation and mobility systems	3
	Climate tech and data	3
	Combinations of frontier technologies	13
Health and biological technologies initiatives	Biotechnology and genomics	10
	Health and drug delivery	14
Energy and material technology initiatives	Renewables and energy storage	12
	Innovation, tech and manufacturing	4
Other technologies	Nuclear	5
	Space	8
	Basic Internet, ICT and cybersecurity	39
	E-commerce	3
Total number of initiatives overall:		287

Source: UN/DESA, based on United Nations System Chief Executives Board for Coordination secretariat (2017).
Note: Initiatives may be double-counted when they belong to more than one category.

Harnessing new technologies: a vision for the future

As indicated in the report of the Secretary-General entitled "Harnessing new technologies to achieve the Sustainable Development Goals" (United Nations, Economic and Social Council, 2018), the United Nations has an important role to play in supporting Member States and other stakeholders in addressing new policy and normative challenges, in particular those directly affecting the central purposes and principles of the Organization and for which collective global responses are necessary.

The United Nations supports Member States and other stakeholders in addressing the challenges that they confront in harnessing new technologies to achieve the SDGs

In this context, the Secretary General has identified five elements central to guiding efforts towards strengthening the engagement of the United Nations system with new technologies in the years ahead:

The Secretary-General has identified five elements central to the engagement of the United Nations system with new technologies

(a) *Protection and promotion of global values.* United Nations engagement with new technologies and the policy issues they raise will be anchored in the values and obligations defined by the Charter of the United Nations and the Universal Declaration of Human Rights[23] and through the realization of the SDGs. At the heart of these standards are values such as equality and equity. These should be the guiding principles in every action undertaken with regard to new technologies;

(b) *Fostering of inclusion and transparency.* Our engagement must ensure that the United Nations remains a trusted venue within which Governments, industry, academia and civil society, among others, can come together to make collective choices regarding new technologies openly, transparently and based on shared values. There must be a greater openness to new ideas and new voices, which challenge institutional business-as-usual reflexes and allow the United Nations to engage credibly with partners. This will include a significant role for youth, who have a unique interest in these choices, building on the work of the Secretary-General's Envoy on Youth;

(c) *Working in partnership.* Effective engagement on new technologies clearly requires close partnership with a range of government, industry, academic and civil society partners. This is especially true, as the private sector is driving much of the progress on development of those technologies;

(d) *Building on existing capabilities and mandates*: Engagement with new technologies should be viewed as a necessary component of successful mandate implementation – not as a new mandate. For this to be achieved, the significant efforts currently under way across the system must be added to and reinforced, alongside ongoing reform efforts;

(e) *Practising humility and engagement in continuous learning*: For many in industry, some in civil society and some Governments, the United Nations is not an obvious interlocutor within the context of emerging technologies. As our collective engagement is broadened and, indeed, even as all actors are being reminded of their shared commitments and obligations, we must be prepared to acknowledge what we do not know in this complex field. We must learn to incentivize an innovative culture in which both successes and failures arising from exposure to new technologies are a source of understanding and a guide to our contribution to policy dialogues. With this goal in mind, we will constantly adjust our actions as we go about learning how we can best engage with technology in support of Member States' technological transformations.

23 General Assembly resolution 217 A (III).

Bibliography

A

Acemoglu, Daron (2000). Labor- and capital-augmenting technical change. *NBER Working Paper*, No. 7544. Cambridge, Massachusetts: National Bureau of Economic Research.

________, and David Autor (2011). Skills, tasks and technologies: Implications for employment and earnings. *Handbook of Labor Economics*, vol. 4B, chap. 12, pp. 1043–1171.

Acemoglu, Daron, and Pascual Restrepo (2017). Robots and jobs: Evidence from US labor markets. *NBER Working Paper*, No. 23285. Cambridge, Massachusetts National Bureau of Economic Research.

________ (2018a). Artificial intelligence, automation and work. *NBER Working Paper*, No. 24196. Cambridge, Massachusetts: National Bureau of Economic Research.

________ (2018b). The race between machine and man: implications of technology for growth, factor shares and employment. *American Economic Review*, vol. 108, No. 6 (June), pp. 1488–1542.

Acemoglu, Daron, and James A. Robinson (2000). Political losers as a barrier to economic development. *American Economic Review*, vol. 90, No. 2 (May), pp.126–130.

Association for Computing Machinery (ACM) US Public Policy Council (USACM) (2017). Statement on algorithmic transparency and accountability. Washington, D.C., 12 January.

Agrawal, Ajay, Christian Catalini and Avi Goldfarb (2014). Some simple economics of crowdfunding. *NBER Innovation Policy and the Economy*, vol. 14, No. 1 (January), pp. 63–97.

Ahlborg, Helene, and Linus Hammar (2014). Drivers and barriers to rural electrification in Tanzania and Mozambique: grid extension, off-grid, and renewable energy technologies. *Renewable Energy*, vol. 61 (January), pp.117–124.

Aker, Jenny C., and Marcel Fafchamps (2015). Mobile phone coverage and producer markets: evidence from West Africa. *World Bank Economic Review*, vol. 29, No. 2 (January), pp. 262–292. Available at https://academic.oup.com/wber/article-abstract/29/2/262/1661486?redirectedFrom=fulltext.

Aker, Jenny C., Christopher Ksoll and Travis J. Lybbert (2012). Can mobile phones improve learning? evidence from a field experiment in Niger. *American Economic Journal: Applied Economics*, vol. 3, No. 4 (October), pp. 94–120. Available at https://www.aeaweb.org/articles?id=10.1257/app.4.4.94.

Ali, Feroz, and Sudarsan Rajagopal (2017). How India rejects bad patents. *Hindu*, 27 December. Available at http://www.thehindu.com/opinion/op-ed/how-india-rejects-bad-patents/article22282403.ece.

Alvaredo, Facundo, and others (2018). *World Inequality Report 2018*. Developed by World Inequality Lab, Paris School of Economics. Available at http://wir2018.wid.world/.

Angwin, Julia, and Terry Parris, Jr. (2016). Facebook lets advertisers exclude users by race. ProPublica. 26 October. Available at www.propublica.org/article/facebook-lets-advertisers-exclude-users-by-race.

Angwin, Julia, Ariana Tobin and Madeleine Varner (2017). Facebook (still) letting housing advertisers exclude users by race. ProPublica. 21 November. Available at https://www.propublica.org/article/facebook-advertising-discrimination-housing-race-sex-national-origin.

Angwin, Julia, and others (2016). Machine bias. Propublica. 23 May. Available at https://www.propublica.org/article/machine-bias-risk-assessments-in-criminal-sentencing.

Arntz, Melanie, Terry Gregory and Ulrich Zierahn (2016). The risk of automation for jobs in OECD countries: a comparative analysis. *OECD Social, Employment and Migration Working* Paper, No. 189. Paris: OECD.

Aron, Jacob (2015). Forget the Turing test: there are better ways of judging AI. *New Scientist*, Technology news. September 21, 2015. Available at www.newscientist.com/article/dn28206-forget-the-turing-test-there-are-better-ways-of-judging-ai/.

Arpaia, Alfonso, Esther Pérez and Karl Pichelmann (2009). *Understanding Labour Income Share Dynamics in Europe. European Economy Economic Paper,* No. 379 (May). Brussels: European Commission Directorate-General for Economic and Financial Affairs.

Artificial Intelligence Index (2017) *2017 Annual Report.* November. Available at https://aiindex.org.

Atkin, David, and others (2017). Organizational barriers to technology adoption: evidence from soccer-ball producers in Pakistan. *Quarterly Journal of Economics*, vol. 132, No. 3 (1 August), pp. 1101–1164.

Aubert, Jean-Eric (2005). Promoting innovation in developing countries: a conceptual framework. World Bank Policy Research Working Paper, No. 3554. Washington, D.C.

Aubin, Charlotte (2018). Accelerating Africa's energy transition. Project Syndicate, 11 January. Available at https://www.project-syndicate.org/commentary/africa-renewables-solar-economic-incentives-by-charlotte-aubin-2018-01.

Aunemo, Helga (2015). *Implementing Off-Grid Solar Solutions in Southeast Asia. A CSR-based Approach to Rural Development.* Trondheim, Norway: Norwegian University of Science and Technology. July.

Autor, David H. (2015). Why are there still so many jobs? the history and future of workplace automation. *Journal of Economic Perspectives*, vol. 29, No. 3, (summer), pp. 3–30.

________, and David Dorn (2013). The Growth of low-skill service jobs and the polarization of the US labor market. *American Economic Review*, vol. 103, No. 5, pp. 1553–1597.

Autor, David H., Lawrence F. Katz and Melissa S. Kearney (2006). The polarization of the U.S. labor market, *American Economic Review*, vol. 96, No. 2 (February), pp. 189–194.

Autor, David H., Frank Levy and Richard J. Murnane (2003). The skill content of recent technological change: an empirical exploration. *Quarterly Journal of Economics*, vol. 118, No. 4, pp. 1279–1333.

Autor, David, and others (2017). The fall of the labor share and the rise of superstar firms. *NBER Working Paper*, No. 23396. Cambridge, Massachusetts: National Bureau of Economic Research. May.

Azadi, Hossein, and Peter Ho (2010). Genetically modified and organic crops in developing countries: a review of options for food security. *Biotechnology Advances*, vol. 28, No. 1 (January-February), pp. 160–168.

B

Baidawi, Adam (2017). Australia powers up the world's biggest battery - courtesy of Elon Musk. *New York Times*, 30 November. Available at www.nytimes.com/2017/11/30/world/australia/elon-musk-south-australia-battery.html.

Baker, Dean, Arjun Jayadev and Joseph Stiglitz (2017). *Innovation, Intellectual Property, and Development: A Better Set of Approaches for the 21st Century*. AccessIBSA: Innovation & Access to Medicines in India, Brazil & South Africa. July.

Bala, Venkatesh, and Sanjeev Goyal (2001). Conformism and diversity under social learning. *Economic Theory*, vol. 17, No. 1 (January), pp. 101–120.

Baldwin, Richard (2016). *The Great Convergence: Information Technology and the New Globalization*. Cambridge, Massachusetts: Belknap Press.

Ball, Philip (2018). How afraid of human cloning should we be? *Guardian*, 25 January.

Barry, Marie-Louise, Herman Steyn and Alan Brent (2011). Selection of renewable energy technologies for Africa: eight case studies in Rwanda, Tanzania and Malawi. *Renewable Energy*, vol. 36, No. 11 (November), pp. 2845–2852.

Baumol, William J. (1986). Productivity growth, convergence, and welfare: what the long-run data show. *American Economic Review*, vol. 76, No. 5 (December), pp. 1072–1085.

Beatty, John (2011). The European patent office 'Raising the Bar' initiative. *World Patent Information*, vol. 33, No. 4 (December), pp. 355–359. Available at www.sciencedirect.com/science/article/pii/S0172219011001001.

Beaudry, Paul, David A. Greeny and Benjamin M. Sand (2013). The great reversal in the demand for skill and cognitive tasks. *NBER Working Paper*, No. 18901. Cambridge, Massachusetts: National Bureau of Economic Research. March.

Behavioural Insights Team. 2016. *The Behavioural Insights Team Update Report 2016–17*. London.

Bell, Alexander M., and others (2017). Who becomes an inventor in America? the importance of exposure to innovation. *NBER Working Paper*, No. 24062. Cambridge, Massachusetts: National Bureau of Economic Research. November.

BenYishay, Ariel, and A. Mushfiq Mobarak (2014). Social learning and communication. *NBER Working Paper*, No. 20139. Cambridge, Massachusetts: National Bureau of Economic Research. May.

________ (2015). Social learning and incentives for experimentation and communication. *Review of Economic Studies*, 30 July.

Benhabib, Jess, Jesse Perla and Christopher Tonetti (2017). Reconciling models of diffusion and innovation: a theory of the productivity distribution and technology frontier. *NBER Working Paper*, No. 23095. Cambridge, Massachusetts: National Bureau of Economic Research.

BEPS Monitoring Group (2017). Comments on the tax challenges of digitilisation, submitted in response primarily to the request for inputs, part I, issued by the Task Force on the Digital Economy, set up under the G20/OECD project on Base Erosion and Profit Shifting (BEPS). 17 October. Available at https://bepsmonitoringgroup.files.wordpress.com/2017/10/digital-economy.pdf. Comments of all submitting organizations are contained in the document entitled *Tax Challenges of Digitilisation: Comments Received on the Request for Input: Part I.* 25 October. Available at www.oecd.org/tax/beps/tax-challenges-digitalisation-part-1-comments-on-request-for-input-2017.pdf.

Berger, T., and C. Frey (2016). Structural transformation in the OECD: digitalisation, deindustrialisation and the future of work. *OECD Social, Employment and Migration Working Papers*, No. 193. Paris: OECD.

Berman, Eli, and Stephen Machin (2000). Skill-biased technology transfer around the world. *Oxford Review of Economic Policy*, vol. 16, No. 1, pp. 12–22.

Blair, Roger D., and Sokol D. Daniel (2013). Welfare standards in U.S. and E.U. antitrust enforcement. *Fordham Law Review*, vol. 81, No. 5, art. 12.

Blomström, Magnus, and Ari Kokko (1998). Multinational corporations and spillovers. *Journal of Economic Surveys*, vol. 12, No. 3 (July), pp. 247–77.

Bloom, Nicholas, and John Van Reenen (2007). Measuring and explaining management practices across firms and countries. *Quarterly Journal of Economics*, vol. 122, No. 4 (November), pp.1351–1408.

Bond, Eric W., and Kamai Saggi (2016). Compulsory licensing and patent protection: a North-South perspective. *Economic Journal*, vol. 128, No. 610 (May), pp. 1157–1179.

Brody, Ben (2018). Google topped peers in lobbying as Washington beat up tech. Bloomberg, 24 January. Available at https://www.bloomberg.com/news/articles/2018-01-24/google-outspends-tech-rivals-on-washington-lobbying-in-2017.

Brousseau, Eric, Tom Dedeurwaerdere and Bernd Siebenhüner (2012). Knowledge matters: institutional frameworks to govern the provision of global public goods. In *Reflexive Governance and Global Public Goods*, Eric Brousseau, Tom Dedeurwaerdere and Bernd Sebenhüner, eds. Cambridge, Massachusetts: MIT Press. Chap. 13, pp. 243–282.

Brown, Julia K., Tetyana Zelenska and Mushfiq A. Mobarak (2013). Barriers to adoption of products and technologies that aid risk management in developing countries. Background paper prepared for *World Development Report 2014*.

Bruckner, Matthias, Marcelo LaFleur and Ingo Pitterle (2017). The Impact of the technological revolution on labour markets and income distribution. Frontier Issues. Department of Economic and Social Affairs of the United Nations Secretariat. Available at www.un.org/development/desa/dpad/publication/frontier-issues-artificial-intelligence-and-other-technologies-will-define-the-future-of-jobs-and-incomes/.

Bruckner, Thomas, and others (2014). Energy systems. In *Climate Change 2014: Mitigation of Climate Change*. Working Group III Contribution to the Fifth Assessment Report of the Intergovernmental Panel on Climate Change, Ottmar Edenhofer and others, eds., Cambridge, United Kingdom: Cambridge University Press

Bryane, Michael (2013). Emerging market winners and losers in manufacturing. IEMS Emerging Market Brief, vol. 13-06 (August). Moscow School of Management (SKOLKOVO) Institute for Emerging Market Studies (IEMS).

Brynjolfsson, Erik (2011). ICT, innovation and the e-economy. *EIB Papers*, vol. 16, No. 2, pp. 60–76. Luxembourg: European Investment Bank.

________, and Andrew McAfee (2011). *Race against the Machine: How the Digital Revolution is Accelerating Innovation, Driving Productivity, and Irreversibly Transforming Employment and the Economy*. Lexington, Massachusetts: Digital Frontier Press.

________ (2014). *The Second Machine Age: Work, Progress, and Prosperity in a Time of Brilliant Technologies*. New York: W.W. Norton.

________ (2017). The business of artificial intelligence. *Harvard Business Review*. July 2017.

Bugaje, I.M. (2006). Renewable energy for sustainable development in Africa: a review. *Renewable and Sustainable Energy Reviews*, vol. 10, No. 6 (December), pp. 603–612.

Burrone, Esteban (n.d.). Standards, intellectual property rights (IPR) and standards-setting process. Geneva: World Intellectual Property Organization. Available at http://www.wipo.int/sme/en/documents/ip_standards_fulltext.html.

C

Campolo, Alex, and others (2017). *AI Now 2017 Report*. New York: AI Now Institute, *New York University*.

Chakravorti, Bhaskar, and Ravi Shankar Chaturvedi (2017). *Digital Planet 2017: How Competitiveness and Trust in Digital Economies Vary Across the World*. Medford, Massachusetts: Institute for Business in the Global Context, Fletcher School. Tufts University. July.

Cirera, Xavier, and William F. Maloney (2017). *The Innovation Paradox: Developing-Country Capabilities and the Unrealized Promise of Technological Catch-Up*. Washington, D.C.: World Bank.

Citi GPS and Oxford Martin School (2017). *Technology at Work v3.0. Automating e-Commerce from Click to Pick to Door*. August.

Ciurzyńska, Agnieszka, and Andrzej Lenart (2011). Freeze-drying: application in food processing and biotechnology – a review, in *Polish Journal of Food and Nutrition Sciences,* vol. 61, No. 3, pp. 165–171.

Cohn, Pamela, and others (2017). Commercial drones are here: the future of unmanned aerial systems. McKinsey & Company. Available at www.mckinsey.com/industries/capital-projects-and-infrastructure/our-insights/commercial-drones-are-here-the-future-of-unmanned-aerial-systems.

Collumbien, Martine, Makeda Gerressu and John Cleland (2004). Non-use and use of ineffective methods of contraception. In *Comparative Quantification of Health Risks: Global and Regional Burden of Disease Attributable to Selected Major Risk Factors*, Majid Ezzati and others, eds. Geneva: World Health Organization. Vol. 2, chap. 15.

Comin, Diego, and Bart Hobijn (2004). Cross-country technology adoption: making the theories face the facts. *Journal of Monetary* Economics, vol. 51, No. 1 (January), pp. 39–83.

________ (2010). An exploration of technology diffusion. *American Economic Review,* vol. 100. No. 5 (December), pp. 2031–2059.

Comin, Diego, and Martí Mestieri Ferrer (2010). The intensive margin of technology adoption. Harvard Business School Working Paper, No. 11-206.

________ (2013). If technology has arrived everywhere, why has income diverged? *NBER Working Paper,* No. 19010. Cambridge, Massachusetts: National Bureau of Economic Research.

________ (2014). Technology diffusion: measurement, causes, and consequences. In *Handbook of Economic Growth,* vol. 2, Philippe Aghion and Steven Durlauf, eds. Pp. 565–622.

Conley, Timothy G., and Christopher R. Udry (2010). Learning about a new technology: pineapple in Ghana. *American Economic Review,* vol. 100, No. 1 (March), pp. 35-69.

Conte, Andrea, and Marco Vivarelli (2011). Imported skill-biased technological change in developing countries. *Developing Economies,* vol. 49, No. 1 (March), pp. 36–65.

Cortez, Ana Luiza, and Mehmet Arda (2015). Global trade rules for supporting development in the post-2015 era. In *Global Governance and Rules for the* Post-*2015 Era: Addressing Emerging Issues in the Global Environment,* Jose Antonio Alonso and José Antonio Ocampo, eds. New York: Bloomsbury.

Crescenzi, Riccardo, and Andrés Rodríguez-Pose (2017). The geography of innovation in China and India. *International Journal of Urban and Regional Research,* vol. 41, No. 6 (November), pp. 1010–1027.

D

Daar, Abdallah S., and others (2007). How can developing countries harness biotechnology to improve health? *BMC Public Health,* vol. 7, No. 1 (February), pp. 1–9.

Derviş, K. (2012). World economy convergence, interdependence, and divergence: growth in emerging market and developing economies is less dependent on advanced economies over the long run, but in the short run they dance together. *Finance and Development*, vol. 49, No. 3 (September), pp. 10–14.

Diouf, Boucar, and Ramchandra Pode (2015). Potential of lithium-ion batteries in renewable energy. *Renewable Energy*, vol. 76 (April), pp. 375–380.

Domingos, Pedro (2015). *The Master Algorithm: How the Quest for the Ultimate Learning Machine Will Remake Our World*. New York: Basic Books.

Dormehl, Luke (2017). *Thinking Machines. The Quest for Artificial Intelligence and Where It's Taking Us Next*. New York: Tarcher Perigee.

Dosi, Giovanni, Luigi Marengo and Corrado Pasquali (2007). Knowledge, competition and innovation: is strong IPR protection really needed for more and better innovations? *Michigan Telecommunications and Technology Law. Review*, vol. 13, No. 2.

E

The Economist (2015). Africa: a brightening continent – solar is giving hundreds of millions of Africans access to electricity for the first time. 17 January. Available at https://www.economist.com/special-report/2015/01/15/a-brightening-continent.

________ (2017). 3D printers start to build factories of the future. 29 June. Available at https://www.economist.com/briefing/2017/06/29/3d-printers-start-to-build-factories-of-the-future.

El-Bermawy Mostata M. (2016). Your filter bubble is destroying democracy. *Wired* opinion. Available at https://www.wired.com/2016/11/filter-bubble-destroying-democracy/.

Ellabban, Omar, Haitham Abu-Rub and Frede Blaabjerg (2014). Renewable energy resources: current status, future prospects and their enabling technology. *Renewable and Sustainable Energy Reviews*, vol. 39 (November), pp. 748–764.

Eller, Alex, and Dexter Gauntlett (2017). *Energy Storage Trends and Opportunities in Emerging Markets*. Conference edition report, commissioned by International Finance Corporation, World Bank Group; and Energy Sector Management Assistance Program. Boulder, Colorado: Navigant Consulting. Available at https://www.ifc.org/wps/wcm/connect/ed6f9f7f-f197-4915-8ab6-56b92d50865d/7151-IFC-EnergyStorage-report.pdf?MOD=AJPERES.

Eubanks, Virginia (2018). *Automating Inequality: How High-Tech Tools Profile, Police, and Punish the Poor*. New York: St. Martin's Press.

EUGDPR (n.d.). GDPR key changes: an overview of the main changes under GDPR and how they differ from the previous directive. Available at https://www.eugdpr.org/key-changes.html.

European Commission (2016). Policy labs: innovative take of public administrations for better policies. EU Science Hub. Available at https://ec.europa.eu/jrc/en/news/policy-labs-innovative-take-public-administrations-better-policies.

________ (2018). 2018 reform of EU data protection rules: stronger rules on data protection mean people have more control over their personal data and businesses benefit from a level playing field. Available at https://ec.europa.eu/commission/priorities/justice-and-fundamental-rights/data-protection/2018-reform-eu-data-protection-rules_en.www.eugdpr.org/key-changes.html.

Ezrachi, Ariel, and Maurice E. Stucke (2016). *Virtual Competition: The Promise and Perils of the Algorithm-Driven Economy.* Cambridge, Massachusetts: Harvard University Press.

F

Fagerberg, Jan, and Manuel M. Godinho (2006). Innovation and catching-up. In *The Oxford Handbook of Innovation*, Jan Fagerberg and David C. Mowery, eds. Oxford: Oxford University Press.

Falcão, Tatiana (2018a). New technologies and international tax cooperation. Background Paper prepared for *World Economic and Social Survey 2018*.

________ (2018b). Taxing the digital economy: policy considerations and how to advance the debate. *Tax Notes International*, 12 February 2018, p. 623.

Feenstra, Robert, Robert Inklaar and Marcel Timmer (2015). The next generation of the Penn World Table. *American Economic Review*, vol. 105. No.10, pp. 3150–3182.

Food and Agriculture Organization of the United Nations (FAO) (2011). *Biotechnologies for Agricultural Development: Proceedings of the FAO International Technical Conference on "Agricultural Biotechnologies in Developing Countries: Options and Opportunities in Crops, Forestry, Livestock, Fisheries and Agro-industry to Face the Challenges of Food Insecurity and Climate Change"*. Rome.

Frey, Carl Benedikt, and Michael A. Osborne (2013). The future of employment: how susceptible are jobs to computerisation? Oxford: Oxford Martin School, University of Oxford. 17 September.

Fu, Xiaolan, Carlo Pietrobelli and Luc Soete (2011). The role of foreign technology and indigenous innovation in the emerging economies: technological change and catching-up. *World Development*, vol. 39, No. 7 (July), pp.1204–1212.

Fu, Xiaolan, and Jing Zhang. (2011). Technology transfer, indigenous innovation and leapfrogging in green technology: the solar-PV industry in China and India, *Journal of Chinese Economic and Business Studies*, vol. 9, No. 4, pp. 329–347.

Fujii, Hemichi, and Shunsuke Managi (2017). Trends and priority shifts in artificial intelligence technology invention: a global patent analysis. RIETI Discussion Paper. No. 17-E-066. Tokyo: Research Institute of Economy, Trade and Industry.

Fukase, Emiko, and Will Martin (2017). Economic growth, convergence, and world food demand and supply. World Bank Policy Research Working Paper, No. 8257. Washington, D.C.

Furman, Jason, and others (2016). *Artificial Intelligence, Automation, and the Economy.* Washington, D.C.: Executive Office of the President of the United States. Available at https://obamawhitehouse.archives.gov/sites/whitehouse.gov/files/documents/Artificial-Intelligence-Automation-Economy.PDF.

Future of Privacy Forum (2017). Unfairness by algorithm: distilling the harms of automated decision-making. Washington, D.C. Available at https://fpf.org/2017/12/11/unfairness-by-algorithm-distilling-the-harms-of-automated-decision-making/.

G

Gal, Michal S. (2013). Merger policy for small and micro jurisdictions. In *More Pros and Cons of Merger Control.* Stockholm: Swedish Competition Authority.

Gay, Daniel (2018). Pharmaceutical dreams: TRIPS and drugs policy in Bangladesh. Available at https://emergenteconomics.com.

Gerschenkron, Alexander (1962). *Economic Backwardness in Historical Perspective: A Book of Essays.* Cambridge, Massachusetts: Belknap Press

Ghosh, Jayati (2016). Ideas on the future of work. Presentation at a discussion organized by the International Labour Organization on the future of work and the implications of technology on jobs. YouTube. 5 February 2016. Available at www.youtube.com/watch?v=L5W-iJyzBMY.

Goñi, Edwin, and William Maloney (2017). Why don't poor countries do R&D? varying rates of factor returns across the development process. *European Economic Review,* vol. 94, Issue C (May): pp. 126–147.

Goos, Maarten, Alan Manning and Anna Salomons (2014). Explaining job polarization: routine-biased technological change and offshoring. *American Economic Review,* vol. 104, No. 8 (August), pp. 2509–2526.

Görg, Holger, and Eric Strobl (2001). Multinational companies and productivity spillovers: a meta-analysis. *Economic Journal,* vol. 111, No. 475 (November), pp. F723–F739.

Graedel, T. E., and others (2015). On the materials basis of modern society. *Proceedings of the National Academy of Sciences of the United States* of *America,* vol. 112, No. 20 (19 May), pp. 6295–6300.

Graetz, Georg, and Guy Michaels (2015). Robots at work. CEPR Discussion Paper, No. 10477. London: Centre for Economic Policy Research. March.

Gruber, Harald, and Pantelis Koutroumpis (2010). Mobile communications: diffusion facts and prospects. *Communications and Strategies,* No. 77, pp. 133–145.

Guerreiro, Joao, Sergio Rebelo and Pedro Teles (2018). Should robots be taxed? *NBER Working Paper,* No. 23806. Cambridge, Massachusetts: National Bureau of Economic Research.

Gupta, Sanjeev, and others (2017). *Digital Revolutions in Public Finance.* Washington, D.C.: International Monetary Fund.

Gurib-Fakim, Ameenah, and Jacobus Nicolaas Eloff, eds. (2013). *Chemistry for Sustainable Development in Africa.* Heidelberg, Germany: Springer-Verlag.

H

Haider, Alexander (2018). Potentials and perils of new technologies in poor and vulnerable countries on their path to sustainable development. Background paper prepared for *World Economic and Social Survey 2018*.

Halberstam, Yosh, and Brian Knight (2014). Homophily, group size, and the diffusion of political information in social networks: evidence from Twitter. *NBER Working Paper*, No. 20681. Cambridge, Massachusetts: National Bureau of Economic Research. November.

Hall, Bronwyn H. (2006). Innovation and diffusion. In *The Oxford Handbook of Innovation*, Jan Fagerberg and David C. Mowery, eds. Oxford: Oxford University Press.

Hallward-Driemeier, Mary, and Gaurav Nayyar (2018). *Trouble in the Making? The Future of Manufacturing-Led Development.* Washington, D.C.: World Bank.

Harney, Kenneth R. (2008). Zip code "redlining": a sweeping view of risk. *Washington Post.* 2 February.

Hausmann, Ricardo (2017). Making the future work for us. Project Syndicate, 29 September 29. Available at https://www.project-syndicate.org/commentary/technology-future-of-work-by-ricardo-hausmann-2017-09.

Hawkins, Troy R., Ola Moa Gausen and Anders Hammer Strømman (2012). Environmental impacts of hybrid and electric vehicles: a review. *International Journal of Life Cycle Assessment*, vol. 17, No. 8 (September), pp. 997–1014. Available at https://www. epa.gov/ghgemissions/understanding-global-warming-potentials.

Heacock, Michelle, and others (2016). E-waste and harm to vulnerable populations: a growing global problem. *Environmental Health Perspectives*, vol. 124, No. 5 (May), pp. 550–555.

Helmy, Mohamed, Mohamed Awad and Kareem A. Mosa (2016). Limited resources of genome sequencing in developing countries: challenges and solutions. *Applied and Translational Genomics*, vol. 9 (Supplement C): pp. 15–19.

Hempling, Scott (2014), "Regulatory capture": sources and solutions. *Emory Corporate Governance and Accountability Review*, vol. 1, No. 1. Available at http://law.emory.edu/ecgar/content/volume-1/issue-1/essays/regulatory-capture.html.

Henna, Rema, Sendhil Mullainathan and Joshua Schwartzstein (2014). Learning through noticing: theory and evidence from a field experiment. *Quarterly Journal of Economics*, vol. 129, No. 3 (1 August), pp. 1311-1353.

Hidalgo, César A., and Ricardo Hausmann (2009). The building blocks of economic complexity. *Proceeding of the National Academy of Sciences of the United States of America*, vol. 106, No. 26 (30 June), pp. 10570-10575.

Hindu (2017). How India rejects bad patents. 27 December. Available at http://www.thehindu.com/opinion/op-ed/how-india-rejects-bad-patents/article22282403.ece.

Hutchinson, John, and Damiaan Persyn (2012). Globalisation, concentration and footloose firms: in search of the main cause of the declining labour share, *Review of World Economics*, vol. 148, No. 1 (April), pp. 17–43.

I

IEEE Global Initiative for Ethical Considerations in Artificial Intelligence and Autonomous Systems (2018). *Ethically Aligned Design: A Vision for Prioritizing Human Well-being with Autonomous and Intelligent Systems, Version 2.* Available at https://standards.ieee.org/develop/indconn/ec/autonomous_systems.html.

Ince, David, Harrie Vredenburg and Xiaoyu Liu (2016). Drivers and inhibitors of renewable energy: a qualitative and quantitative study of the Caribbean, *Energy Policy*, vol. 98 (C), pp. 700–712.

Innovations for Poverty Action (2011). Increasing demand for hygienic latrines in Bangladesh. Policy brief. New Haven, Connecticut.

Intergovernmental Panel on Climate Change (IPCC) (2014a). *Climate Change 2014: Synthesis Report.* Contribution of Working Groups I, II and III to the Fifth Assessment Report of the Intergovernmental Panel on Climate Change, Rajendra K. Pachauri and Leo Mayer, eds. Geneva. Available at www.ipcc.ch/pdf/assessment-report/ar5/syr/SYR_AR5_FINAL_full.pdf.

________ (2014b). Summary for Policymakers. In *Climate Change 2014: Mitigation of Climate Change.* Contribution of Working Group III to the Fifth Assessment Report of the Intergovernmental Panel on Climate Change, O. Edenhofer and others, eds. Cambridge, United Kingdom: Cambridge University Press.

International Council on Clean Transportation (2016). Proposed temporary management regulation for corporate average fuel consumption and new-energy vehicle credits for new passenger cars in China. Policy update. October, Available at http://www.theicct.org/sites/default/files/publications/China%20CAFC%20and%20NEV%20credits_policy-update_vF_06102016.pdf.

International Energy Agency (IEA) (2016). *Global EV Outlook 2016: Beyond One Million Electric Cars.* Paris: OECD/IEA Available at https://www.iea.org/publications/freepublications/publication/Global_EV_Outlook_2016.pdf.

________ (2017). *Global EV Outlook 2017: Two Million and Counting,* Paris: OECD/IEA. Available at https://www.iea.org/publications/freepublications/publication/GlobalEVOutlook2017.pdf (accessed on 17 November 2017).

________ (2018a). *Energy Access Outlook 2017: From Poverty to Prosperity.* Paris: OECD/IEA.

________ (2018b). *Global EV Outlook 2018: Towards Cross-modal Electrification.* Paris: OECD/IEA. Available at https://webstore.iea.org/download/direct/1045?filename=global_ev_outlook_2018.pdf.

International Labour Organization (ILO) (2011). *World of Work Report 2011: Making Markets Work for Jobs.* Geneva: International Labour Office.

________ (2014). *World Social Protection Report 2014/15: Building Economic Recovery, Inclusive Development and Social Justice.* Geneva: International Labour Office.

________ (2015). *Global Wage Report 2014/15: Wages and Income Inequality.* Geneva: International Labour Office.

________ (2017). *World Employment and Social Outlook: Trends 2017.* Geneva: International Labour Office.

________ (2018). The impact of technology on the quality and quantity of jobs. Issue brief No. 6, prepared for the second meeting of the Global Commission on the Future of Work, 15–17 February 2018. Cluster 3: Technology for social, environmental and economic development.

________ and Organization for Economic Cooperation and Development (2015). The labour share in G20 economies. Report prepared for the G20 Employment Working Group. Antalya, Turkey, 26 and 27 February 2015.

International Monetary Fund (IMF) (2016). *Fiscal Monitor April 2016: Acting Now, Acting Together.* Washington, D.C.

________ (2017). Understanding the downward trend in labor income shares (chap. 3), In *World Economic Outlook, April 2017: Gaining Momentum?* Washington, D.C.

J

Jackson, Matthew O., Brian W. Rogers and Yves Zenou (2017). The economic consequences of social-network structure. *Journal of Economic Literature*, vol. 55, No. 1 (March), pp. 49–95.

Jaffe, Adam. B. (2015). Technology diffusion. In *Emerging Trends in the Social and Behavioral Sciences: Interdisciplinary Directions*, Robert. A. Scott and Stephen. M. Kosslyn, eds. Thousand Oaks, California: SAGE Publications.

Jambeck, Jenna R. (2017). Role of technology in reducing plastic waste and pollution. Background paper prepared for *World Economic and Social Survey 2018*.

Jansen, Kees, and Aarti Gupta (2009). Anticipating the future: "biotechnology for the poor' as unrealized promise? iFutures vol. 41, No. 7 (September), pp. 436–445.

Jensen, Lars (2018). Digitally enabled financial services: how digital technology is driving financial inclusion. United Nations Development Programme, Bureau for Policy and Programme Support (BPPS) Strategic Policy Unit. December.

Juma, Calestous, and Ismail Serageldin (2007). *Freedom to Innovate: Biotechnology in Africa's Development.* Report of the High-level African Panel on Modern Biotechnology. Addis Ababa and Pretoria: African Union and New Partnership for Africa's Development.

K

Kahneman, Daniel (2011). *Thinking, Fast and Slow.* New York: Farrar, Straus and Giroux.

Kamperman Sanders, Anselm (2018). International incentives and obstacles for technology creation and diffusion. Background paper prepared for *World Economic and Social Survey 2018*

Karabarbounis, Loukas, and Brent Neiman (2013). The global decline of the labor share. *Quarterly Journal of Economics*, vol. 129, No. 1 (January), pp 61–103.

Karachalios, Konstantinos (2017). Advancing technology for humanity: the human standard and artificial intelligence. IEEE Standards University. Available at https://www.standardsuniversity.org/e-magazine/march-2017/advancing-technology-humanity-human-standard-artificial-intelligence/.

Kaufmann, Daniel, Aart Kraay and Massimo Mastruzzi (2011). The worldwide governance indicators: methodology and analytical issues. *Hague Journal on the Rule of Law*, vol. 3, No. 2 (June), pp. 220–246.

Kaul, Inge, Isabelle Grunberg and Marc A. Stern, eds. (1999). Global Public Goods: International Cooperation in the 21st Century. New York: Oxford University Press. See www.oxfordscholarship.com/view/10.1093/0195130529.001.0001/acprof-9780195130522-Chapter-1.

Kaul, Inge, and others (2003). Why do global public goods matter today. In *Providing Global Public Goods: Managing Globalization*. Oxford: Oxford University Press. Pp. 2–20.

Kawamura, Hiroshi (2017). Significant uptake of electrical vehicles and its socio-economic and environmental impacts. Background paper prepared for *World Economic and Social Survey 2018*.

Keller, Wolfgang (2004). International technology diffusion. *Journal of Economic Literature*, vol. 42, No. 3 (September), pp.752–782.

Knowledge@Wharton (2017). What will happen if the FCC abandons net neutrality? 5 December. Available at http://knowledge.wharton.upenn.edu/article/net-neutrality-debate/.

Koeniger, Winfried, Marco Leonardi and Luca Nunziata (2007). Labor market institutions and wage inequality. *ILR Review*, vol. 60, No. 3 (April), pp. 340–356.

Korinek, Anton, and Joseph E. Stiglitz (2017). Artificial intelligence and its implications for income distribution and unemployment. *NBER Working Paper*, No. 24174. Cambridge, Massachusetts: National Bureau of Economic Research.

Krause, Eleanor, and Isabel V. Sawhill (2017). What we know and don't know about declining labor force participation: a review. Washington, D.C.: Brookings Institution. May.

Kshetri, Nir (2010). Diffusion and effects of cyber-crime in developing economies. *Third World Quarterly*, vol. 31, No. 7 (October), pp. 1057–1079.

L

LaFleur, Marcelo, Kenneth Iversen and Lars Jensen (2018). Unlocking the potential of knowledge and technology for all. Frontier Issues. 1 April. Department of Economic and Social Affairs of the United Nations Secretariat.

LaFleur, Marcelo, and Ingo Pitterle (2017). Global context for achieving the 2030 Agenda for Sustainable Development: Low growth with limited policy options? secular stagnation - causes, consequences and cures. Policy note. DSP Development Issues No. 9. 1 March. Available at https://www.un.org/development/desa/dpad/publication/development-issues-no-9-low-growth-with-limited-policy-options-secular-stagnation-causes-consequences-and-cures/.

The Lancet (2017). Artificial intelligence in health care: within touching distance. Correspondence. Vol. 390, No. 10114 (23 December).

Lang, Jianlei, and others (2013). Energy and environmental implications of hybrid and electric vehicles in China. *Energies*, vol. 6, pp. 2662–2685.

LaPointe, Cara (2018), The ethics of emerging technologies: an overview of key ethical implications of leveraging emerging technologies for sustainable development. Background paper prepared for *World Economic and Social Survey 2018.*

Larsen, Peter Bjørn, Toni Ahlqvist and Karl Friðriksson (2009). Applying technology convergence for innovation in Nordic regions. Oslo: Nordic Innovation Centre.

Larson, Selena (2017). Massive cyberattack targeting 99 countries causes sweeping havoc. CNN Tech Cyber-Safe. 13 May. Available at http://money.cnn.com/2017/05/12/technology/ransomware-attack-nsa-microsoft/index.html.

Lee, Kai-Fu (2017). A blueprint for coexistence with AI. *WIRED*, 12, July. Available at www.wired.com/story/a-blueprint-for-coexistence-with-artificial-intelligence/.

Lee, Kenneth, Edward Miguel and Catherine Wolfram (2016). Experimental evidence on the demand for and costs of rural electrification. *NBER Working Paper*, No. 22292. May. Available at http://www.nber.org/papers/w22292.pdf.

Lee, Keun (2013). *Schumpeterian Analysis of Economic Catch-Up*. Cambridge, United Kingdom: Cambridge University Press.

________ (2016). *Economic Catch-up and Technological Leapfrogging: The Path to Development and Macroeconomic Stability in Korea*. Cheltenham, United Kingdom: Edward Elgar.

________, and John Mathews (2013). Science, technology and innovation for sustainable development. CDP Background Paper, No. 16 (April). ST/ESA/2013/CDP/16. Prepared as an input to the discussion at the fifteenth session of the Committee for Development Policy, 18-22 March 2013. Available at https://www.un.org/development/desa/dpad/wp-content/uploads/sites/45/publication/CDP-bp-2013-16.pdf.

Lewis, Seth C., and Oscar Westlund (2015). Big data and journalism: epistemology, expertise, economics, and ethics. *Digital Journalism*, vol. 3, No. 3, pp. 447–466.

Liverpool-Tasie, L.S.O., and Alex Winter-Nelson (2012). Social learning and farm technology in Ethiopia: impacts by technology, network type, and poverty status. *Journal of Development Studies*, vol. 48, No. 10, pp.1505–1521.

Lowrey, Annie (2013). The inequality of climate change. *New York Times*, 12 November.

Lugard, Paul, and Lee Roach (2017). The era of "big data" and EU/U.S. divergence for refusals to deal. *Antitrust*, vol. 31, No.2 (spring).

Lum, Kristian, and William Isaac (2016). To predict and serve? *Significance*, vol. 13, No. 5 (October), pp. 14–19.

M

Ma, Julian K-C., and others (2005). Plant-derived pharmaceuticals: the road forward. *TRENDS in Plant Science*, vol.10, No.12 (December), pp. 580–585.

Maddison, Angus (2004). Contours of the world economy and the art of macro-measurement 1500-2001. Ruggles Lecture, presented at the 28th General Conference of the International Association for Research in Income and Wealth, Cork, Ireland. August. Available at http://citeseerx.ist.psu.edu/viewdoc/download?doi=10.1.1.694.2406&rep=rep1&type=pdf.

Mandelli, Stefano, and others (2014). Sustainable energy in Africa: a comprehensive data and policies review. *Renewable and Sustainable Energy Reviews*, vol. 37 (September), pp.656–686.

Mathews, John A. (2001). National systems of economic learning: the case of technology diffusion management in East Asia. *International Journal of Technology Management*, vol. 22, Nos. 5/6, pp. 455–479.

Mazzucato, Mariana (2011). *The Entrepreneurial State: Debunking Public vs. Private Sector Myths*. Demos. Available at www.demos.co.uk/files/Entrepreneurial_State_-_web.pdf.

McAfee, Andrew, and Erik Brynjolfsson (2017). *Machine, Platform, Crowd: Harnessing Our Digital Future*. New York: W.W. Norton.

McKinsey Global Institute. (2016). *Digital Finance for All: Powering Inclusive Growth in Emerging Economies*. McKinsey & Company. September. Available at www.mckinsey.com/~/media/McKinsey/Global%20Themes/Employment%20and%20Growth/How%20digital%20finance%20could%20boost%20growth%20in%20emerging%20economies/MGI-Digital-Finance-For-All-Executive-summary-September-2016.ashx.

________ (2017a). *A Future that Works: Automation, Employment, and Productivity*. McKinsey & Company. January.

________ (2017b). *Jobs Lost, Jobs Gained: Workforce Transitions in a Time of Automation*. McKinsey & Company. December.

McMullen, David P., and others (2014). Demonstration of a semi-autonomous hybrid brain-machine interface using human intracranial EEG, eye tracking, and computer vision to control a robotic upper limb prosthetic. *IEEE Transactions on Neural Systems and Rehabilitation Engineering*, vol. 22, No. 4 (July) pp. 784–796.

McNeil, Donald G., Jr. (2018). W.H.O. approves a safe, inexpensive typhoid vaccine. *New York Times*, 3 January Global Health. Available at www.nytimes.com/2018/01/03/health/typhoid-vaccine-who.html.

Melaas, Aaron, and Fang Zhang (2016). National innovation systems in the United States and China: a brief review of the literature. Paper No. 011 (March). Medford, Massachusetts: Center for International Environment and Resource Policy; Energy, Climate and Innovation Program, Fletcher School, Tufts

University.

Metcalfe, Stan (1995). The economic foundations of technology policy: equilibrium and evolutionary perspectives (chap. 11). In *Handbook of the Economics of Innovation and Technological Change*, Paul Stoneman, ed. Oxford: Blackwell.

Meyer, Klaus E. (2004). Perspectives on multinational enterprises in emerging economies. *Journal of International Business Studies*, vol. 35, No.4 (July), pp. 259–276.

Michaels, Guy, Ferdinand Rauch and Stephen J. Redding (2013). Task specialization in U.S. cities from 1880-2000. *NBER Working Paper*, No. 18715. Cambridge, Massachusetts: National Bureau of Economic Research.

Milanovic, Branko (2016). *Global Inequality: A New Approach for the Age of Globalization*. Cambridge, Massachusetts: Harvard University Press.

Miller, Grant, and A. Mushfiq Mobarak (2013). Gender differences in preferences, intra-household externalities, and low demand for improved cookstoves. *NBER Working Paper*, No. 18964. Cambridge, Massachusetts: National Bureau of Economic Research.

MIT Technology Review Custom and Oracle (2016). The rise of data capital. MIT Technology Review.

Moretti, Enrico (2010). Local multipliers, *American Economic Review*, vol. 100, No. 2 (May), pp. 373–377.

Munshi, Kaivan (2004). Social learning in a heterogeneous population: technology diffusion in the Indian Green Revolution. *Journal of Development Economics*, vol. 73, No. 1 (February), pp. 185–213.

Muro, Mark, and others (2017). *Digitalization and the American Workforce*. November. Available at www.brookings.edu/wp-content/uploads/2017/11/mpp_2017nov15_digitalization_full_report.pdf. Metropolitan Policy Program. Washington, D.C.: Brookings.

N

Nakamoto, Satoshi (2008). Bitcoin: a peer-to-peer electronic cash system. Available at https://bitcoin.org/bitcoin.pdf.

National Human Genome Research Institute (2017). Cloning. Fact sheet. Available at www.genome.gov/25020028/cloning-fact-sheet.

National Institute of Standards and Technology (NIST) (2000). The role of standards in today's society and in the future. Testimony of Raymond G. Kammer before the House Committee on Science, Subcommittee on Technology. Available at https://www.nist.gov/speech-testimony/role-standards-todays-society-and-future.

National Institute on Aging, National Institutes of Health and World Health Organization (2011). Global health and aging. NIH publication No. 11-7737. October. Available at www.who.int/ageing/publications/global_health.pdf.

National Science Board (2016). Science and Engineering Indicators 2016. Alexandria, Virginia. Available at https://www.nsf.gov/statistics/2016/nsb20161/#/.

Nelson, Richard, and Sidney G. Winter (2009). *An Evolutionary Theory of Economic Change*. Cambridge, Massachusetts: Harvard University Press.

Neslen, Arthur (2017). Electric cars emit 50% less greenhouse gas than diesel, study finds. *Guardian*, 25 October.

Newman, Lily Hay (2018). The ransomware that hobbled Atlanta will strike again. *Wired*, 30 March. Available at https://www.wired.com/story/atlanta-ransomware-samsam-will-strike-again/.

Nguyen, Khanh Q. (2007). Alternatives to grid extension for rural electrification: decentralized renewable energy technologies in Vietnam. *Energy Policy*, vol. 35, No. 4 (April), pp. 2579-2589.

Nicas, Jack (2018). How YouTube drives people to the Internet's darkest corners. *Wall Street Journal*, 7 February.

Noble, Safiya. Umoja (2018). *Algorithms of Oppression: How Search Engines Reinforce Racism*. New York: New York University Press.

O

O'Neill, Daniel W., and others (2018). A good life for all within planetary boundaries. *Nature Sustainability*, vol. 1 (February), pp. 88–95.

Odagiri, Hiryuki, and others (2010). Conclusion. In *Intellectual Property Rights, Development, and Catch-up: An International Comparative Study*, Hiryuki Odagiri, and others, eds. Oxford: Oxford University Press. Pp. 412–430.

Organization for Economic Cooperation and Development(OECD) (1997). National Innovation Systems. Paris.

________ (2010). *Competition, patents and innovation II*. Proceedings of the Roundtable on Competition, Patents and Innovation (II), held by the OECD Competition Committee in June 2009. DAF/COMP (2009)22.1 April.

________ (2011). *Demand-side Innovation Policies*. Paris.

________ (2012). *OECD Employment Outlook 2012*. Paris.

________ (2014). *Challenges of International Co-operation in Competition Law Enforcement*. Paris.

________ (2015). *OECD Science, Technology and Industry Scoreboard 2015Innovation for Growth and Society*. Paris.

________ (2016). *OECD Science, Technology and Innovation Outlook 2016*. Paris.

________ (2017a). *Algorithms and Collusion: Competition Policy in the Digital Age*. Paris.

________ (2017b). Big data: bringing competition policy to the digital era. Executive summary. Key findings from the discussion held by the Competition Committee on 29 November 2016. DAF/COMP/M(2016)2/ANN4/FINAL. Paris. 26 April.

________ (2017c). *Fixing Globalisation: Time to Make It Work for All*. Paris

________ (2017d). *OECD Compendium of Productivity Indicators 2017*. Paris.

________ (2017e). *OECD Employment Outlook 2017*. Paris.

________ (2018a). OECD Tax Talk No. 9. YouTube. 16 March.

________ (2018b). *Tax Challenges Arising from Digitalisation: Interim Report 2018 – Inclusive Framework on BEPS*. Paris.

Oster, Emily, and Rebecca Thornton (2012). Determinants of technology adoption: peer effects in menstrual cup take-up. *Journal of the European Economic Association*, vol. 10, No. 6 (December), pp. 1263–1293.

P

Peplow, Mark (2016). The plastics revolution: how chemists are pushing polymers to new limits. *Nature News*, vol. 536, No. 7616 (17 August), pp. 266–268.

Plane, Angelisa, and others (2017). Exploring user perception of discrimination in online targeted advertising. In *Proceedings of the 26th USENIX Security Symposium, Vancouver, BC, Canada, August 16–18, 2017.*

Police Executive Research Forum (2014). *The Role of Local Law Enforcement Agencies in Preventing and Investigating Cybercrime.* Critical Issues in Policing Series. Police Washington, D.C.

Pritchett, Lant (1997). Divergence, big time. *Journal of Economic Perspectives*, vol. 11, No. 3 (summer), pp. 3–17.

Q

Quattrociocchi, Walter, Antonio Scala and Cass R. Sunstein (2016). Echo chambers on Facebook. Available at SSRN: https://ssrn.com/abstract=2795110.

R

Raney, Terri (2006). Economic impact of transgenic crops in developing countries. *Current Opinion in Biotechnology*, vol. 17. No. 2 (April), pp. 174–178.

Reisman, Dillon, and others (2018). Algorithmic impact assessment: a practical framework for public agency accountability. New York: AI Institute, New York University. *April.*

Rieke, Aaron, Miranda Bogen and David G. Robinson (2018). Public scrutiny of automated decisions: early lessons and emerging methods. Report of Omidyar Network and Upturn. Available at https://www.omidyar.com/insights/public-scrutiny-automated-decisions-early-lessons-and-emerging-methods.

Ross, Alec (2017). *The Industries of the Future.* New York: Simon & Schuster.

Rotolo, Daniele, Diana Hicks and Ben R. Martin (2015). What is an emerging technology? *Research Policy*, No. 44, No. 10 (December), pp. 1827–1843. https://doi.org/10.1016/j.respol.2015.06.006.

Royal Society (2012) *Science as an Open Enterprise.* London. June.

Ruane, John, and Andrea Sonnino (2011). Agricultural biotechnologies in developing countries and their possible contribution to food security. *Journal of*

Biotechnology, vol. 156, pp. 356–363.

S

Sabalza, Maite, Paul Christou and Teresa Capell (2014). Recombinant plant-derived pharmaceutical proteins: current technical and economic bottlenecks, in *Biotechnology Letters*, vol. 36, No. 12 (Decenmber), pp. 2367–2379.

Salicrup, Luis A., and Lenka Fedorková (2006). Challenges and opportunities for enhancing biotechnology and technology transfer in developing countries, in *Biotechnology Advances*, vol. 24, No. 1 (February), pp. 69–79.

Schön, Wolfgang (2018). Ten questions about why and how to tax the digitalized economy. IBFD *Bulletin of International Taxation*, vol. 72, No. 4/5 (6 March).

Schwab, Klaus. (2016). *The Fourth Industrial Revolution*. New York: Crown Business.

________, with Nicholas Davis (2018). *Shaping the Fourth Industrial Revolution*. Geneva: World Economic Forum.

Schwebel, Frank J., and Mary E. Larimer (2018). Using text message reminders in health care services: a narrative literature review. *Internet Interventions*. June.

Sen, Rohit and Subhes C. Bhattacharyya (2014). Off-grid electricity generation with renewable energy technologies in India: an application of HOMER. *Renewable Energy*, vol. 62, No. 1 (February) pp.388–398.

Shambaugh, Jay, Ryan Nunn and Becca Portman (2017). Eleven facts about innovation and patents. Washington, D.C.: Hamilton Project.

Shankar, Maya, and Lori Foster (2016). Behavioural insights at the United Nations: achieving Agenda 2030. Available at www.undp.org/content/undp/en/home/librarypage/development-impact/behavioural-insights-at-the-united-nations--achieving-agenda-203.html.

Shirley, Rebekah, and Daniel Kammen (2013). Renewable energy sector development in the Caribbean: current trends and lessons from history. *Energy Policy*, vol. 57 (June), pp. 244–252.

Shum, Paul K.C., and others (2016). Globalization and the role of multinational corporations (chap. 4). In *International Economic Development. Leading Issues and Challenges*, Fu Lai Tony Yu, Wai Kee Yuen and Diana S. Kwan, eds. Abingdon, United Kingdom: Routledge.

Smith, Aaron, and Monica Anderson (2017). Automation in everyday life. Washington, D.C.: Pew Research Center. 4 October. Available at www.pewinternet.org/2017/10/04/automation-in-everyday-life/.

Speicher, Till, and others (2018). Potential for discrimination in online targeted advertising. In *Proceedings of Machine Learning Research*, vol. 81: Conference on Fairness, Accountability and Transparency, 23–24 February 2018, New York, pp. 5–19.

Stucke, Maurice E. (forthcoming). Should we be concerned about data-opolies? *Georgetown Law Technology Review*.

________, and Allen Grunes (2016). *Big Data and Competition Policy.* Oxford: Oxford University Press.

Sundararajan, Arun (2016). *The Sharing Economy. The End of Employment and the Rise of Crowd-based Capitalism.* Cambridge: MIT Press.

Sunstein, Cass R. (2007). The polarization of extremes. *Chronicle of Higher Education: Chronicle Review.* 14 December.

Suri, Tavneet, and William Jack (2016). The long-run poverty and gender impacts of mobile money. *Science,* vol. 354, No. 6317 (9 December), pp. 1288–1292. Available at http://science.sciencemag.org/content/354/6317/1288.full.

Susswein, Ruth. (2018). New data protection rights…for Europeans. *Consumer Action* Data Protection Issue (Spring).

T

't Hoen, Ellen F. M., Pascale Boulet and Brook K. Baker (2017). Data exclusivity exceptions and compulsory licensing to promote generic medicines in the European Union: A proposal for greater coherence in European pharmaceutical legislation. *Journal of Pharmaceutical Policy and Practice,* vol. 10, p. 19.

Taylor, Linnet (2016). The ethics of big data as a public good: which public? whose good? Philosophical Transactions of the Royal Society A, vol. 374, No. 2083 (28 December).

Tegmark, Max (2017). *Life 3.0: Being Human in the Age of Artificial Intelligence.* New York: Alfred A. Knopf.

Thaler, Richard H. (1999). Mental accounting matters. *Journal of Behavioral Decision Making,* vol. 12, No. 3 (September), pp.183–206.

________, and Cass R. Sunstein (2008). *Nudge: Improving Decisions about Health, Wealth, and Happiness.* New Haven, Connecticut: Yale University Press.

Thiel, Christian, Jette Krause and Panagiota Dilara (2015). Electric Vehicles in the EU from 2010 to 2014: Is Full Scale Commercialisation Near? *JRC Science and Policy Report,* No. 27417. Luxembourg: Publications Office of the European Union.

Timilsina, Govinda R., and Kalim U. Shah (2016). Filling the gaps: policy supports and interventions for scaling up renewable energy development in Small Island Developing States. *Energy Policy,* vol. 98 C (November), pp. 653–662.

Tonukari, Nyerhovwo J., and Douglason G. Omotor (2010). Biotechnology and food security in developing countries. *Biotechnology and Molecular Biology Reviews,* vol. 5, No. 1 (February), pp. 013–023.

Tribunal Administratif Paris, 12 June 2017, No. 1505178/1-1, summary by Bob Michel, Tax Treaty Case Law IBFD.

U

UBS Limited (2017). Q-Series: UBS evidence lab electric car teardown – disruption ahead? Global Research. 18 May Available at https://static1.squarespace.com/static/5959484578d17192407068e4/t/5a42996a53450ae78ed86dbb/1514314095552/Report-UBS-Model-3-Bolt-EVV.pdf.

United Kingdom, Department for Environment, Food and Rural Affairs, and Department for Transport (2017a). UK plan for tackling roadside nitrogen dioxide concentrations: an overview. July. Available at https://assets.publishing.service.gov.uk/government/uploads/system/uploads/attachment_data/file/633269/air-quality-plan-overview.pdf.

United Kingdom, Department for Environment, Food and Rural Affairs, and Department for Transport (2017b). UK plan for tackling roadside nitrogen dioxide concentrations: detailed plan. July. Available at https://assets.publishing.service.gov.uk/government/uploads/system/uploads/attachment_data/file/633270/air-quality-plan-detail.pdf.

United Nations (2011). *World Economic and Social Survey 2011: The Great Green Technological Transformation*. E/2011/50/Rev.1-ST/ESA/333. Sales No. E.11.II.C.1.

________ (2012). *Road Map on Building a Green Economy for Sustainable Development in Carriacou and Petite Martinique, Grenada*. Product of an international study led by the Division for Sustainable Development of the Department of Economic and Social Affairs of the United Nations Secretariat, in cooperation with the Ministry of Carriacou and Petite Martinique Affairs and the Ministry of Environment, Foreign Trade and Export Development of Grenada.

________ (2013). *Report on the World Social Situation 2013: Inequality Matters*. ST/ESA/345. Sales No. E.13.IV.2.

________ (2014). *United Nations E-Government Survey 2014: E-Government for the Future We Want*. Sales No. 14.II.H.1.

________ (2016a). *Report on the World Social Situation 2016: Leaving No One Behind – The Imperative of Inclusive Development*. ST/ESA/362. Sales No. E.16.IV.1.

________ (2016b). *World Economic and Social Survey 2016: Climate Change Resilience – An Opportunity for Reducing Inequalities*. E/2016/50/Rev.1-ST/ESA/363. Sales No. E.16.II.C.1.

________ (2017a). Remarks of the Secretary-General, António Guterres, delivered on 6 November at the 2017 Web Summit, held in Lisbon from 6 to 9 November 2017. Available at https://www.un.org/sg/en/content/sg/speeches/2017-11-06/secretary-generals-remarks-web-summit.

________ (2017b). *Financing for Development: Progress and Prospects*. Report of the Inter-agency Task Force on Financing for Development 2017. Sales No. E.17.I.5.

________ (2017c). *The Sustainable Development Goals Report 2017.* Sales No. E.17.I.7.

________ (2018a). *Financing for Development: Progress and Prospects 2018.* Report of the Inter-agency Task Force on Financing for Development. Sales No. E.18.I.5.

________ (2018b). *World Public Sector Report 2018: Working Together—Integration, Institutions and the Sustainable Development Goals.* Sales No. E.18.II.H.1.

________, Department of Economic and Social Affairs, Economic Analysis and Policy Division (2017). World Economic Situation and Prospects monthly briefing. 102. 8 May. Available atwww.un.org/development/desa/dpad/publication/world-economic-situation-and-prospects-may-2017-briefing-no-102/.

United Nations, Department of Economic and Social Affairs, Population Division (2017). *World Population Prospects: The 2017 Revision - Key Findings and Advance Tables.*" ESA/P/WP/248. Available at https://esa.un.org/unpd/wpp/Publications/Files/WPP2017_KeyFindings.pdf.

United Nations, Economic and Social Council (2017). Report of the Secretary-General on progress towards the Sustainable Development Goals. E/2017/66. Available at https://unstats.un.org/sdgs/files/report/2017/secretary-general-sdg-report-2017--EN.pdf.

________ (2018). Report of the Secretary-General on harnessing the Sustainable Development Goals. 21 May. E/2018/66.

United Nations, Economic Commission for Europe (ECE) (2009). *Policy Options and Instruments for Financing Innovation: A Practical Guide to Early-Stage Financing.* Sales No. 09.II.E.3.

United Nations, United Nations System Chief Executives Board for Coordination secretariat (2017). *Compendium of Responses to the CEB Survey on Frontier Issues.* 27 October. Available https://www.unsceb.org/CEBPublicFiles/CEB_Survey_Compendium.pdf.

United Nations Conference on Trade and Development (UNCTAD) (2017). *Trade and Development Report 2017: Beyond Austerity – Towards a Global New Deal.* Sales No. E.17.II.D.5.

________ (2018). *World Investment Report, 2018: Investment and New Industrial Policies.* Sales No: E.18.II.D.4.

________, Trade and Development Board (2017). Note by the UNCTAD secretariat on enhancing international cooperation in the investigation of cross-border competition cases: tools and procedures. 26 April. TD/B/C.I/CLP/44.

United Nations Educational, Scientific and Cultural Organization (UNESCO) (2015). *UNESCO Science Report: Towards 2030.* Paris.

United Nations Environment Programme, International Resource Panel (2017). *Assessing Global Resource Use: A Systems Approach to Resource Efficiency and Pollution Reduction.* Nairobi: United Nations Environment Programme.

United Nations Framework Convention on Climate Change (UNFCCC) (2015). *Report of the Conference of the Parties on its twenty-first session, held in Paris from 30 November to 13 December 2015, Part two: Action taken by the Conference of the Parties at its twenty-first session* (FCCC/CP/2015/10/Add.1, decision 1/CP.21, annex)

United Nations University/Step Initiative 2014. (2014). *Solving the E-Waste Problem (Step) White Paper: One Global Definition of E-waste.* Available at http://www.step-initiative.org/files/step/_documents/StEP_WP_One%20Global%20Definition%20of%20E-waste_20140603_amended.pdf.

United States Standards Strategy Committee (2016). *United States Standards Strategy.* Washington, D.C.: American National Standards Institute.

University of Minnesota, Center for Sustainable Polymers (2018). Sustainable polymers 101. Available at https://csp.umn.edu/sustainable-polymers-101.

Urmee, Tania, David Harries and August Schlapfer (2009). Issues related to rural electrification using renewable energy in developing countries of Asia and Pacific. *Renewable Energy,* vol. 34, No. 2 (February), pp. 354–357.

United States Environmental Protection Agency (2017) Greenhouse gas emissions: understanding global warming potentials. 14 February. Available at https://www.epa.gov/ghgemissions/understanding-global-warming-potentials.

V

Varblane, Urmas, David Dyker and Dorel Tamm (2007). How to improve the national innovation systems of catching-up economies? *Trames,* vol. 11, No. 2, pp. 106–123.

Vickers, Chris, and Nicolas L. Ziebarth (2017). Lessons for today from past periods of rapid technological change. Background paper prepared for *World Economic and Social Survey 2018.*

Vidican Auktor, Georgeta (2017). Renewable energy as a trigger for industrial development in Morocco. In *Green Industrial Policy: Concepts, Policies, Country Experiences,* Tilman Altenburg and Claudia Assmann, eds. Geneva: UN Environment; and Bonn: German Development Institute.

Viitamo, Esa (2003). Knowledge-intensive services and competitiveness of the forest cluster: case of Finland. ETLA Discussion Paper, No. 845. Helsinki: Research Institute of the Finnish Economy.

Vosoughi, Soroush, Deb Roy and Sinan Aral (2018). The spread of true and false news online. *Science,* vol. 359, No. 6380 (9 March), pp. 1146–1151.

W

Wallace, Nick, and Daniel Castro (2018). The impact of the EU's new data protection regulation on AI. Center for Data Innovation. 27 March.

Weinberger (2018). Don't make AI artificially stupid in the name of transparency. *Wired.* Opinion. Available at https://www.wired.com/story/dont-make-ai-artificially-stupid-in-the-name-of-transparency/.

Wiesser, Daniel (2004). On the economics of electricity consumption in small island developing states: a role for renewable energy technologies? *Energy Policy,* vol. 32, No. 1 (January), pp.127–140.

Wolf, Steven, David Just and David Zilberman (2001). Between data and decisions: the organization of agricultural economic information systems. *Research Policy,* vol. 30, No, 1 (January), pp. 121–141.

Wong, Poh Kam, and Annette Singh. (2008). From technology adopter to innovator: Singapore. In *Small Country Innovation Systems: Globalization, Change and Policy in Asia and Europe*, Charles Edquist and Leif Hommen, eds. Cheltenham, United Kingdom: Edward Elgar. Pp. 71–112.

World Bank (2015). *World Development Report 2015: Mind, Society, and Behavior.* Washington, D.C.

________ (2016). *World Development Report 2016: Digital Dividends.* Washington, D.C.

World Economic Forum (2017). *The Global Risks Report 2017,* 12th ed. Geneva. Available at www3.weforum/org/docs/GRR17_Report_web.pdf.

________ (2018). *The Global Risks Report 2018,* 13th ed. Geneva. Available at www.weforum.org/reports/the-global-risks-report-2018.

World Energy Council (2016). *World Energy Resources 2016.* London. Available at www.worldenergy.org/publications/2016/world-energy-resources-2016/.

World Health Organization (WHO) (2009). *Global Health Risks: Mortality and Burden of Disease Attributable to Selected Major Risks.* Geneva.

________ (2017). *World Health Statistics 2017: Monitoring Health for the SDGs.* Geneva. Available at www.who.int/gho/publications/world_health_statistics/2017/en/.

________ (2018). Essential medicines and health products: typhoid vaccine prequalified. Available at www.who.int/medicines/news/2017/WHOprequalifies-breakthrough-typhoid-vaccine/en/.

World Wide Web Foundation (2017). Algorithmic accountability: Applying the concept to different country contexts. Washington, D.C. July.

World Trade Organization (WTO) (2015). TRIPS: WTO members agree to extend drug patent exemption for poorest members. 6 November. Available at https://www.wto.org/english/news_e/news15_e/trip_06nov15_e.htm.

________ (2017). *World Trade Statistical Review 2017.* Geneva.

Z

Zahra, Shaker A., and Gerard George (2002). Absorptive capacity: a review, reconceptualization, and extension. *Academy of Management Review*, vol. 27, No. 2 (April), pp. 185–203.

Zettler, Erik R., Tracy J. Mincer and Linda A. Amaral-Zettler (2013). Life in the "plastisphere": microbial communities on plastic marine debris. *Environmental Science and Technology*, vol. 47, No. 13, pp. 7137–7146.

Zgrzebnicki, Pawel (2017). Selected ethical issues in artificial intelligence, autonomous system development and large data set processing. *Studia Humana*, vol. 63, No. 3, pp. 24–33.

Databases

Conference Board Total Economy Database
www.conference-board.org/data/economydatabase/

FAOSTAT [Food and Agriculture Organization of the United Nations (FAO)] database
www.fao.org/faostat/en/

ILOSTAT: International Labour Organization labour statistics database
www.ilo.org/ilostat

National Renewable Energy Laboratory website (United States); "Photovoltaic Research" page
www.nrel.gov/pv

OECD.Stat: Main Science and Technology Indicators
https://stats.oecd.org/Index.aspx?DataSetCode=MSTI_PUB

Partnership on AI website
www.partnershiponai.org/

UIS.Stat: United Nations Educational, Scientific and Cultural Organization (UNESCO) Institute for Statistics (UIS) database
http://data.uis.unesco.org/

World Development Indicators: primary World Bank collection of development indicators
https://data.worldbank.org/products/wdi